OPACITY
AND THE CLOSET

OPACITY
AND THE CLOSET

Queer Tactics in Foucault, Barthes,
and Warhol

NICHOLAS DE VILLIERS

University of Minnesota Press
Minneapolis
London

An earlier version of chapter 1 was published as "Confessions of a Masked Philosopher: Anonymity and Identification in Foucault and Guibert," *symplokē* 16, nos. 1–2 (2009): 75–91.

An earlier version of chapter 4 was published as "Unseen Warhol/Seeing Barthes," *Paragraph: A Journal of Modern Critical Theory* 28, no. 3 (2005): 21–35.

Published by the University of Minnesota Press
111 Third Avenue South, Suite 290
Minneapolis, MN 55401–2520
http://www.upress.umn.edu

Library of Congress Cataloging-in-Publication Data

de Villiers, Nicholas.
    Opacity and the closet : queer tactics in Foucault, Barthes, and Warhol / Nicholas de Villiers.
    Includes bibliographical references and index.
    ISBN 978-0-8166-7570-8 (hc : acid-free paper)
    ISBN 978-0-8166-7571-5 (pb : acid-free paper)
1. Queer theory. 2. Self in literature. 3. Homosexuality in literature. 4. Foucault, Michel,
1926–1984—Criticism and interpretation. 5. Barthes, Roland—Criticism and interpretation.
6. Warhol, Andy—Criticism and interpretation. I. Title.
    PN56.H57D43 2012
    809'.93353—dc23

                                        2011052483

Printed in the United States of America on acid-free paper

The University of Minnesota is an equal-opportunity educator and employer.

20 19 18 17 16 15 14 13 12   10 9 8 7 6 5 4 3 2 1

The other is not to be known; his opacity is not the screen around a secret, but, instead, a kind of evidence in which the game of reality and appearance is done away with.
—Roland Barthes, "The Unknowable,"
A Lover's Discourse: Fragments

Contents

Bartleby's Queer Formula

Nothing so aggravates an earnest person as a passive resistance.

—Herman Melville, "Bartleby, the Scrivener: A Story of Wall Street"

HERMAN MELVILLE'S SHORT STORY "Bartleby, the Scrivener: A Story of Wall Street" explicitly concerns itself with the problem of biography regarding the "opaque" subject of the narrative: a pale, mechanical lawyer's copyist named Bartleby. The narrator, Bartleby's employer, begins with this "problem": "I waive the biographies of all other scriveners, for a few passages in the life of Bartleby. . . . While of other law copyists, I might write the complete life, of Bartleby nothing of that sort can be done. I believe that no materials exist, for a full and satisfactory biography of this man. It is an irreparable loss to literature."[1] The overt problem that the narrator encounters with his employee is a perceived refusal to do odd jobs around the office: whenever Bartleby is asked to perform a task, he responds, in a passive yet contradictorily firm manner, "I would prefer not to." This mantra increasingly frustrates the narrator, who rather than dismissing Bartleby outright, resolves to reason with Bartleby and "understand" him on the basis of his personal history. When he puts a few questions to Bartleby regarding his origins, he meets with the same passive resistance:

> "Bartleby," said I, in a still gentler tone, "come here; I am not going to ask you to do anything you would prefer not to do—I simply wish to speak to you."
>
> Upon this he noiselessly slid into view.
>
> "Will you please tell me, Bartleby, where you were born?"
>
> "I would prefer not to."
>
> Will you tell me *anything* about yourself?"

"I would prefer not to."

"But what reasonable objection can you have to speak to me? I feel friendly towards you." . . .

"What is your answer, Bartleby," said I. . . .

"At present I prefer to give no answer," he said.[2]

Bartleby's apparent refusal to disclose anything about his background, we might surmise, is why the narrator feels there are no materials with which to write the biography of Bartleby. But the larger problem is his resistance to what the narrator perceives to be "friendly feeling" and intersubjectivity, of what the narrator thinks to be his compassion, charity, sympathy, and understanding. The narrator justifies to himself every attempt to help Bartleby when he discontinues his work and even invites him home to live with him after learning that Bartleby has no home and has been living in the office. This gesture of friendship, perhaps even of love, which manifests itself as curiosity about Bartleby's mysterious activities when he is alone in the office and about his life in general, constitutes *understanding* in the fully humanist sense. But as Jacques Lacan insists, "We place no trust in altruistic feeling, we who lay bare the aggressivity that underlies the activity of the philanthropist."[3] At the end of the narrative, after recounting the sad death of Bartleby alone in a prison yard, and speculating further about his origins as an employee of the Dead Letter office, the narrator concludes his "little narrative" with the cry, "Ah, Bartleby! Ah, humanity!" thus finally trying to possess the unpossessable Bartleby in the human community of sympathy. Humanist understanding therefore seeks intersubjectivity, a reflection of similarity in the other. It looks for psychological depth, motives, and personal history, and it ceaselessly performs a hermeneutic operation of making transparent the resistances it encounters. But at moments it is frustrated, aggravated, "unmanned" in Melville's terms, by a passive resistance that appears as an opacity.

Bartleby's formula—"I would prefer not to"—is neither an affirmation nor a negation, it has an ambiguous linguistic status. In "Bartleby; or, The Formula," Gilles Deleuze has elaborated on this formula that "drives everyone crazy":

We immediately notice a certain mannerism, a certain solemnity: *prefer* is rarely employed in this sense, and neither Bartleby's boss, the attorney, nor his clerks normally use it ("queer word, I never use it myself"). The usual formula would instead be *I had rather not.* But the strangeness of the formula goes beyond the word itself. Certainly it is grammatically correct, syntactically correct, but its abrupt termination, NOT TO, which leaves what it rejects undetermined, confers upon it the character of a radical, a kind of limit-function. Its repetition and its insistence render it all the more unusual, entirely so. Murmured in a soft, flat, and patient voice, it attains to the irremissible, by forming an inarticulate block, a single breath. In all these respects, it has the same force, the same role as an *agrammatical* formula.[4]

This strange and unusual formula marks a limit of articulation that is correctly identified as producing "queer" effects—not the least of which that it begins to infect the speech of the attorney and his clerks, contaminating their language.[5] According to Deleuze, the formula is ravaging, devastating:

> The formula I PREFER NOT TO excludes all alternatives, and devours what it claims to conserve no less than it distances itself from everything else. It implies that Bartleby stop copying, that is, that he stop reproducing words; it hollows out a zone of indetermination that renders words indistinguishable, that creates a vacuum within language. But it also stymies the speech acts that a boss uses to command, that a kind friend uses to ask questions or a man of faith to make promises. If Bartleby had refused, he could still be seen as a rebel or insurrectionary, and as such would still have a social role. But the formula stymies all speech acts, and at the same time it makes Bartleby a pure outsider to whom no social position can be attributed. This is what the attorney glimpses with dread.[6]

This "stymieing" of command, of paternalistic philanthropy, and of socialization is indeed *queer*: the strangeness of the formula frustrates both grammatical and social normativity, including the social role of rebellious refusal. Bartleby is unpossessable by the narrator's philanthropy and charity—what Deleuze calls "all the masks of the paternal function"—so the cry "Ah, Bartleby! Ah, humanity!" is not simply (or not only) a homoerotic identification of the narrator with Bartleby.[7] Rather, according to Deleuze, this "does not indicate a connection, but rather an alternative in which he has had to choose the all-too-human law over Bartleby" and thereby remain a witness, interpreter, and narrator.[8]

In "Bartleby, or On Contingency," Giorgio Agamben follows Deleuze in treating Bartleby less as a psychological double of the narrator and more as a conceptual persona for a philosophical concept: "The scribe who does not write (of whom Bartleby is the last, exhausted figure) is perfect potentiality, which a Nothing alone now separates from the act of creation."[9] Agamben observes that the man of the law honestly tries to understand the scrivener, but he uses concepts of will and necessity that are not the same as potentiality and impotentiality: "Bartleby calls into question precisely this supremacy of the will over potentiality."[10] Rather, the formula that he obstinately repeats "destroys all possibility of constructing a relation between being able and willing. . . . It is the formula of potentiality."[11] Agamben proposes that "only inside an experience that has thus retreated from all relation to truth, to the subsistence or nonsubsistence of things, does Bartleby's 'I would prefer not to' acquire its full sense (or, alternatively, its nonsense)" since "potentiality, insofar as it can be or not be, is by definition withdrawn from both truth conditions and, prior to the action of 'the strongest of all principles,' the principle of contradiction."[12] Agamben thus sets up our difficult task: to think potentiality and contingency apart from will and necessity, and to enter into an experience that has retreated from the conditions of truth and the law of noncontradiction. A queer formula, a queer task, indeed.

Opacities
Queer Strategies

Veiling and unveiling: isn't that what interests them? What keeps them busy? Always repeating the same operation, every time.

—Luce Irigaray, "When Our Lips Speak Together"

Writing is that neutral, composite, oblique space where our subject slips away, the negative where all identity is lost, starting with the very identity of the body writing.

—Roland Barthes, "The Death of the Author"

IN AN INTERVIEW TITLED "The End of the Monarchy of Sex," Michel Foucault diagnoses a movement "taking shape today which seems to be reversing the trend of . . . 'always more truth in sex,' a trend which has doomed us for centuries. . . . I have the impression of an 'anti-sex' grumbling . . . as if a thorough effort were being made to shake this great 'sexography' which makes us decipher sex as the universal secret."[1] While Foucault was perhaps optimistic in his estimation (circa 1977), this book will assess such efforts to shake the dominant hermeneutic of "the closet." It will also consider the creative and collaborative queer work of "fabricating other forms of pleasure, of relationships, of coexistences, attachments, loves, intensities" that Foucault posits as an alternative.[2]

The metaphor of "coming out of the closet" is indeed hegemonic—propounded not just as a manner of being truthful but also as the quintessential gesture of acknowledging who one is. To "come out" is first and foremost to locate identity not just in a speech act but in a speech act by which one presumably discloses a previously closeted "secret."[3] "Coming

1

out of the closet" is thus the seemingly ubiquitous metaphor for understanding the connection between homosexuality, identity, and speech (usually conceived as authentic, true, and free expression of a formerly repressed
sexuality). Foucault has detailed the manifold ways in which sexuality has
become "the truth" of a person, a truth that must be *made to speak*, ceaselessly, in ever-new permutations of the confessional.[4] Christian confessional
and modern psychoanalysis both take on the task of deciphering sexuality
through the medium of speech. There is a fundamental connection between
the "hermeneutics of suspicion," which distrusts appearances, and the
suspicious hermeneutic impulse whereby sexuality is understood as concealed meaning that can nonetheless be made transparent to scrutiny.[5] The
operation described by Eve Kosofsky Sedgwick as "the epistemology of
the closet" makes sexuality into a secret that can be known, causing certain types of privileged "knowingness" to circulate.[6] (Think for example
of the *Saturday Night Live* cartoon sketch "The Ambiguously Gay Duo,"
in which homoerotic sexual ambiguity gives rise to virulent speculation
and the exchange of rumor, seeking confirmation of a unanimous suspicion.)[7] The closet and coming out, in fact, expose the double binds and
incoherence of the structure of public and private. In this regard, legal
trials have proven that homosexuality can have neither the privilege of
being public nor of being private.[8] Privileged knowingness might best be
understood as reserving the right to speak (even if confidentially) about
another's sexuality, and this is indeed what acts of coming out are intended to disrupt (with varying degrees of success). While I do not wish to
downplay the importance of such speech acts as coming out, Sedgwick
and others have indicated the ways in which this is by no means a simple
operation of truth telling, and such critics as David Van Leer have ques-
tioned the privilege accorded to the metaphor itself in its emphasis on self-
revelation, conversion, and confession.[9]

Why might someone refuse to tell the truth of his or her sexuality?
According to the dominant logic of the closet, such behavior can only
betoken closetedness, a lack of truthfulness-to-oneself and a crippling
complicity with homophobia. Therefore, it is worth asking, first of all, if
homophobia is always a will-to-ignorance and silence, and whether it
might in fact include a fear of *not* knowing everything about a person's

sexuality. It is important to consider the ways that homophobia often insists on knowing rather than refusing to know about the sexuality of gay people. Indeed, as Sedgwick points out in *Epistemology of the Closet*, the subject can be faulted for not disclosing enough rather than disclosing too much about her or his sexuality. This disclosure is "at once compulsory and forbidden."[10] "Outing" has been criticized for its controlling impulse, whereby, as Silvia Bovenschen has argued, "Someone who refuses to render himself universally accessible and classifiable, even though according to general opinion he belongs to a type that may become an object of a discussion, is suspect. In outing he is categorically categorized."[11] Roland Barthes, in his preface to *Tricks*, Renaud Camus's novel of gay cruising, claims that there is one thing that "society will not tolerate," namely, that "I should be . . . *nothing*, or, more precisely, that the *something* I am should be openly expressed as provisional, revocable, insignificant, inessential, in a word irrelevant."[12] This emphasis on "insignificance" has been critiqued by those who see Barthes and others as complicit with a homophobic logic of erasure and absence.[13] But what if we were to take seriously these "intolerable" and "suspect" behaviors and consider them distinctly queer strategies, strategies of *opacity*, not necessarily of silence or invisibility? Barthes clarifies that the problem is not that I should be *nothing*, but rather that the *something* I am might be *impertinent*. Following Foucault's remarks in "The Subject and Power," I see this as a struggle against subjection *(assujetissement)* and against a form of power that "categorizes the individual, marks him by his own individuality, attaches him to his own identity, imposes a law of truth on him that he must recognize and others have to recognize in him."[14] This form of power makes individuals into recognizable subjects by imposing a categorizing and interpretive regime of truth.

Michel Foucault, Roland Barthes, and the Pop artist Andy Warhol each made sustained efforts in their lives and works to "shake off" the closet and the epistemological, ontological, and political presuppositions on which it is based. These three important queer figures in postwar French and American culture were responding critically to the discursive formation of the closet, and all found ways to vitalize its critique through creative self-enactments by which they relocated themselves against the massively overdetermined rhetoric of the truth, of secrets revealed, of bringing into the light, of clarity, of transparency, hence of confessional self-inspection, of self-rectification.

Saint Augustine's *Confessions*—often seen as prefiguring modern auto-biography—is perhaps one of the best illustrations of this rhetoric. Addressing himself directly to God—but with his contemporary readership in mind—Augustine proclaims, "What could be hidden within me, even if I were unwilling to confess it to you? I would be hiding you from myself, not myself from you. Now, however, my groaning is witness that I am displeased with myself."[15] In "Technologies of the Self," Foucault explains the ideal of permanent verbalization espoused by Cassian: "self-examination is subordinated to obedience and the permanent verbalization of thoughts."[16] Foucault shows the consequences of this approach, "Confession is a mark of truth. This idea of the permanent verbal is only an ideal: it is never completely possible. But the price of the permanent verbal was to make everything that could not be expressed into a sin," hence what is known as "the sin of omission."[17]

Foucault explains that "from the eighteenth century to the present, the techniques of verbalization have been reinserted in a different context by the so-called human sciences in order to use them without renunciation of the self but to constitute, positively, a new self. To use these techniques without renouncing oneself constitutes a decisive break."[18] A striking example of the technique of verbalization without self-renunciation appears in the *Confessions* of Jean-Jacques Rousseau. Rousseau asserts that "as we have seen, never throughout the whole of my life has my heart, as transparent as crystal, been able to hide for a single moment any feeling of any intensity that has taken refuge there."[19] According to Paul de Man's deconstruction of Rousseau in "Excuses *(Confessions)*," "shame is primarily exhibitionistic" and this (literary) structure is self-perpetuating: as we move toward deeper shame, each confession gets harder to tell and more necessary and satisfying to confess.[20] Ironically, then, "the excuse consists in recapitulating the exposure in the guise of concealment," and "guilt is forgiven because it allows for the pleasure of revealing its repression."[21] This self-perpetuating operation, whereby shame allows for the satisfaction of self-exposure through confession, has a mechanical quality about it to de Man. He therefore insists that "the text is not a figural body but a machine."[22] He argues that writing or language as mechanical (grammar) threatens the autobiographical subject, and that this points to "a radical estrangement between the meaning and the performance of any text."[23] He points out that the machine performs anyway, so we supply the guilt to make the excuse meaningful: "Excuses generate the very guilt they exonerate, though always in excess or by default."[24] De Man calls this excess that results from Rousseau's use of figural language "irony," and notes that, "far from closing off the tropological system, irony enforces the repetition of its aberration."[25]

The common tropes of confession found in Augustine and Rousseau are chiefly those of transparency (to God or the reader's gaze), the ideal of continual self-disclosure through verbalization, and the way in which the confession quickly becomes an excuse or justification of one's shameful behavior displayed exhibitionistically for others. But beyond this, I would like to follow de Man's critique of Rousseau in examining whether we might consider confessional discourse a "machine" that exceeds the auto-biographical subject.

The closet as a modern form of confessional discourse strikes me as particularly "mechanical" in its operations. The guilt and shame associated with sexual secrets often seem to be supplied in order to make the closet meaningful, which distracts us from the way it "performs any-way" (as de Man puts it). Foucault famously voiced his doubts about the Repressive Hypothesis, asking, "Suppose the obligation to conceal it was but another aspect of the duty to admit to it (concealing it all the more and with greater care as the confession of it was more important, requiring a stricter ritual and promising more decisive effects)? What if sex in out society, on a scale of several centuries, was something that was placed within an unrelenting system of confession?"[26] Both de Man and Foucault acknowledge the way in which this operation is like an unrelent-ing machine. So the question then becomes how to throw a spanner in the machine of confessional discourse?

What if we were to look at speech as nonrevelatory, outside the param-eters of confession and truth, the humanist desire for *reflection,* and the ideal of *transparency?* What if we were to attend to its *opacity?* What would such an opacity look or sound like, and what would be its function? This book interrogates the viability of the metaphor of the closet and puts forth a concept of "opacity" as an alternative queer strategy or tactic that is not linked to an interpretation of hidden depths, concealed meanings, or a neat opposition between silence and speech.[27] To this end I examine queer appropriations of forms typically linked to truth telling, the revelation of secrets, authenticity, and transparency, namely, the interview, the autobiography, the diary, and the documentary.[28]

I use the term "strategy" here to indicate a certain relation to particular "games of truth" and to indicate the simultaneously ludic and regulated nature of language. Strategies are specific to particular historical, cultural, and discursive situations and can have different intentions and effects. It may well be that a strategy's "motivation" is part and parcel of a homophobic logic of shame, self-loathing, and a petit-bourgeois concern for privacy.[29] But this does not prohibit its *effects* from being productively queer. This tension may, in fact, be the enabling condition for any consideration of queer opacity whatsoever. It is my conviction that strategies should be considered less for their reactive or protective abilities (that is, a reading in terms of the closet, in terms of what the strategy is intended to prevent or protect against), but rather more for what they might enable, creatively and politically. Indeed, what is remarkable about opacity as a discursive strategy is its productivity (including the remarkable number of attempts to make sense of it, which perhaps makes it an ironic productivity).[30]

The figure of Bartleby with which I began exemplifies what I suggest is a queer strategy of opacity.[31] What follows is an elaboration of three other instances of opacity, designated by proper names that refer to actual historical individuals, but I am using those names here as figures indicating specific *strategies:* Michel Foucault, Roland Barthes, and Andy Warhol. My readings of these figures suggest that they invent and deploy different strategies and tactics for specifically resisting both the closet and the confessional discourse associated with it. They also suggest alternatives to the essentialist concepts of the subject and the author on which these depend.[32] These figures are in fact the strategies of opacity they perform, strategies that like Bartleby's linguistic formula are not quite affirmations or quite completely negations, but rather indicate resistances to a type of epistemology that can only seek the truth. Like Bartleby's formula, these linguistic strategies stymie the speech acts used to interrogate the person that might otherwise seem to be behind them.

One problem I can foresee here is delimiting the difference between what I am calling opacity and the (modernist) strategy of "myth-making." For example, if we were to consider the persona of Oscar Wilde, it is difficult to separate out the cult image of the mythic figure (as emphasized in Todd Haynes's *Velvet Goldmine* [1998]), the actual historical individual (which is sought by the film *Wilde* [1997], in an ironic but effective search for truth), and the strategies of opacity that can be found in the Wilde trials, precisely at that moment in which the categorizing homophobic impulse wishes to play the mythic persona off against or alongside the civic individual, and wherein it became increasingly obvious that telling the truth does not set you free.[33]

The notion of being "on trial" (and thus of answering for oneself) will therefore be a recurring motif.[34] I suggest that there is in fact a structural homology between the trial and the interview (and in some cases the biography) insofar as that each of them consists of operations that have as their goal the production of truth. Brian Winston has traced how the interview is "causally related to Benthamite legal reforms because, almost as soon as the new 'natural' legal interrogatory was in place in the courts, it was borrowed for journalism," noting that "newspaper interviews were to become common practice in the 1870s, the word itself with this specific journalistic connotation being dated to 1869," and that this interrogatory was also used "for social science, and then borrowed again for radio and the cinema."[35] In *Giving an Account of Oneself,* Judith Butler likewise identifies what she calls the "juridical model" of self-narrative, though she speaks of the subject's opacity to itself, in a different sense than I am using the term.[36]

This homology between the interview and the trial is especially evident in the interviews and posthumous "trials" of Foucault, Barthes, and Warhol. I have chosen to focus on a rather narrow but pivotal moment in postwar U.S. and French history, both the history of "out" gay politics (post-Stonewall, post-'68), and the evolution of mass-media communications featuring the celebrity and intellectual interview (plus the formation of a "gay press" in France and the United States, which combines these two historical strands).[37] Indeed, mediation is a major theme in what follows, particularly in the conclusion. I emphasize these figures' collaborations (some posthumous or not fully voluntary) with biographers, interviewers, and literary or visual artists, as well as their individually authored publications, in order to link opacity with technological mediation. I consider them both in their original historical context and in terms of their transatlantic circulation, translation, and "afterlife."

In his *Media Manifestos*, Régis Debray identifies the particular milieu of their emergence:

> 1950–1980: the boom in semiotic cults sees itself stimulated by the concomitant one in "mass culture." . . . Without passing through linguistics at all, Norbert Wiener (inventor of cybernetics) had already as early as 1948 defined man without reference to interiority as a communication machine. . . . While resolutely unaware of it, French semiology was metaphorizing and "culturalizing" the American mechanist paradigm. From the domains of metaphor to immediate surroundings, all aspects of social life soon came under the empire of signs.[38]

Debray periodizes a shift between what he calls "the *graphosphere*, when printed text imposes its rationality on the whole of the symbolic milieu" and "*the videosphere*, with its devitalization of the book via audiovisual media," but he notes that "mediaspheres have not succeeded one another as substitutions, but rather as complications in a perpetual game of mutual reactivation."[39] Foucault, Barthes, and Warhol straddle these two mediaspheres, with Warhol clearly exemplifying the videosphere while nonetheless publishing several printed texts.

Identifying a similar phenomenon and set of figures, Peter Wollen points out that "the arrival of pop art in the early sixties was just one element in a much more general cultural shift: Warhol and Lichtenstein should be seen alongside cultural critics such as McLuhan (or Eco or Barthes), writers like Burroughs, obsessed by advertising, the image bank, the word virus and the 'Reality Studios,' and of course, filmmakers like Godard." According to Wollen, "Artists had to come to terms with the new images, whether through irony, celebration, aesthetic enhancement, or *détournement*."[40] The transatlantic connection made by Debray and Wollen is also important to my own project of connecting Foucault,

Barthes, and Warhol. For instance, it was in Paris in 1965 that Warhol announced his intention of giving up painting and going into film and the world of music and performance, and, as we will see, Warhol became a kind of conceptual persona in texts by Foucault and Barthes.[41]

As works by Foucault and Barthes circulate in translation and edited collections, prefaced by Americans (such as Susan Sontag's *A Barthes Reader*), they are provided with new contexts.[42] In *French Theory: How Foucault, Derrida, Deleuze, & Co. Transformed the Intellectual Life of the United States,* François Cusset examines the "creative misreadings" and different ideological purposes to which works by these French philosophers were put in the American academy, quite removed from their dialogue with Marxism, in courses taught in departments of literature, in women's studies, and in gay, lesbian, and queer studies as they emerged in the 1980s and 1990s.[43] Unfortunately, since he sometimes uses as his sources the venomous critiques (American and French) of cultural studies and multiculturalism, Cusset sometimes too quickly conflates "identity politics" with the critique or subversion of identity advanced by queer theory.[44]

I must, however, address this issue of identity politics. I focus on three white gay men as case studies and forecast the critique that their positions (as prominent, "famous" figures with creative agency) owe a great deal to "white male privilege." While recognizing Marlon Ross's critique, in "Beyond the Closet as Raceless Paradigm," of "the closet" as a primarily white European discourse, I would like not only to move "beyond" the closet as metaphor but also to consider how Foucault, Barthes, and Warhol repudiate both the privileges associated with the closet (and "outness") and what is presumed to be a "modern homosexual identity."[45] There is indeed something quite *untimely* about each of them.[46]

I also do not want to be too quick to decide that the figures I am treating are matter-of-factly "male" or "masculine" in their identifications. Indeed, Barthes was well aware that, like Marcel Proust's character Charlus, his tastes declared him a woman. Barthes did not seem to protest much against this identification. Likewise, Hilton Als has suggested that accounts of Andy Warhol's status as "father figure" to the Factory are greatly mistaken and that "Warhol as She" or "Warhol as Mother" applies more frequently, especially in Warhol's relationship to transsexual superstar Candy Darling.[47] While Mary Harron's film *I Shot Andy Warhol* (1996) certainly reveals the male privilege and misogyny of the "bitchy" gay men at Warhol's Factory, it remains an open question whether any "genderqueer" solidarity is finally created between Candy Darling (poorly cast as obviously male) and spokeswoman for the "Society for Cutting Up Men," Valerie Solanas.[48] We should recall that Ondine declared that Warhol's initials "A.W." meant "All Woman," and Warhol did not object.[49] While this might be seen as merely stereotypically woman-identified yet woman-hating camp, what if we were to take it seriously? Following from Laura Mulvey's suggestion that the position of the woman in Hitchcock and noir films is "guilty" (associated with castration) and thus that the sadistic erotic drive of the male hero (aligned with the law) is "to break her down and force her to tell by persistent cross-questioning," it is possible to conjecture that the position of being thusly interrogated is therefore structurally "feminine."[50] Like Melanie in Hitchcock's *The Birds* (1963), I find Warhol's resistance to telling the truth even when cross-questioned in interviews to be particularly "feminizing" as well as "queer."[51]

The End of the Family Line

I propose that a great deal lies behind the potential double-entendre of "getting the story straight" when it comes to questions of biography. Biographies have a largely normalizing function regarding their subject. The subject's life is read in terms of conventional codes of narrative development and is situated in the context of his or her family—even when he or she might represent an end to the family line.[52] A resistance to biographical identifications challenges heterocentric and psychologistic attempts to place and fix these figures according to their family background (the typical "biopic" eureka: "that explains everything"). This is not, however, to argue that Foucault, Barthes, or Warhol denied the importance of his upbringing, ethnicity, class, or mother (both Barthes and Warhol spent much of their adult lives living with their mothers).[53] But the posthumous oedipalization of their biographies has been too swiftly accomplished without acknowledging the possibility of what Barthes, in a caption to a family photo from *Roland Barthes by Roland Barthes,* calls "family without familialism."[54]

Two of the major Warhol film biographies—Kim Evans's *Andy Warhol* (1987) and Chuck Workman's *Superstar: The Life and Times of Andy Warhol* (1990)—familiarize and *familialize* their queer subject.[55] Warhol wittily expressed horror after being shot at the thought of his two worlds colliding (Family and Factory): "If you value your privacy, don't ever get shot, because your private life turns into an open house very quickly."[56] The Warhol documentaries treat Warhol's biography as providing an explanation for his work and demonstrate how the interview usually functions within the documentary genre to produce truth and authenticity. Far more than his biographers, Warhol rigorously scrutinized the production of personality and celebrity. Warhol's films (especially the "Screen Tests") and film appearances reveal a unique example of the negotiation of gay identity in the media and the creation of queer tactics of resistance to the search for a hidden, closeted truth.[57] Rather than reading each of these figures in terms of the closet (their "private" versus "public" life), I suggest that they present a set of productive strategies for the creation of public personas that in fact resist homophobia and heteronormativity.[58]

Biography also presents a specific problem in its attempt to describe and explain gay lives, often in a way that privileges the objectivity and authority of the biographer (simultaneously discrediting the biographical subject while crediting the biographer). David Halperin suggests that "the perennial threat of discreditation through biographical description becomes painfully acute, and the need to resist it becomes pressingly urgent, when the biographical subject is gay. The struggle for interpretive authority . . . intrinsic as it may be to the biographical situation in general, acquires an absolutely irreducible political specificity when it is waged over a gay life."[59] Homosexuality is treated as an object of knowledge, something spoken about, rather than as a positionality from which it is possible to know and to speak.[60] A *queering* of biographical forms is therefore a crucial strategy for each of these figures, which is what makes them troubling and fascinating objects of study. To reverse these positions of speaking authority—subject and object—means a reauthorization of gay subjectivity. It also allows us to scrutinize the role of the biographer

in attempting to describe and produce knowledge about the homosexuality of that subject. Foucault has rightly noted in an interview the difficulty
of giving meaning to a phrase such as "Proust was a homosexual." He
points out that the term "homosexuality" is inadequate as a descriptive
category on the one hand and a means of restoring a type of experience
on the other.[61] In his oral biography of Warhol with the tongue-in-cheek
title *The Autobiography and Sex Life of Andy Warhol,* John Wilcock
makes the remarkable point that "even after all these years, I could not
say to you with certainty Andy Warhol is homosexual because I no longer
even know what the definition of that word is. It is not so narrow as I once
believed it to be, and I think Andy might partly be responsible for that
attitude growing in society, too. A lot of things around him, which you
would ask questions about anywhere else, somehow become irrelevant.
You never think of them."[62] Rather than seeing this as evidence of "de-
gaying" mystification, I find it quite congruent with comments by Barthes
and Foucault.

An Art of Living

In the postscript interview to the English translation of Foucault's *Raymond Roussel,* translator Charles Ruas asks Foucault: "The phenomenon
of an artist obscured by his own work—do you think that it is related to
his sexual identity?" Foucault responds with a sketch of the gay literary
conundrum:

> Between cryptography and sexuality is a secret, there is certainly a direct rela-
> tionship. Let's take three examples: When Cocteau wrote his works, people said,
> "It's not surprising that he flaunts his sexuality and his sexual preferences with
> such ostentation since he is a homosexual." Then Proust, and about Proust they
> said, "It's not surprising that he *hides* and *reveals* his sexuality, that he lets it
> appear clearly while also hiding it in his work, since he is a homosexual." And it
> could also be said about Roussel, "It's not surprising that he hides it completely
> since he is a homosexual." In other words, of the three possible modes of behav-
> ior—hiding it entirely, hiding it while revealing it, or flaunting it—all can appear
> as a result of sexuality, but I would say that it is related to a *way of living*. It's a
> choice in relation to what one is as a sexual being and also as a writer. It's a
> choice made in the relationship between the style of sexual life and the work.[63]

Foucault's analysis of Proust and Cocteau is significant since both authors played with the distinction between the life and the work, the author and the narrator. Proust's "Marcel" both is and is clearly not Marcel Proust.[64] When he published the 1957 English edition of his blatantly homoerotic *Le Livre blanc* with an enigmatic preface, Cocteau was making precisely the same point about himself: "Who wrote it? Did I? Another? Probably. Are we not become others the moment after we've done writing? A posthumous book? That too is possible; are we not today yesterday's dead? . . . Therefore be not uneasy if you find it in you to attribute this book to me. I'd not be in the least bit ashamed of it. And I simply beg the unknown author's forgiveness for thus taking unfair usurping advantage of his anonymity."[65] This strategy, which is closer to Foucault's "hiding it while revealing it" mode of behavior, demonstrates the immense power of anonymity to both confound and transform notions of the self.[66] The important point, however, is not to get caught in the game of sexual cryptography but to move toward an understanding of the writer's *life as work*, the relation to oneself taken as a creative activity. I will also be applying this to Foucault's friend Hervé Guibert, but Jean Genet could also easily be included here,[67] along with Samuel R. Delany, Yukio Mishima, Severo Sarduy, Quentin Crisp, and Oscar Wilde (who famously claimed, "I have put all my genius into my life; I have put only my talent into my works").[68] Foucault suggests, "Therefore, I believe that it is better to try to understand that someone who is a writer is not simply doing his work in his books, in what he publishes, but that his major work is, in the end, himself in the process of writing his books. The private life of an individual, his sexual preference, and his work are interrelated *not* because his work translates his sexual life, but because the work includes the whole life as well as the text."[69] As I will discuss in chapter 1, Foucault's biographer James Miller slightly misinterprets this conclusion as a justification for his book *The Passion of Michel Foucault,* which clearly reads Foucault's books as translations of his psyche and sexuality.[70] Rather, the concerns expressed here about the stylization of life, including sexuality and writing, are significantly related to late Foucault interviews, such as "On the Genealogy of Ethics: An Overview of a Work in Progress," in which Foucault asks: "Couldn't everyone's life become a work of art?

Why should the lamp or our house be an art object but not our life?" He remarks that although "Sartre refers the work of creation to a certain relation to oneself—the author to himself—which has the form of authenticity or inauthenticity. I would like to say exactly the contrary: we should not have to refer the creative activity of somebody to the kind of relation he has to himself, but should relate the kind of relation one has to oneself to a creative activity."[71] Thus, it is not a question of authenticity but an art of living that concerns Foucault.

What we should note in Foucault's tone when describing the gay literary predicament is the exhaustion of the phrase "since he is a homosexual": the dull predestination of the biographical "fact" of sexuality. In the first volume of *The History of Sexuality*, Foucault explains that for the personage of the nineteenth-century homosexual, "nothing that went into his total composition was unaffected by his sexuality. It was everywhere present in him: at the root of all of his actions because it was their insidious and indefinitely active principle; written immodestly on his face and body because it was a secret that always gave itself away."[72] Against a notion of the indiscreet legibility of written homosexuality, Foucault shifts his account to the *writing* homosexual, refusing to read the latter as the former, or even refusing the very category of "the homosexual writer."

A similar tone of exhaustion appears in Foucault's treatment of the Sartrean opposition of authenticity to inauthenticity. We should recall that Sartre's treatment of Genet in his study *Saint Genet* caused Genet intense suffering. In his 1964 *Playboy* interview with Madelein Gobeil, when asked, "What did you feel while reading the book he devoted to you?" Genet responds:

> A kind of disgust—because I saw myself naked and stripped by someone other than myself. In all my books I strip myself but at the same time I disguise myself with words, choices, attitudes, magic. I take pains not to damage myself too much. Sartre stripped me without mercy. He wrote about me in the present tense. My first impulse was to burn the book. Sartre had handed me the manuscript. I finally allowed him to publish it because I've always felt compelled to be responsible for what I evoke.[73]

Foucault's desire "to say exactly the contrary" to Sartre, to "relate the kind of relation one has to oneself to a creative activity," points in a more productive direction for understanding the relationship between the author's life and work: *the strategy of a writer is the work of transforming the self.* Genet's "words, choices, attitudes, magic" might be seen as a disguise, but what if we instead see them as a stylization of the self?[74]

Foucault's desire to imagine a person's life becoming a work of art will therefore govern my own approach to Foucault himself (though not in the manner of James Miller), to Barthes, and to Warhol. Éric Marty has argued that Barthes should be understood as manifesting a desire for a type of writing whose object is "the biographical," with multiple variations in position and strategy without adopting any one definitively.[75] Barthes's *Roland Barthes by Roland Barthes* should be understood as demystifying autobiographical discourse—for example, by playing games with the pronouns I/you/he—while at the same time exploring the idea of the author as an object of desire, an idea that informs my treatment of critical and biographical studies of Barthes, Foucault, and Warhol.[76] Andy Warhol will be examined less in terms of the art objects he produced, rather more in terms of the work of art he made of his life, of his persona, which emerges in his collaborative efforts as a writer. Following Foucault, I believe that for each of these figures "his major work is, in the end, himself in the process of writing his books." This is not to explain the work as a translation of the life and sexuality of the author, but rather the reverse, to see the life, self, and sexuality in terms of a performative process.

This is why I regard these writers as using "queer" discursive strategies in their works and interviews, taking *queer* not as an a priori but as a process itself, following Sedgwick's definition: "That's one of the things that 'queer' can refer to: the open mesh of possibilities, gaps, overlaps, dissonances, and resonances, lapses and excesses of meaning when the constituent elements of anyone's gender, of anyone's sexuality aren't made (or *can't be* made) to signify monolithically."[77] This experimental and open process is one Sedgwick explicitly links to epistemology and representation, to meaning, but I would also like to allow for the possibility of nonmeaning and nonknowledge as "queer" strategies (as she alludes to when she speaks of gaps and lapses of meaning).[78] This is what I am calling *queer opacity.* Against the hermeneutics of sex as a field of meaning to be deciphered and interpreted, the oeuvre is not decrypted for the secret truth of sexuality or seen as simply a result of sexuality. Rather, the strategies in each of the following texts should be understood as indicating a style of living, what homophobic political reactionaries call "chosen lifestyle." This is one of those terms, so stigmatized among gay people trying to claim civil rights, that Foucault's ethics insist on reappropriating.

In an insistence on "Camp" as a *queer* strategy of political resistance, Moe Meyer clarifies his use of the term in the following way: "What 'queer' signals is an ontological challenge that displaces bourgeois notions of the Self as unique, abiding, and continuous while substituting instead a concept of the Self as performative, improvisational, discontinuous, and processually constituted by repetitive and stylized acts."[79] Therefore, queer is not a sexual identity based on material sexual practices but is closer to performative theories of gender.[80] Meyer is here explaining why "queer" is different from "gay" identity, but Foucault made a similar differentiation between "gay" and "homosexual." When an interviewer suggests a connection between homosexual style and lying, Foucault responds:

> I don't think it makes much sense to talk about a homosexual style. . . . One could perhaps say that there is a "gay style" or at least that there is an ongoing attempt to recreate a certain style of existence, a form of existence or art of living, which might be called "gay." In answer to the question about dissimulation, it is true that, for instance, during the 19th century it was, to a certain degree, necessary to hide one's homosexuality. But to call homosexuals liars is equivalent to calling the resistors under a military occupation liars.[81]

This distinction between homosexuality and "gay style" as an art of living is immensely productive. While Foucault's periodization of the closet might appear quaintly optimistic, his connection between dissimulation and resistance against military occupation is a fortuitous one for problematizing the closet.[82]

Foucault's discussion above of secrecy and disclosure with regard to one's sexuality—and the various modes one might adopt to manage it—intersects with Sedgwick's discussion of the simultaneously compulsory and forbidden disclosures of sexuality demanded by the closet. In *Epistemology of the Closet,* Sedgwick claims that "the gay closet is not a feature only of the lives of gay people. But for many gay people it is still the

fundamental feature of social life; and there can be few gay people, however courageous and forthright by habit . . . in whose lives the closet is not
still a shaping presence."[83] However, Sedgwick notes the inherent dangers
in this hypothesis: "There are risks in making salient the continuity and
centrality of the closet, in a historical narrative that does not have as a ful-
crum a saving vision—whether located in past or future—of its apocalyptic rupture. A meditation that lacks that particular utopian organization
will risk glamorizing the closet itself, if only by default; will risk presenting as inevitable or somehow valuable its exactions, its deformations, its
disempowerment and sheer pain."[84] The same could be said of the risks
taken in this present study, which are the same risks of glamorization but
are run because of *a refusal to value and present as inevitable the centrality of the closet.*

Cesare Casarino has suggested the possibility of "the sublime of the
closet" as a potential overcoming of the closet through a kind of implosion:

> The sublime of the closet is *not a coming* out. It is rather, an overcoming of the
> closet: a coming pure and simple. This is not to underestimate the immense force
> and dire necessity of coming out for any queer politics. This is merely to under-
> stand the act of coming out of the closet as that political scenario which the
> powers that keep one shut up in there can already foresee and hence prepare for
> accordingly—such a scenario, after all, is their worst nightmare. To the extent to
> which the act of coming out is regulated by the same dialectics of incarceration
> and liberation already implicit in the functioning of the closet, such an act is pre-
> cisely that form of resistance that has been recorded a priori in the heteronorma-
> tive social contract. To come out of the closet also reaffirms the effectiveness and
> *raison d'être* of the closet. . . . This is to say that if to come out of the closet may
> turn out to be also the proverbial solution that feeds back into the very problem
> it was meant to solve, as it locks one into the vicious circle of a perpetually self-
> reproducing dialectical relay, other types of solutions need to be pursued at the
> same time.[85]

Casarino therefore acknowledges the political continuity and centrality
of the closet as outlined by Sedgwick yet allows for the simultaneous pur-
suit of "other types" of (nondialectical) solutions to the problem than the
always already foreseen "coming out." This is also where I situate my
own attempt to examine queer strategies and processes that might overcome the vicious circularity of the dialectic of the closet. Indeed, this is to

take risks—risks of glamorization, of illusions of transcendence, of political naïveté—but as Sedgwick seems to acknowledge with difficulty, an
apocalyptic vision is not necessarily a saving vision. Sedgwick explains
that if these risks are worth running, "it is partly because the nonutopian
traditions of gay writing, thought and culture have remained so inex-
haustibly and gorgeously productive for later gay thinkers, in the absence
of a rationalizing or even of a forgiving reading of their politics."[86] But
do we need a rationalizing or forgiving reading of the politics of earlier
gay writing, thought, and culture?

We might want to trouble this opposition between nonutopian and
utopian traditions of gay writing. For example, Diana Knight has suggested that utopia is an overlooked but crucial dimension of Barthes's
writing:

> Barthes always accepted the necessity of political engagement with this war of
> meanings. . . . However, much of Barthes's writing testifies to his longing for a
> realm beyond such meanings, and this largely metaphorical space is invariably
> identified with utopia. Barthes often insisted on the beyondness of this utopian
> realm, somewhere on the far side rather than the near side of meaning, and there-
> fore to be distinguished from any pre-semiological golden age . . . hence Barthes's
> discussions of an outplaying of meaning in terms of its suspension or even of
> its theft.[87]

But this utopianism, traversing meaning in order to exempt it, is a matter
of tactics. As Knight points out, Barthes accepts the necessity of political
engagement, and I would argue that his "longing for a realm beyond"
might actually be a political tactic with regard to meaning itself. Barthes
imagines a "post-meaning: one must traverse . . . the whole meaning, in
order to be able to extenuate it, to exempt it. Whence a double tactic:
against *Doxa* [naturalized common sense], one must come out in favor of
meaning, for meaning is the product of History, not of Nature; but against
Science (paranoiac discourse), one must maintain the utopia of suppressed
meaning."[88] Against a *scientia sexualis* that turns sexuality into an object
of paranoiac knowledge, the suppression of the signified of homosexuality
maintains a utopian potential and a tactical advantage (where suppression
is not the same as repression or denial). In *Epistemology of the Closet*,
Sedgwick refers to Barthes's utopia as "at least premature," but since she

is primarily attentive there to what happens "in the vicinity of the closet," she tends to read all forms of silence, suppression, and opacity as signs of "closetedness" and ignorance, something she shares with her interlocutor D. A. Miller.[89] Following Sedgwick's later writing in which she critically reflects back on the "paranoid reading" mode of Miller's and her own earlier work, my approach to Barthes is more akin to what she calls "reparative reading."[90]

For my purposes, discourse and strategy must be considered together. Foucault considers "discursive formations" in terms of a field of strategic possibilities "within a particular set of concepts, to play different games."[91] He argues that "it is in discourse that power and knowledge are joined together. And for this very reason, we must conceive of discourse as a series of discontinuous segments whose tactical function is neither uniform nor stable" and as "a multiplicity of discursive elements that can come into play in various strategies."[92] Foucault defines power in dynamic, productive terms as a field of force-relations rather than in terms of stratified, juridical, or State Power. Where there is power, there is resistance, and "this resistance is never in a position of exteriority in relation to power."[93] Foucault explains in "The Subject and Power" that every power relationship implies "a strategy of struggle" and clarifies his use of the term "strategy" (from a context of war or a game) as employed in three ways:

> First, to designate the means employed to attain a certain end. . . . Second, to designate the way in which a partner in a certain game acts with regard to what he thinks should be the action of others and what he considers others think to be his own. . . . Third, to designate the procedures used in a situation of confrontation to deprive the opponent of his means of combat and to reduce him to giving up the struggle.[94]

What, then, is the difference between Foucault's definition of the term "strategy" and his use of the term "tactic" or "tactical"? We might find that tactics appear specific and local but function within larger strategies.

A more detailed juxtaposition of "strategies" with "tactics" can be found in the work of Michel de Certeau, who argues that strategies always imply a spatial position of power or property (thus calculation from a safe position), whereas tactics are dependent on time and seizing the right moment, "on the wing" as it were.[95] I consider Warhol's interviews as precisely such a "tactical" situation for improvisation, collaboration, evasion, and "perversion" of the goals of the interview. Certeau's phrasing fits Warhol well: "Whatever it wins, it does not keep. It must constantly manipulate events in order to turn them into 'opportunities.'"[96] I will therefore apply the term "tactic" to Warhol's "opaque" interview persona. (The words "opacity" and "opaque" appear frequently throughout Certeau's *The Practice of Everyday Life,* often linked to "tactics" and opposed to Foucault's description of the ideal of panopticism.)

A more pronounced rejection of the term "strategy" can be found in *Roland Barthes by Roland Barthes,* where in characterizing his own work Barthes distinguishes between *Tactique/Strategie* as follows: "The movement of his work is tactical: a matter of displacing himself, of obstructing, as with bars, but not of conquering. . . . This work would therefore be defined as: a tactics without strategy."[97] Elsewhere, Barthes characterizes his work (in the third person) as "a kind of intellectual 'sport': he systematically goes where there is a solidification of language, a consistency, a stereotypy. Like a watchful cook, he makes sure that language does not thicken, that it doesn't stick. This movement, one of pure form, accounts for the progressions and regressions of the work: it is a pure language tactic, which is deployed in the air, without any strategic horizon."[98] In Barthes's affirmation of a formal and linguistic "tactics without strategy,"[99] one notices an alternation between the valences of "cooking" and "sport," whereas in Foucault's consideration of strategies of struggle we have a different sort of athleticism, related to the "agonism" of wrestlers.[100] In his introductory chapter to *Textual Strategies,* Josué V. Harari considers Derridean and Barthesian textuality *as a strategy* that has the advantage of cutting across the traditional distinctions between reading and writing, criticism and literature, and juxtaposes their supposed textual isolationism to Foucault's consideration of discourse in terms of power as a strategic situation.[101] Harari points to the connection between "strategy" and "strategem" as artifice or trick.[102] We are not far from the register of camp, a strategy of artifice that David Halperin has defined as "a form of cultural resistance that is entirely predicated on a shared consciousness of being inescapably situated within a powerful system of social and sexual meanings" that resists the power of that system from within.[103]

One of the most successful interventions in the field of thinking about supposedly "closeted" (pre-Stonewall) gay textual production and the confused field of sexual politics is David Van Leer's *The Queening of America: Gay Culture in Straight Society.* Van Leer argues against a militarist model in which gays and straights constitute consciously opposed armies:

> Although there is no reason to deny the pervasiveness of homophobia, it is important to see . . . that confrontation is only one of the many avenues to power[;] . . . often minorities speak most volubly between the lines, ironically reshaping dialogues the oppressor thinks he controls or even finding new topics and modes of speaking to which the oppressor himself lacks access. . . . The sexual character of language is rarely direct, and post-Stonewall criticism has occasionally stigmatized such writing as "closeted." But just as invisibility does not impede all forms of speech, so the refusal to identify one's personal interests can facilitate other kinds of gay statements.[104]

Van Leer opens up a field of inquiry that is often foreclosed by accepting too readily a neat opposition between invisibility and visibility in language. Indeed, here we run into an interesting slippage in gay political thought regarding "visibility" and "speech," "audibility" or "readability." Van Leer is right to point out that the sexual character of language is rarely direct. Post-Stonewall gay politics has tended to prefer purity of communication whereby a fixed meaning is carried smoothly from sender to receiver, preferring the closure of denotation instead of the perpetual play of connotation. In a discussion of the connotative logic of bisexuality that is indebted to Barthes's *S/Z,* Jo Eadie points to how "Barthes describes this reductive [denotative] process in terms resonant of homosexuality. Describing that reading practice which attempts to contain connotations by gathering them under a single 'name,' he points out that 'when the unnesting of names ceases, a critical level is established, the work is closed, the language by which the semantic transformation is ended becomes nature, truth, the work's secret.'"[105] Eadie suggests that "outing" follows a similar logic of ending connotation with the denotation of homosexuality as a kind of last word, which, of course, then becomes nature, truth, *the* secret.[106]

The closet condenses a number of highly charged cultural dualisms, and certain queer thinkers have already suggested their potential deconstruction. Schematically, the closet suggests—and in some cases takes for granted—the following oppositions: silence/speech, invisible/visible, in/out, private/public, secret/open, disavowal/avowal, negation/affirmation, shame/pride, shyness/exhibitionism, secrecy/disclosure, connotation/denotation, covert/overt, conceal/reveal, deny/admit, dishonesty/honesty, lie/truth, surface/depth, obtuse/obvious, oblique/direct, obscure/illuminated, opaque/transparent.[107] We can see the power of the privileged (right-hand) terms in such journalistic banalities as "openly homosexual." The final few alliterative binaries are what I would like to put pressure on and to deconstruct. But to simply reverse the opposition, to privilege one term over the other, to pick a side, would be merely an initial move, as Jacques Derrida cautioned in "Signature, Event, Context": "Deconstruction cannot be restricted or immediately pass to a neutralization: it must, through a double gesture, a double science, a double writing—put into practice a *reversal* of the classical opposition *and* a general *displacement* of the system."[108] My work is indebted to the Derridean project as queered by Sedgwick, Judith Butler, Lee Edelman, and others, but finally I am more interested in a general displacement of the dualistic conceptual order of the closet.[109]

Opaque and transparent—taken to their limits—don't work as opposites, since for something to be fully transparent it would be invisible, and for something to be completely opaque would mean a complete blockage of vision altogether, another invisibility. So *opacity* is visible only outside of the purity of the opposition opaque/transparent itself. Likewise, the closet is unable to contain the above oppositions but attempts metaphorically to maintain them. Within my project, therefore, Foucault's, Barthes's, and Warhol's strategies and tactics of opacity must be thought separately from the dialectical relays of the closet. I take inspiration from Foucault's clarification of philosophical activity as "the critical work that thought brings to bear on itself . . . the endeavor to know how and to what extent it might be possible to think differently."[110]

Foucault's concept of the "will to truth" undermines a neat opposition between falsehood and truth, looking less at the true or false *content* of a particular discourse but rather at the way it works as a discourse *that demands truth*. In "The Thought of the Outside," Foucault explains that the simple assertion "I lie, I speak" in ancient times was "enough to shake the foundations of Greek truth: 'I lie, I speak,' on the other hand, puts the whole of modern fiction to the test."[111] Foucault's discussion of the experience of language as an "experience of the outside" in fact points to "what precedes all speech, what underlies all silence: the continuous streaming of language. A language spoken by no one: any subject it may have is no more than a grammatical fold. A language not resolved by any silence."[112] This "neutral space" absorbs the seeming paradox of "I lie, I speak" and absorbs the division between speech and silence.[113]

How might Foucault and Barthes share a concern for this *neutral* space, what Barthes calls "the drift far from the all-too-pure pair: *speaking/keeping silent*"?[114]

Silence and Friendship

In *Epistemology of the Closet*, Sedgwick glosses Foucault's remark that "there is no binary division to be made between what one says and does not say; we must try to determine the different ways of not saying such things. . . . There is not one but many silences, and they are an integral part of the strategies that underlie and permeate discourses" by highlighting how silence is a part of the closet's strategy of power, since "closetedness" is, paradoxically enough, "the speech act of a silence."[115] In contrast to this interpretation, in a 1982 interview with Foucault in Toronto, his friend and colleague Stephen Riggins remarks: "One of the many things that a reader can unexpectedly learn from your work is to appreciate silence. You write about the freedom it makes possible, its multiple causes and meanings. For instance, you say in your last book that there is not one but many silences. Would it be correct to infer that there is a strongly autobiographical element in this?" To which Foucault responds:

> I think that any child who has been educated in a Catholic milieu just before or during the Second World War had the experience that there were many different ways of speaking as well as many forms of silence. There were some kinds of silence which implied very sharp hostility and others which meant deep friendship, emotional admiration, even love. . . . Maybe another feature of this appreciation of silence is related to the obligation of speaking. I lived as a child in a petit bourgeois, provincial milieu in France and the obligation of speaking, of

making conversation with visitors, was for me something both very strange and very boring. I often wondered why people had to speak. Silence may be a much more interesting way of having a relationship with people.[116]

Foucault recalls an almost silent day spent with filmmaker Daniel Schmidt that was for him "the first time that a friendship originated in strictly silent behavior."[117] He laments that "silence is one of those things that has unfortunately been dropped from our culture. We don't have a culture of silence; we don't have a culture of suicide either. The Japanese do, I think. Young Romans or young Greeks were taught to keep silent in very different ways according to the people with whom they were interacting. Silence was then a specific form of experiencing a relationship with others. This is something which I believe is really worthwhile cultivating. I'm in favor of developing silence as a cultural ethos."[118] We should then ask: how might friendship entail silence? In Barthes's "Inaugural Lecture" at the Collège de France, he thanks Foucault by similarly connecting silence and friendship: "As for the present, allow me to exempt from the discretion and silence incumbent upon friendship the affection, intellectual solidarity, and gratitude which bind me to Michel Foucault, for it is he who kindly undertook to present this chair and its occupant to the Assembly of Professors."[119] Why is silence "incumbent upon friendship," as Barthes puts it? His remark calls to mind Maurice Blanchot's reflection in "Friendship," wherein "friendship . . . passes by way of the recognition of the common strangeness that does not allow us to speak of our friends but only to speak to them, not to make of them a topic of conversations (or essays), but the movement of understanding in which, speaking to us, they reserve, even on the most familiar terms, an infinite distance, the fundamental separation on the basis of which what separates becomes relation."[120] I would like to briefly trace here how what separates Barthes and Foucault becomes their relation.

When Riggins voices his appreciation for Foucault's discussion of the multiple forms and meanings of silence, he is referring to the first volume of *The History of Sexuality,* where Foucault claims that discourse is not separated from silence, singular or plural, as if from an absolute limit, but rather silences function "alongside the things said, with them and in relation to them within overall strategies."[121] In a section on the "rule of the tactical polyvalence of discourse"—which not incidentally uses the examples of sodomy and homosexuality—Foucault explains, "Discourses are not once and for all subservient to power or raised up against it, any more than silences are. . . . In like manner, silence and secrecy are a shelter for power, anchoring its prohibitions; but they also loosen its holds and provide for relatively obscure areas of tolerance."[122] Thus, we might propose a *tactical polyvalence of silence* as well, which Foucault makes clear in the interview. At the same time, however, Foucault also points to an "obligation to speak," which echoes his larger claim in the *History of Sexuality* that rather than repression, prohibition, and silence characterizing modern Western sexual discourse, there was an "incitement to discourse" beginning with the Christian pastoral, which "prescribed as a fundamental duty the task of passing everything having to do with sex through the endless mill of speech."[123] This insight about the compulsion to speak is echoed by Barthes's "Inaugural Lecture" in which he famously asserts that language "is neither reactionary nor progressive; it is quite simply fascist; for fascism does not prevent speech, it compels speech."[124] While Foucault does not use the word "fascism" here, he often speaks of the "tyranny" or "monarchy" of sex. Thus, we will see that for Barthes and for Foucault, silence might offer an alternative to the *obligation* of speech. But then the open question remains (to borrow Derrida's phrase): "How to Avoid Speaking?"[125]

In *Bringing Out Roland Barthes*, D. A. Miller faults Barthes for the way in which his silence on the subject of his homosexuality has functioned as a closet, and this silence, rather than protecting Barthes, has shielded his critics who "are spared having to show how deeply their attacks are motivated by a name he never claims."[126] However, in his preface to Renaud Camus's *Tricks*, Barthes complicates the issue of *silence* with regard to homosexuality: "To reject the social injunction [of identity] can be accomplished by means of that form of silence which consists of saying things *simply*. . . . Renaud Camus's *Tricks* are simple. This means that they speak homosexuality, but never speak about it: at no moment do they invoke it."[127] Barthes here creates a third term to the binary of silence/speech, namely, "speaking simply," which he nonetheless regards as *a form of silence*.

An amusing contemporary parallel might be drawn between two Bravo television shows (at least their early incarnations): the makeover show *Queer Eye for the Straight Guy*,[128] which obsessively speaks about homosexuality (thereby reifying the homo/hetero binary implicit in the title, which manages to inoculate the public against any threat posed by the activist and conceptual challenge of "queer"), versus the first season of the fashion reality competition *Project Runway*,[129] which never spoke "about" homosexuality but allowed homosexuality to be queerly "spoken" through every flaming camp moment. (The second season of *Project Runway* ruined this analogy, with Daniel Vosevic inaugurating the round of perfunctory comings out.) However, like Barthes with *Tricks*, I do not assume that *Project Runway* was therefore "closeted" (especially Tim Gunn).

With regard to the closet, Foucault fares better on this matter, having in late interviews frequently acknowledged the importance of becoming "gay" not as a form of desire but as something desirable, as a creative force in forming new relationships, in particular forms of *friendship*. But in one of his more frank interviews, the previously mentioned interview with Riggins, it is important to note that he begins with a discussion of silence as it relates to friendship. So here we are presented with a constellation: silence, friendship, homosexuality. Foucault already revealed the important link between homosexuality and friendship in his interview for *Gai Pied*, "Friendship as a Way of Life."[130] But with Riggins we also see silence as "a specific form of experiencing a relationship with others." Both Foucault and Barthes use Antiquity and Japan in their attempt to imagine "silence as a cultural ethos." And both use Christian confessional and psychoanalysis to talk about the obligation to speak.

On this latter point, Barthes makes a similar connection to the one made by Foucault in his *History of Sexuality* between Christian confessional and the birth of psychoanalysis. In an essay entitled "Listening," Barthes explains:

> Auricular confession, from mouth to ear, in the secrecy of the confessional, did not exist in the Patristic age; it was born (around the seventh century) from the excesses of public confession and from the advances of individualist conscience. . . . [P]rivate listening to sin has thus developed. . . . [T]he archetypal instrument of modern listening, the telephone, collects the two partners into an

ideal (and under certain circumstances, intolerable) intersubjectivity, because this instrument has abolished all senses except that of hearing . . . interpellation leads to an interlocution in which the listener's silence will be as active as the locutor's speech: *listening speaks,* one might say: it is at this (either historical, or structural) stage that psychoanalytic listening intervenes.[131]

From Christian confessional via the detour of the phone to the psychoanalyst's couch, Barthes reveals the way in which listening, silence, and speech are interdependent: *interlocution interpellates* the individual as speaking/listening subject. In this same essay, Barthes remarks that "no law is in a position to constrain our listening: freedom of listening is as necessary as freedom of speech."[132] In *Roland Barthes by Roland Barthes,* he remarks that a "uniformly noisy place seems to him unstructured because in this place there is no freedom left to choose silence or speech. . . . [I]t is on the whole a (modest) pledge of freedom: how on such a day can I give meaning to my silence, since, *in any case,* I cannot speak?"[133] All this talk of freedom, this connection to *rights,* to politics, will be further complicated when Barthes calls for a *right to silence.*

In his course at the Collège de France in 1977–78 titled "The Neutral" or, better yet, "The Desire for Neutral," Barthes postulates "a right to be silent—a possibility of keeping silent."[134] In this course, we also see the importance of Antiquity and Japan: Barthes makes multiple references to the Skeptics and Zen Buddhism in his discussion of the "figures" of Silence. But what does Barthes mean by a right to keep silent? In *Roland Barthes by Roland Barthes,* he clarifies, again in the third person, that "he is quite willing to be a political *subject* but not a political *speaker.* . . . And it is because he fails to separate political reality from its general, *repeated* discourse that politics is barred to him. Yet out of this preclusion he can at least make the *political* meaning of what he writes: it is as if he were the historical witness of a contradiction: that of a *sensitive, avid and silent* political subject (these adjectives must not be separated)."[135] This final parenthesis is crucial in understanding why Barthes is not a militant (to D. A. Miller's chagrin it would seem), but he sees his silence as a form of political sensitivity. In the arena of politics, no worse accusation can be launched than that of *quietism,* for it is immediately associated with acquiescence and complicity.[136] And this is no doubt Miller's perception of

Barthes's role as a "closeted" writer. Barthes characterizes himself, or rather his character "R.B.," as a "political misfit" who is "especially intolerant of blackmail (for what underlying reason?), it was above all blackmail that he saw in the politics of states."[137] This coy parenthetical question might be clarified with the help of Sedgwick's concept of the profound _blackmailability_ of Western masculinity, whereby all speech _and_ silence can be related to the suspicion of homosexuality.[138]

Barthes acknowledges that "all my life, politically, I have given myself a bad time. . . . In the name of what does a militant decide to . . . militate?"[139] In his preface to _Tricks,_ Barthes explains: "Speaking of homosexuality permits those who 'aren't' to show how open, liberal, and modern they are, and those who 'are' to bear witness, to assure responsibility, to militate."[140] But it is in this same preface that Barthes proposes a third, complex or neutral, term against the binary speaker/silence(d): "that form of silence which consists of saying things _simply._" This disruption of the opposition must therefore be heard as an echo of his concepts of "active/ avid silence" and "listening [that] speaks." Is there such a thing as an _ethics of silence?_ At one point Barthes mocks himself in his desire to reconnect politics with ethics: "This is a literally _retarded_ notion, for by coupling Ethics and Politics, you are about two hundred years old."[141]

Likewise, Foucault sometimes resisted the position of being a political speaker (making suggestions as to a program, vis-à-vis gay liberation, the antipsychiatry movement, or prison reform) with important exceptions. But Foucault clarifies that _there are several different ways of speaking,_ and likewise _there are several different forms of silence,_ with different ethical and political ramifications. Foucault acknowledges that in his experience growing up in a Catholic milieu just before the Second World War, "there were some kinds of silence which implied very sharp hostility"— this might be called repressive, prohibitive "Power"—but others "meant deep friendship, emotional admiration, even love." This silence of friendship and admiration is the silence to which Barthes is referring in his acknowledgment of Foucault in his "Inaugural Lecture." And hopefully at this point it is clear how much intellectual solidarity can be found between Barthes's work and Foucault's, even when they almost never speak "about" each other.

Interlocution/Interpellation

I have found that in many cases the theories of Foucault and Barthes (and Warhol) can be used to read each other. The structure of *Opacity and the Closet: Queer Tactics in Foucault, Barthes, and Warhol* is therefore staggered, like the "bond" of a brick wall (complete with "queen closers"), such that Barthes overlaps with Foucault and Warhol but never lines up the same in each "course."[142] While I question the assumption that one should go to the source to find the truth (an assumption often built into the interview and the autobiography), I have also found that each figure's moments of autocritique (such as Barthes's book "on" Roland Barthes) are invaluable examples of how to avoid importing an ill-fitting interpretive framework to discuss their particular strategies or tactics of opacity. In "The Foucault Phenomenon," Paul Bové explains that critics of Foucault "blot out the resistance of Foucault's work to being inscribed within networks of discourse and discipline that embody and exemplify the regime of truth it challenges," and in refusing to understand Foucault in his own terms, they "arraign Foucault before a rigged court that has prejudged him."[143]

There is a strange sort of revenge taken by Foucault's biographer James Miller in the name of truth. He uses a fictional short story by Hervé Guibert, "The Secrets of a Man," as if it contains true confessions by Foucault, concluding:

> The "obligation of truth," it seems, really was Foucault's unavoidable fate. . . . Try as he might, the philosopher could not remain silent about who he really was. That is why *all* of Foucault's books, from the first to the last, comprise a kind of involuntary memoir, an implicit confession. And that is why, for all of the "games" that Foucault confessed to playing in these books, they express at least one serious and irrefutable truth—the truth about himself. The self that he spent a lifetime trying to unriddle, renounce, and reinvent, he was never quite able to escape.[144]

Who can miss the relish taken in this revenge in the name of confessional truth? Or, the sense of *inevitability* to this irrefutable, involuntary, implicit confession? Using the rhetoric of coming out (he could not remain silent about who he really was, the truth about himself which he could not renounce), Miller turns Foucault into someone whom it is hard for his readers to recognize as the author of *The History of Sexuality.* Indeed, never has Foucault's phrase "one confesses — or is forced to confess" seemed more apt.[145]

We can also see this operation in the film *Factory Girl* (2006), which, even while it recognizes Warhol's incongruity in the confessional booth, tries to force a confession out of him (for the ruination of Edie Sedgwick).[146] Like Miller, Bob Colacello thinks he is being sympathetic when he explains to *A&E Biography* that although Warhol's affectless, opaque smile worked well for publicity and art, "you can't live your life that way."[147] Debray, in a similarly sympathetic revenge, celebrates the sentimental Barthes in opposition to the great semiologist Barthes, noting that "*Fragments of a Lover's Discourse* or *Camera Lucida* do not seem really to draw from the same wellsprings as the *Elements of Semiology* or *The System of Fashion.* As if whatever depth was contained in the aesthete's humours came to underscore what was superficial in the rigor of the 'scientist.'"[148] Yet while he notes that "it is no slight paradox that these enemies of the ineffable and emotion [Barthes and Eco] owed their brightest prestige, as it turned out, to *literary* ineffableness and emotion," Debray sees this gentle subversion as "perhaps indeed the extreme of elegance, the height of tact and irony."[149]

What then, finally, is the role of the interlocutor in these discursive arenas — the biographer, the interviewer, the critic? Herman Melville (or is it Bartleby's despairing, would-be biographer?) claims, "Nothing so aggravates an earnest person as a passive resistance."[150] We might ask how and why the earnest quality of the interrogator or biographer seems to be resisted by the subjects I am treating here. The difficult role "identification" plays in instances of writing on these opaque subjects also forms an important part of my discussion. If I have chosen not to foreground my personal identifications with these figures (as much as this has been an effective strategy for feminist and queer scholars), it is out of a skepticism regarding the way in which this earnest personalizing might paradoxically function to shield my arguments from criticism. (As Nietzsche put it: "Some people throw a bit of their personality after their bad arguments, as if that might straighten their paths and turn them into right and good arguments — just as a man in a bowling alley, after he has let go of the ball, still tries to direct it with gestures.")[151] I would instead insist that identification with opaque figures could only function in terms of identification with their strategies or tactics. For example, I agree with Barthes's tactic in interviews of insisting that it is after all not up to him to analyze his own unconscious.

Concerning this precarious identification with an author's practice (rather than value), Barthes clarifies that he does not wish to compare himself to Proust: "*Proust and I*. How pretentious! Nietzsche spared no irony about the Germans' use of that conjunction: 'Schopenhauer *and* Hartmann,' he jeered. 'Proust and I' is worse still."[152] He clarifies that in *"identifying [himself] with him,"* he is not "projecting" onto a character or a person, but rather he identifies with Proust's desire to write. He identifies with a modest worker and a divided subject who must choose between writing a commentary (an interpretation) or an affabulation that is capable of thinking incidents.[153]

Each of the following chapters will include a critique of previous treatments of their subject by critics and biographers. My hope is to examine the benefits and pitfalls of different approaches depending on their relation to the problem of opacity. I will often draw attention to the ways in which a paradigm or metaphor has been deployed to make sense of a figure despite the resistance to that paradigm or metaphor expressed by the subject himself. Thus, for instance, the figure of the confessional as used to treat the subject of Foucault's biography, or repression to examine the writings of Roland Barthes, or hidden psychological motivation to analyze Andy Warhol.

While I engage with psychoanalytic theory at certain points in this work—since Barthes and Foucault were both in direct dialogue with Freudian and Lacanian theory, and they also made conscious efforts to reject the scientific normativity of psychoanalysis—I concur with Halperin's and Didier Eribon's recent critiques of the theoretical dominance of psychoanalysis within queer theory, and their desire to locate alternative traditions and discourses for thinking about queer subjectivity.[154] Michael D. Snediker also criticizes the unfortunate preoccupation of psychoanalytic queer theory with a limited range of negative affects (melancholia, self-shattering, and death drive).[155] While I appreciate Snediker's critique of queer theory's embrace of "self-shattering," I am still invested in versions of this found in Foucault and Guibert. However, what I find remarkable is that the self-displacement I find in Warhol and Barthes is not quite so angst ridden; it does not perhaps deserve the name "self-shattering" but is best described by Barthes as a self that is "dispersed," "inconsistent," and "drifting," as I discuss in chapters 3 and 4.

While I attempt to take each writer "at his word," I will also try to point out the ironies implicit in this ethical practice when applied to figures who render concepts of "agency" and "authorial intention" so relative and in some cases irrelevant (since they each see the subject as an effect of language rather than as a locus of intentionality). Therefore, I will also show how the public personas of Foucault, Barthes, and Warhol are the results of mediation and collaboration, some of which is inevitably involuntary and posthumous (as is the case for Foucault and Guibert, discussed in chapter 1).

If my approach is motivated by its own sort of hermeneutics of suspicion, it is a suspicion of the epistemological privilege maintained by those who purport to uncover the secret of someone's sexual identity (biographers, straight and gay).[156] Halperin has aptly characterized the convolutions of the epistemology of the closet as follows: "If you can never be in the closet, you can't ever be out of it either, because those who have once enjoyed the epistemological privilege constituted by their knowledge of your ignorance of their knowledge typically refuse to give up that privilege, and insist on constructing your sexuality as a secret to which they have special access, a secret which always gives itself away to their superior and knowing gaze."[157] Thus, constructing sexuality as a secret maintains the privileges and pleasures of closet knowledge and indeed preserves the closet. My interest in queer appropriations of the diary format has to do with their ironic relation to this structure of secrecy and the contradictions of public and private. As Cecily in Wilde's *The Importance of Being Earnest* explains: "I keep a diary in order to enter the wonderful secrets of my life. If I didn't write them down I should probably forget all about them."[158] When Algernon asks to look in her diary, she refuses, because, "You see, it is simply a very young girl's record of her own thoughts and impressions, and consequently meant for publication."[159] Many of the diary-type works I will be examining were indeed published: Andy Warhol's as *The Andy Warhol Diaries*, Hervé Guibert's *To the Friend Who Did Not Save My Life* and *Le Mausolée des amants, Journal 1976–1991*, and Roland Barthes's *Incidents*.[160] Reading these works as if they give away their authors' secrets, as if against their will, is specious and clearly preserves the privileges of knowingness and actually maintains the closet. If outing oneself (or another) is a performative utterance, then doesn't it follow that asserting that someone was/is closeted is equally performative in its effects?[161]

On the Surface

Barthes indicated in his "Inaugural Lecture" that a "speech-system is defined less by what it permits us to say than by what it compels us to say."[162] Writing this book, especially when dealing with Andy Warhol, I have found it difficult to negotiate the pitfalls of what Rey Chow has called the "ideology of depth."[163] The values accorded to depth—to "profound" and "deep" meaning—are difficult to contradict, and seem built into what counts as a truly intellectual endeavor. I am inspired by Chow's effort to resist both the Repressive Hypothesis and the "deep habits" of intellectual and ideology criticism.[164] This is not an easy argument to make, however, as I have had to catch myself from slipping into these habitual reflexes of language (what Barthes calls "doxa")—using words like "uncover," "reveal," "deeply," "profoundly"—so as not to align myself with those who dismiss Warhol as "shallow" or who defend him by arguing that there is really a hidden intelligence and deep motive driving his work (as in: "he can't possibly mean that there was just a surface reason for doing what he did"—again subscribing to the very criteria by which Warhol was invalidated). Unlike Chow, I am not always translating, per se, but I have often felt as if I were, in trying to find the right words, one of which for me is "opacity." I am also indebted to Barthes's frequent translator Richard Howard, whose care in translating Barthes's texts, especially on the issue of the "suspension" or "exemption" of meaning, has greatly informed my own discussion of how this is not the same as "repression."

Like Chow, Stephen Best and Sharon Marcus make an argument for "surface reading" as an alternative to the dominant mode of "symptomatic reading" advanced by psychoanalysis and Marxism, a form of interpretation that "took meaning to be hidden, repressed, deep, and in need of detection and disclosure by an interpreter."[165] In opposition to this way of reading, they explain that "a surface is what insists on being looked at rather than what we must train ourselves to see through."[166] Surface reading, or what Marcus has called "just reading," therefore, "refuses the depth model of truth, which dismisses surfaces as inessential and deceptive."[167]

Best and Marcus contrast Sedgwick's early reading of "a text's silences, gaps, style, tone, and imagery" as symptoms of the queerness "absent only apparently from its pages" in *Epistemology of the Closet* with her later work on "reparative reading."[168] They also distance themselves from a paranoid reading of repressed meaning, proposing that the surface is rather "what is neither hidden nor hiding," and pointing to an emerging interest in "literal readings that take texts at face value."[169] They highlight how Marcus's "just reading" of female friendship in Victorian novels "highlights something true and visible on the text's surface that symptomatic reading had ironically rendered invisible," and how Best's study of first-person testimony by Caribbean slaves reads their words as they appear, as impossible speech that oscillates between "confession and coercion," noting how "attention to the rumors on the surface of the archive challenges our conception of the latter as a repository of latent voices and 'hidden transcripts.'"[170] They argue that "these understandings of what one can learn from surfaces resonate with a rarely cited statement Foucault made about his relationship to archives."[171] Here they refer to an interview on *The Archaeology of Knowledge* in which Foucault explains what he means by the *archive:* "the set of discourses actually pronounced; and this set of discourses . . . continues to function, to be transformed through history, and to provide the possibility of appearing in other discourses."[172] Foucault says that the term "archaeology" bothers him a bit, since he is skeptical of both the search for foundations/beginnings (the Greek *arché*)[173] and the idea of excavation: "What I'm looking for are not relations that are secret, hidden, more silent or deeper than the consciousness of men.

I try on the contrary to define the relations on the very surface of discourse; I attempt to make visible what is invisible only because it's too much on the surface of things."[174] This resonates with my own approach to archives, beginning with the Foucault archive and the critical problem of whether to approach his work and his life in terms of secret or hidden relations or, instead, those on the very surface of discourse.

ONE

Confessions of a Masked Philosopher
Anonymity and Identification in Foucault and Guibert

Hence I cannot give you what I thought I was writing for you—that is what I must acknowledge: the amorous dedication is impossible (I shall not be satisfied with a worldly or mundane signature, pretending to dedicate to you a work which escapes us both). The operation in which the other is to be engaged is not a signature. It is, more profoundly, an inscription. . . . [I]n [Pasolini's] Teorema the "other" does not speak, but he inscribes something within each of those who desire him—he performs what the mathematicians call a catastrophe (the disturbance of one system by another): it is true that this mute figure is an angel.

—Roland Barthes, "The Dedication," *A Lover's Discourse: Fragments*

Betrayal, theft, and homosexuality are the basic subjects of this book. There is a relationship among them which, though not always apparent, at least, it seems to me, recognizes a kind of vascular exchange between my taste for betrayal and theft and my loves.

—Jean Genet, *The Thief's Journal*

IN ONE OF THE MANY DIALOGUES with a fictional interlocutor in the works of Michel Foucault, in this case *The Archaeology of Knowledge*, Foucault addresses critical suspicions regarding his "moveable thought":

"Are you already preparing the way out that will enable you in your next book to spring up somewhere else and declare as you're now doing: no, no, I'm not where you are lying in wait for me, but over here, laughing at you?"

"What, do you imagine that I would take so much trouble and so much pleasure in writing, do you think that I would keep so persistently to my task, if I were not preparing—with a rather shaky hand—a labyrinth into which I can venture . . . in which I can lose myself and appear at last to eyes that I will never have to meet again. I am no doubt not the only one who writes in order to have no face. Do not ask who I am and do not ask me to remain the same: leave it to our bureaucrats and our police to see that our papers are in order. At least spare us their morality when we write."[1]

Many of Foucault's biographers find here the irony of Foucault's fame, yet his desire for anonymity. (Here, Foucault no doubt references Maurice Blanchot, as perhaps the most famously "faceless" French writer.) Against a writing style that seems self-effacing, they attempt to put a face to the name Foucault, to undertake the difficult task of locating Foucault's "identification papers." This *morality* of writing stands in opposition to Foucault's reference to eyes he will never have to meet again: this is a text that *cruises* us.[2] This morality is met with Foucault's famous laughter. This laughter is a prominent feature in many Foucault biographies, such as James Miller's *The Passion of Michel Foucault*, as well as in the works of Foucault's friends Hervé Guibert and Gilles Deleuze (both of whom have expressed the difficulty of transcribing Foucault's laugh).[3] These accounts vary in terms of how they present and invoke the more "personal" Foucault. As Eleanor Kaufman has pointed out: "With respect to this 'personal' Foucault, it is interesting to note the prodigious industry of Foucault biographies. In contrast to the overwhelming surplus of details that these biographies provide, the details that Deleuze proffers—and they are generally the same gestural tracings (the eyes, the voice, the laugh) repeated over and over again—seem paradoxically more revelatory. . . . While the biographies would present a Foucault laid bare, Deleuze presents a Foucault who haunts."[4] This laughter also haunts Hervé Guibert in his roman à clef, *To the Friend Who Did Not Save My Life*, in which the narrator describes his relationship to a fictionalized version of Foucault named "Muzil," and recounts Muzil's death from AIDS-related illness.[5] (When Hervé tells Muzil about this "famous disease," "My friend fell off the sofa in a paroxysm of laughter. 'A cancer that would hit only homosexuals, no, that's too good to be true, I could just die laughing!' As it happened, Muzil was already infected with the retrovirus.")[6] One passage recalls the night of his death when Hervé watches a rerun clip from an intellectual television show *Apostrophes*,[7] of one huge, endless fit of Muzil's laughter:

> literally cracking up at a moment when everyone expected him to be as serious as the pope and pontificate about one of the tenets of his subversive history of behavior, and that burst of hilarity warmed my heart at a time when I though it had turned to ice. . . . That was the last tape of Muzil I ever watched, for since then I have refused, from fear of the pain it would cause me, to face any other images of his presence, save those of dreams, and his great shout of laughter, which I've preserved forever in freeze frame.[8]

This ambivalent affective documentation—one of many "freeze frame" moments in Guibert's book—can be productively juxtaposed against what Kaufman rightly identifies as the prodigious industry of Foucault biographies.

James Miller's biography *The Passion of Michel Foucault* is an exhaustive account of the details of Foucault's life, but in particular his sexuality and his alleged obsession with madness and death (an obsession perhaps more properly attributable to Miller himself). In his preface, Miller justifies his biographical project and acknowledges the dilemma of "trying to write a narrative account of someone . . . who raised the gravest doubts about the character of personal identity as such; someone who, as a matter of temperament, distrusted prying questions and naked honesty; someone, finally, who was nevertheless inclined to see his own work as, on some level, autobiographical."[9] Miller here reduces Foucault's quite studied rejection of confessional discourse to a matter of temperament and implicitly justifies what will be his own reading of Foucault's theoretical work as autobiographical. While he claims that Foucault spoke frankly about his exploration of "the esoteric form of sado-masochistic eroticism," Miller wonders whether in writing his biography he "was behaving like some not-so-Grand Inquisitor."[10] He explains that "that was not the end of the problems raised by telling the truth": AIDS also entered into the story, "casting a pall over every page I wrote, giving this life a twist that was not at all the twist that I would have hoped for."[11] Here again we see the force of narrative for Miller, and his investment in telling the truth. Miller is at pains to justify his project: "Despite the many dangers, of scandal and reductionism, of unconscious stereotyping and prurient sensationalism . . . I have gone ahead, and tried to tell the whole truth, as best I could."[12] In a shocking footnote, Miller claims, "That it is worth struggling for objectivity (problematic though this ideal obviously is) I take to be confirmed by the modern experience with unchecked myth-mongering: for example, in Russia between 1917 and 1989; and in Germany under Hitler."[13] Thus, implicitly, to tell the truth about Foucault, against all odds, is a *heroic* (and supposedly antidictatorial) project.

Thus, an ethical problem confronts those who write about Foucault in a biographical way. This problem is often put in terms of a *betrayal*. For example, David Halperin considers his book *Saint Foucault: Towards a Gay Hagiography* as an intervention in the discourses surrounding Foucault, and it features an extended analysis and denunciation of Miller's biography. In his brilliantly titled chapter "The Describable Life of Michel Foucault," Halperin focuses in on the postscript to Miller's book, in which Miller explains the reasons he felt drawn to write about Foucault's life and sexuality. Halperin explains:

> It is the evident determination to *appear* ingenuous that compromises Miller's attitude of candor and suggests that the purpose behind his abandonment of authorial invisibility in the postscript is not in fact to disclose 'the truth' about his obsession with Foucault so much as to construct a cover for the motives that actuated the writing of his biography—and thereby to safeguard the invisibility and objectivity of his authorial persona. Miller's confession of the secret of his interest in the details of Foucault's sexual practices, far from clarifying the nature of his personal and political investments in the project of describing them, seems carefully staged so as to betray signs of what can finally be interpreted only as his own cluelessness.[14]

Halperin analyzes Miller's gesture of saying he knew *less than virtually nothing* about sadomasochistic practices for how it functions to shield Miller from scrutiny. Halperin juxtaposes this with another text that "deals with the problem of specifying the gay identity of a dead French theorist": D. A. Miller's *Bringing Out Roland Barthes*.[15] By contrast, D. A. Miller highlights his own personal, political, and erotic investments in writing about Roland Barthes's homosexuality within the complex, self-reflexive prose of *Bringing Out Roland Barthes* (about which I will have more to say in the following chapter). Halperin's own technique for refusing authorial invisibility is by beginning his own book with the revelation of a complex identification with Foucault, writing for "those who feel ourselves to be in Foucault's embattled position, or who share his political vision."[16] Echoing Sartre's claim in *Saint Genet* (in fact echoing Flaubert), Halperin declares, "In short, *Michel Foucault, c'est moi.*"[17]

But I am rather uneasy with such a gesture, the way in which it consumes the other into the self, thus cannibalizing it.[18] Yet Halperin clearly establishes a strategic identification with Foucault's positionality and politics. I appreciate Halperin's attention to the issue of authorial invisibility (especially as it bears on the example of Melville's narrator discussed in my preface). He is right to note the way in which authorial gestures of self-disclosure are not always invitations to scrutinize the author's motives, but can in fact function as disavowals and reinstatements of objectivity.

In contrast to these accounts of Foucault's position as a gay thinker who died from AIDS-related illness, Hervé Guibert's fictionalized representation of Foucault in his character "Muzil" in *To the Friend Who Did Not Save My Life* poses a possible challenge to traditional forms of biography (Miller), "hagiography" (Halperin), and autobiography (Guibert's account of Foucault and his own experience of seropositivity and AIDS takes the form of a "journal"). In each of these works, the problem of Foucault's sexuality, his "private" and "public" life, his interest in the possibility of anonymity, and his resistance to confessional modes of discourse is articulated and grappled with differently. Unlike other biographical works, Guibert's is faced with a crisis of representation and self-presentation (biography and autobiography) brought about by the AIDS crisis. Guibert's text is unique in that it is at the same time a biography and an autobiography (or—more precisely—*autofiction*) of death from AIDS.[19]

Muzil

In ways that are significantly different from both Miller and Halperin, Guibert's narrator is painfully aware of each instance of betrayal in his relation to Muzil. When he visits Muzil in the hospital, he takes notes on their conversations and the details of Muzil's gestures:

> This daily activity relieved and disgusted me; I knew that Muzil would have been so hurt if he had known I was writing reports of everything like a spy, like an adversary, all those degrading little things in my diary, which was perhaps destined

(that was the worst of it) to survive him, to bear witness to a truth he would have liked to erase around the periphery of his life, to leave only the well-polished bare bones enclosing the black diamond—gleaming and impenetrable, closely guarding its secrets—that seemed destined to form his biography, a real conundrum chock-full of errors from end to end.[20]

I wish to draw attention to the way in which the diary bears "witness to a truth" that is in fact considered degrading and peripheral to the stunning metaphor of the "black diamond" of Muzil/Foucault's biography. Is documenting these facts an alternative to this conundrum of errors, or a betrayal of Muzil's wishes? Both James Miller and Guibert are obsessed with the notion of the impenetrable, secretive biography and its errors, but in his "search for truth" Miller seems unaware of the affective significance and ambivalence of betrayal. Betrayal is at one and the same time relieving and disgusting; its affective register encompasses both pleasure and shame. At another point, the narrator kisses Muzil's hand in the hospital, then washes his lips "with a feeling of shame and relief":

> I was so ashamed and relieved that I got out my diary to make an entry, just as I had after all my other visits. But I felt even more ashamed and relieved after describing this nasty gesture. What right did I have to record all that? What right did I have to use friendship in such a mean fashion? And with someone I adored with all my heart? And then I sensed—it's extraordinary—a kind of vision, or vertigo, that gave me complete authority, putting me in charge of these ignoble transcripts and legitimizing them by revealing to me (so it was what's called a premonition, a powerful presentiment) that I was completely entitled to do this since it wasn't so much my friend's last agony I was describing as it was my own, which was waiting for me and would be just like his, for it was now clear that besides being bound by friendship, we would share this same fate in death.[21]

Here, the love for a friend does not exclude the ambivalence of betrayal, as in Genet's books (*Querelle*, for instance),[22] it is only at the most shameful of moments (moments of betrayal) that love and complicity are revealed, though we should not miss the thoroughly Catholic tonality of this Judas's kiss. Like Miller's preface, here we find an elaborate justification of his authority and right to record, and Guibert was often asked by the press after the publication of his book what right he had to recount Foucault's "last agony." On Guibert's own appearance on *Apostrophes*, the host Bernard Pivot cites the above passage and says "c'est terrible d'écrire ça" ("it's terrible to write that"), and Guibert freely agrees "oui, c'est terrible" ("Yes, it's terrible").[23] He acknowledges that keeping the journal was truly a kind of betrayal, and that Foucault would have been furious. But he defends his writing, claiming: (1) that it is not as if Foucault was a "closet queen" (significantly using the English argot), and that to maintain privacy about Foucault's death is a form of hypocrisy; (2) that when he keeps a journal it is so that he can *forget,* that he writes in order to forget; and (3) that writing in the journal about Foucault's "last agony" was like a vision of his "propre destin" ("own destiny") and his "propre mort" ("own death"). As was the case in Halperin, in some ways this represents an eclipsing of the other by the self, but this familiar mode of identification does not account for the *vertigo,* the premonition of that which awaits him. The notion of a shared fate in death intersects with the documentary impulse in a form reminiscent of the AIDS documentary/ video-diary *Silverlake Life: The View from Here* (1993), in which the two men who nurse one another share both illness and the space of the documentary.[24] However, like *Silverlake Life,* this is not a synchronized sharing, which is both painful and inevitable, and produces a sort of *vertigo of identification.*

Later in the novel, the narrator and his friend and lover Jules (another character whom the narrator sees as sharing the fate of seropositivity) go to get anonymously tested by Médecins du Monde. They see

> one boy come out again absolutely in shock, as though the sidewalk on the Boulevard Saint Marcel had actually opened beneath his feet and the earth had whirled around him in a flash, leaving him no longer certain either where to go or what to do with his life, paralyzed by the news written all over his face, which he lifted suddenly to heaven, where no answer appeared. It was a terrifying vision for Jules and me, which projected us one week into the future, and at the same time relieved us by showing us the worst that could happen, as though we were living it at the same time, precipitously, second-hand, a cheap exorcism at the expense of that poor wretch.[25]

This passage both underscores and complicates the notion of shared fate as it relates to Muzil: again there is relief and shame in witnessing another's agony, again a vertigo at the world whirling around the boy who has an *atheistic epiphany* at the moment of diagnosis (almost a cliché of AIDS narrative). This is vertigo at the precipice of precipitous vision. However, here the identification is revealed as a cheap exorcism at the expense of another.

The most painful aspect of the narrator's relieving and disgusting practice of keeping a diary is the way in which the diary will survive Muzil after his death. Thus, Guibert expresses his own affective ambivalence about the journal-within-a-journal: "I'm probably leaving some things out, but I've no desire to look in that diary now, five years later, since I'd rather spare myself the pain of being nastily reminded of this sad time in such vivid detail."[26] This sentence indicates both the document and its erasure, juxtaposing the vivid detail (the diary in which not the slightest word, gesture, or detail was left out) with another journal in which some things are left out. As Guibert told the host of *Apostrophes*, returning to the journal was almost too painful. And the journal is for Guibert a way to forget. On another television appearance after the publication of *The Compassion Protocol*,[27] on the program *Ex libris*,[28] Guibert tells the host Patrick Poivre D'Arvor that he never rereads his books, that in particular he does not have the courage to reread *To the Friend Who Did Not Save My Life* "parce que c'est le sida" ("Because it is AIDS"). Jean-Pierre Boulé, in a discussion of Guibert's video autoportrait *La Pudeur ou l'Impudeur* (1990–91),[29] reveals that Guibert says he never viewed any of the more than ten hours of film that he recorded, "Once *La Pudeur ou l'Impudeur* had been completed, he had no desire to see the film; nor did he insist that the film be broadcast in his lifetime. This was by no means a new attitude on his part, and the concept of exorcism is the key to an understanding of his work."[30] Exorcism is therefore a crucial function of Guibert's writing.

Thus, significantly, the journal that betrays Muzil's opacity (the black diamond, around which everything else must be erased) itself anticipates its own erasure, and we are presented only with the opacity of the narrator's novel. To complicate matters further, the journal is almost always a fictional form (a literary copy of a copy, as Barthes revealed in his essay for *Tel Quel*, "Deliberation").[31] While Guibert indicates that there indeed was such a diary, it is still made into fiction. Boulé explains, "In fact, all Guibert's work springs from his private diary, from which he sometimes transferred passages to his books. In *Le Protocol Compassionel*, he says: 'C'est quand ce que j'écris prend la forme d'une journal que j'ai la plus grande impression de fiction' ['It is when what I write takes the form of a journal that I have the greatest impression of fiction.'].[32] The posthumous publication of Guibert's *Le Mausolée des amants, Journal 1976–1991* further complicates this productive indeterminacy.

In his book *Death and the Labyrinth: The World of Raymond Roussel*, Foucault puzzles over the curious fact that "Roussel, whose language is extremely precise, said that *How I Wrote Certain of My Books* was a 'secret and posthumous text.' No doubt he meant several things other than the obvious meaning, which is secret until death: that death was a ritual part of the secret, its prepared threshold and its solemn exclusion . . . or even better, death would reveal that there is a secret without showing what it hides, only what makes it *opaque* and *impenetrable*."[33] This "perplexing indiscretion" is at the heart of Guibert's own project in paradoxically revealing that which is most impenetrable and opaque about Muzil, after his death, and Guibert's book is paradoxically also a "secret and posthumous text" in taking part in the *ritual of secrecy* itself.

There are then several texts at play in this novel. At least one other book is gestured to within *To the Friend Who Did Not Save My Life*: "I'd given my editor a manuscript in which I admitted I was ill, and an item like that, falling into the hands of an editor like him, would race around town—under the seal of secrecy—like wildfire, which I expected, calmly and with a kind of indifference, because it was only natural to betray my secrets, since I'd always done that in all my books, even though his genie could never be stuffed back into its bottle, and I would never again be a part of the human community."[34] Following D. A. Miller's definition, knowledge of the illness acts as an "open secret" that circulates under the seal of secrecy.[35] This form of betrayal is in some senses more familiar; as Guibert notes, it is the *modus operandi* of all of his books, such as the staged *familiar* confessional/betrayal of *My Parents*.[36] But this betrayal of oneself as one betrays another is uncannily present in all gay biography; both Halperin and D. A. Miller acknowledge this in their books (D. A. Miller claims that any gay knowledge he produces about Barthes will be *of them both*);[37] James Miller stands out for precisely this reason.

Guibert has explained in an interview that "every book carries with it a crime. . . . I am very upset when the time comes to dedicate my books: each time they betray secrets, and these secrets are not only mine. To write is to betray, to commit a crime."[38] Leo Bersani has much to say about betrayal in the works of Jean Genet—and the connections between betrayal, mourning, and homosexuality—which speaks to Guibert's situation. Bersani claims that "*betrayal is an ethical necessity.* This difficult and repugnant truth is bound to be the major stumbling block for anyone interested in Jean Genet."[39] Bersani argues that Genet betrays his lover in *Funeral Rites* as a way to refuse conventional forms of mourning. But to view betrayal as an original act of mourning risks "ethical kitsch," and Bersani takes his argument further in an attempt to explain the relationship between betrayal and homosexuality in Genet: "Much more interesting is how betrayal is inscribed within homosexual love itself."[40] Betrayal allows Genet to not simply invert the social hierarchy that sees both homosexuality and betrayal as negative and shameful (which would be simple resignification, following Sartre's argument in *Saint Genet*), but to reject society itself (including the entire field of the transgressive). Bersani argues that Genet imagines a kind of "nonrelational betrayal" that allows him solitude from the social injunction of heterosociality.[41] Guibert, like Genet, might be seen as using betrayal to refuse conventional forms of mourning. But Guibert's book is also, following Bersani, a radical refusal of social positioning. Guibert writes his book in a desire for solitude:

> I'm alone here and they feel sorry for me, they worry about me, they think I'm not taking good care of myself, so these friends . . . telephone me regularly, compassionately, me—a man who has just discovered that he doesn't like his fellow men, no, I definitely don't like them, I rather hate them instead, and this would explain everything, that stubborn hatred I've always felt, and I'm beginning a new book to have a companion, someone with whom I can talk, eat, sleep, at whose side I can dream and have nightmares, the only friend whose company I can bear at present.[42]

It is hard to miss the parallels here to Genet's novels, which act as his companions in prison, at whose side he can dream and have nightmares (especially *Our Lady of the Flowers*).[43] Sartre claimed that "the craft of writing appears first as a means of communication. But Genet began to write in order to affirm his solitude."[44] This also allows us to understand why Guibert sees his books as a way to "never again be a part of the human community."[45] In fact, Guibert's *My Parents* begins with the disinheriting dedication "*To nobody.*"

To dedicate a book involves *the betrayal of secrecy itself.* The closet structure that in some ways rematerializes (or compounds) within discussions of AIDS allows for a limited range of strategies. Guibert claims that "there's a stage in this sickness when keeping it a secret just doesn't matter anymore, it even becomes hateful and burdensome."[46] However, this attitude can be compared to that of Muzil, who did keep the secret until his death, even from his lover Stéphane. Stéphane and Muzil's sister find out that Muzil's illness had been AIDS the day *after* he dies, when they read in the hospital register: "Cause of death: AIDS." Here, as at other moments, Guibert distances his intimate knowledge of Muzil's illness from Stéphane's knowledge of Muzil. What follows is a remarkable "closet" moment: "The sister had demanded that they cross this out, that they blacken it completely, or scratch it out if they had to, or even better, tear out the page and redo it, for while these records are of course confidential, still, you never know, perhaps in ten or twenty years some muckraking biographer will come and Xerox the entry, or X-ray the impression still faintly legible on the next page."[47] This Freudian logic of negation involves an overcanceling: cross, blacken, scratch, tear, for fear of Xerox and X-ray (a cross— "X"—that exposes). This muckraking biographer could be either Guibert or James Miller, neither of whom waited ten years. The secrecy surrounding Muzil's death begs several questions: Is Muzil set up as a strategy not taken by the narrator? Does Muzil's keeping his family in the dark correspond with the narrator's desire not to tell his family, so as to be free from their gaze and their obligation? Whose shame is involved here? Is this a case of shame on Muzil's part, or on the part of his sister?

David Macey, in *The Lives of Michel Foucault* (the plural speaks volumes), explains that during his lifetime,

> Foucault was sometimes criticised for not being more openly gay. . . . In death, he was to be criticised for not "coming out" about his illness. The first French intellectual to "come out" about AIDS was Jean-Paul Aron. . . . Aron comments [on Foucault]: "He was . . . homosexual. He was ashamed of it, but he lived it,

sometimes in demented fashion. His silence in the face of his illness upset me because it was a shameful silence, not the silence of an intellectual. It went quite against everything he had always defended. It seemed ridiculous to me." [. . .] Aron's comments aroused [Foucault's partner Daniel] Defert's anger [. . .] Commenting on Aron's remarks, he said: "Jean-Paul Aron seems to be saying: 'I am speaking because Foucault did not dare to speak.' . . . I shared Foucault's life and moral choices for twenty-three years. If we had, as Aron says, been ashamed of being homosexual, I would never have created AIDES [a major advisory organization for PWAs]."[48]

I quote at length to show how vexed the logic of the closet—with its mantra of a name one must "dare to speak"—becomes when tangled up with AIDS. Jean-Paul Aron claims that to be silent about AIDS is to be ashamed of homosexuality (there are no doubt many instances of this, though Foucault seems a poor example). Daniel Defert's rebuttal is to claim that to speak out about AIDS proves retroactively that one is not ashamed of homosexuality. Aron's comments are from his article for *Le Nouvel Observateur,* which makes conspicuous use of the possessive in its title: "Mon SIDA."[49] Whereas Defert's provocative title probes the queer affect of shame: "Plus on est honteux, plus on avoue."[50] The title might be translated as "The more ashamed one is, the more one admits/claims."

Guibert's book stages many similar confrontations with Defert through his fictionalized representative Stéphane. After Muzil's death, an interaction with Stéphane illuminates Guibert's ambivalence about the documentary impulse. Stéphane, toward whom the narrator reveals a rather jealous contempt, asks Hervé to document Muzil's apartment with his camera:

> Stéphane insisted that I photograph Muzil's bed, which Muzil had never allowed me to see, being always careful to shut the door behind him. . . . Unwillingly, nudged in the back by Stéphane, who saw the scene as a priceless research document, I framed the poor mattress lying on the floor, even though there wasn't enough depth of field and I knew from experience that the picture wouldn't turn out, but the shutter didn't click: no more film. Through that series of photographs—which I never had printed, simply giving Stéphane a copy of the negatives—I freed myself like a magician from what haunted me, by drawing a circle around the ruined stage where my friendship had been played out.[51]

What is most remarkable about this passage is not only its ethical ambivalence (wherein the blame for the documentary impulse is placed on

Stéphane instead of Hervé), but also its "kettle logic." Here I refer to a passage in Sigmund Freud's *The Interpretation of Dreams,* in which he recalls the defense put forward by a man who was charged by one of his neighbors with having given him back a borrowed kettle in damaged condition.[52] The defendant asserted first, that he had given it back undamaged; second, that the kettle had a hole in it when he borrowed it; and third, that he had never borrowed a kettle from his neighbor at all. If a single one of these lines of defense were to be accepted as valid, the man would have to be acquitted. Like Freud's defendant, in Guibert's account a plethora of failures result in no picture being taken, or developed. In "Traces and Shadows," Ralph Sarkonak argues that "Guibert's writing about photography emphasizes the photos that were taken but didn't turn out, the photos that should or could have been taken."[53] Guibert's *Ghost Image* describes a series of such absent, but nonetheless haunting "ghost" images, where "the text would not have existed if the picture had been taken . . . this text is the despair of the image."[54] The above passage is literally a "negative" of the passages confessing the relief and the shame of the diary, and we again find a form of exorcism of the haunting power of Muzil. This bespeaks a recurrent anxiety about documentation (especially the diary and the photograph as posthumous documents) and about representing the unrepresentable.

Guibert concludes, "AIDS will have been my paradigm in my project of self-revelation and the expression of the inexpressible."[55] The expression of the inexpressible is a project that uses AIDS as its paradigm; it is AIDS that has challenged forms of expression and representation. In exploring the connections among the title elements in "AIDS, Homophobia, and Biomedical Discourse," Paula Treichler has argued that "AIDS is a nexus where multiple meanings, stories, and discourses intersect and overlap, reinforce and subvert each other. Yet clearly this mysterious male homosexual text has figured centrally in generating what I call here an *epidemic of signification.*"[56] Within public discourse, the morbid and fatalistic tone I have been employing along with Guibert has been replaced by "People Living with AIDS," but the AIDS crisis has not only caused a crisis in positive and negative *representations of* AIDS, it has brought about a crisis of representation itself. Against the regretful tone of Miller's biography, in which AIDS is a narrative twist that he would not have hoped for, Guibert's book attests to a crisis of narrative itself. There are several different forms of "narrative time" at play in the book. The subject and the object in this book become confused, but never fully eclipse one another in the "totemic" identification of mourning.[57] Thus, Muzil/Foucault is inscribed in the work as a *catastrophe:* not only his death, but also his thought disturbs the system of Guibert's novel.

The Inscription of Michel Foucault

Foucault's thought is engaged in several passages that bring us back to his statement with which I began this chapter. Foucault's facelessness and desire for anonymity find expression in Muzil's conversations with the narrator, which in many ways mirror significant late Foucault interviews. While being "faceless" should not immediately be confused with being "nameless," the two are obviously related, as the face and the name are undoubtedly the two most privileged markers of identity in modern Western culture (they are what our identification papers consist of). The relationship between the two is explicitly addressed in a passage that nonetheless focuses more on the problem of how to be "faceless":

> Just as he was careful, beyond the limits he established for his oeuvre, to erase that name made inordinately famous throughout the world, he tried to make his face invisible, although he was particularly easy to recognize thanks to several distinctive features and the many pictures of him published by the press over the previous decade. Whenever he invited out to dinner one of the few friends he still enjoyed seeing . . . as soon as he entered the restaurant . . . he'd make a beeline for a chair that would allow him both to sit with his back to the other patrons and to avoid facing a mirror. . . . The public would see only the gleaming and self-contained enigma of that skull he took care to shave every morning.[58]

As with the cover of the volume of collected interviews *Foucault Live,* we are presented with an image of the back of Foucault's shaved skull. And perhaps like Roland Barthes's critique of the myth of "The Brain of Einstein" in *Mythologies,* the image of Foucault's head stands in for the enigma of his thought and identity (we see where his thought supposedly occurs, yet we see it from the back, without a face).[59] This fixation on

Foucault's brain is the subject of Guibert's short story "Les secrets d'un homme" ("The Secrets of a Man") in which Guibert imagines the trepanation of a brilliant philosopher and the childhood secrets buried deep within the "polished diamond" of the brain tissue, safe from the imbecility of interpretation.[60] These "secrets" James Miller then cites as reliable biographical anecdotes.[61]

As in Barthes's "Soirées de Paris" in his posthumously published *Incidents,* we find here a desire for anonymity felt by the writer in Paris: the small circle of friends, the desire not to be identified as a famous author, a certain sympathy with Maurice Blanchot. James Miller has noticed the irony of Foucault's desire to be like Blanchot. Miller explains that Blanchot created a mystique by

> making a fetish of anonymity. He permitted no photographs of himself to circulate. He never lectured or read his work in public. He granted no interviews, though he did make a habit of "interviewing" himself. Foucault found Blanchot's mystique irresistible. "At the time, I dreamt of being Blanchot," he confided to one friend years later. A close student of Blanchot's critical theories, he also studied his rhetoric, using the device of "interviewing" himself in his book *Raymond Roussel* and also at the end of *The Archaeology of Knowledge.* In a touching homage to the faceless author, he even turned down an invitation to meet Blanchot over dinner, remarking to Daniel Defert that he knew the writing—and had no need to know the writer.[62]

But both Barthes and Foucault declined Blanchot's strategy of nonpublicity. Barthes, in an interview with Pierre Boncenne, addresses the problem of the interview itself:

> Generally speaking, I don't enjoy interviews, and at one point I wanted to stop giving them. I had even decided upon a kind of "last interview." And then I realized that this was an excessive attitude: the interview belongs, to put it casually, to an inescapable social game, or, to put it more seriously, to a solidarity of intellectual work between writers and the media. . . . Now, why don't I enjoy interviews? The basic reason has to do with my ideas on the relationship between speech and writing. I love writing. I love speech only within a very specific framework, one that I establish myself, for example in a seminar, or in a course. I'm always uneasy when speech is used somehow to repeat writing, because then I have an impression of uselessness: I could not say what I want to say any better than by writing it. . . . That's the essential reason for my reticence. There is another reason that has more to do with the mood of an interview: . . . very

often, you know, in interviews for the major media, a somewhat sadistic relationship is established between the interviewer and the interviewee, where it's a question of ferreting out some kind of truth from the latter by asking aggressive or indiscreet questions to get a reaction out of him. . . . Your question brings to mind a general study that has yet to be made, one that I have always wanted to take as the subject of a course: a vast schematic analysis of the activities of contemporary intellectual life.[63]

Like Barthes, Foucault did not refuse to do interviews, and perhaps better than Barthes, he used his interviews to say things that his books did not (it is difficult to say whether Guibert achieves this or not; like Barthes, he often seems to quote himself in interviews). The many interviews in *Foucault Live* are indeed a testimony to Foucault's attention to the specific opportunity of the interview (an opportunity to say something *other than* his books, see especially his actual appearance on *Apostrophes,* in which—as Guibert noted—he refuses to "pontificate about one of the tenets of his subversive history" of sexuality). Also, an attitude of friendship governs many of the interviews Foucault gave to the gay press, though he is careful not to use his name to plot out any sort of program for gay liberation and often uses these interviews to question the assumed goals of gay liberation. James Miller explains that it was only after 1978 that Foucault began to comment on the culture and politics of the gay community directly, and claims that "by speaking out on such matters, he was, in effect, 'coming out'—belatedly, perhaps, but also decisively."[64] While I am uneasy with this application of the discourse of "the closet" to Foucault (as he himself was ambivalent about such a politics of sexual identity), Miller is helpful in his chronology of the relationship between North American and French gay political organizing (the Gay Liberation Front and the Front Homosexuel d'Action Révolutionnaire) and the formation of a gay press.[65] He quotes Jean Le Bitoux, who in 1979 founded the gay journal *Gai Pied:* "'Foucault and I often discussed his reservations about the problematic necessity of "coming out," Le Bitoux has recalled. 'These personal reservations never stopped Foucault from fighting for gay rights'—or for [*sic*] helping Le Bitoux launch *Gai Pied,*" which Foucault named.[66] Miller explains that in its first issue, "*Gai Pied* featured a short essay by Foucault. And in 1981, the magazine published a longer interview, billed as 'A Conversation with a Fifty-year-old Reader,' who is otherwise unnamed—though, at the end, his interlocutors discreetly say, 'Thank you, Michel Foucault.'"[67]

Anonymity and facelessness are strategies that allow for particular experiences and possibilities. Miller is perhaps not wrong in placing an emphasis on Foucault's interest in San Francisco gay bathhouses as a space of experimentation with desubjectification. Foucault explained to Jean Le Bitoux: "I think that it is politically important that sexuality is able to function as it functions in the bathhouses. You meet men there who are to you as you are to them: nothing but a body with which combinations and productions of pleasure are possible. You cease to be imprisoned in your own face, in your own past, in your own identity."[68] William Haver has suggested that Foucault's "disappearance" in the *Archaeology* quote with which I began points to the possibility of a "coincidence of a destitute being-in-common of whatever singularities with the vulnerable, anonymous encounters of erotic nomads. This would constitute what counts as disappearance . . . in Foucault, not as a sacrificial invisibility in a communitarian aesthetic sublime, but as an aesthetic from within which, and as which, the figure of the ethico-perverse might appear."[69] These erotic possibilities are also critical possibilities; anonymity affords specific possibilities for the author in the space of the interview.

The absence of the name in the interview becomes a much more central problematic in an interview for *Le Monde* conducted by Christian Delacampagne in which Foucault opted for the mask of anonymity: "The Masked Philosopher."[70] Even the phrase "the mask of anonymity" reveals the confusion between the face and the name. Foucault explains: "Why did I suggest that we use anonymity? Out of nostalgia for a time when, being quite unknown, what I said had some chance of being heard. . . . A name makes reading too easy."[71] But Foucault's interview is remarkably un-nostalgic and unpolemical regarding the supposed problems of publishing, the media, and the situation of intellectuals suggested by the interviewer. Foucault responds: "I've met a lot of people who talk about 'the intellectual.' And, listening to them, I've got some idea of what such an animal could be. It's not difficult—he's quite personified. He's guilty of pretty well everything: of speaking out and keeping silent, of doing nothing and of getting involved in everything. . . . In short, the intellectual is raw material for a verdict, a sentence, a condemnation, an exclusion."[72] This astute observation of the double binds inherent in being a public intellectual marks the dilemma of "speaking out and keeping silent" and is remarkably in line with Barthes's predicament (Barthes acknowledges that he is a "*sensitive, avid and silent* political subject [these adjectives must not be separated]" but that "All my life, politically, I have given myself a bad time").[73] However, against this juridical, condemnatory, or critical tone, Foucault's statements are quite optimistic and affirmative of the necessity of philosophy and the positive value of "curiosity." For Foucault, curiosity evokes "a readiness to find what surrounds us strange and odd; a certain determination to throw off familiar ways of thought and to look at the same things in a different way."[74] This is then linked to his definition of philosophy as "the displacement and transformation of frameworks of thinking, the changing of received values and all the work that has been done to think otherwise, to do something else, to become other than what one is."[75] The work of thinking otherwise, of reconceptualizing a framework of thinking, of working in the midst of uncertainty, is also evoked in Foucault's introduction and conclusion to *The Archaeology of Knowledge* and his introduction to volume 2 of his *History of Sexuality, The Use of Pleasure.* In the latter, a segment entitled "Modifications," Foucault explains: "As for what motivated me, it is quite simple. . . . It was curiosity—the only kind of curiosity, in any case, that is worth acting upon with any degree of obstinacy: not the curiosity that seeks to assimilate what is proper for one to know, but that which enables one to get free of oneself."[76] This introduction explains the gap between the first and second volumes of *The History of Sexuality,* in which Foucault felt he had to undertake a theoretical shift, a recentering of his study, turning from modernity to antiquity, in order to analyze "the games of truth in the relationship of self to self and the forming of oneself as a subject."[77]

Foucault recognized the risks in upsetting the publication schedule he had projected, and Guibert incorporates this anxiety over Foucault's potentially endless book into his own equally anxious, potentially endless book, which he fears is closing in on him.[78] In a passage that echoes the labyrinthine opening of *The Archaeology of Knowledge,* Guibert explains:

He'd announced the titles of the following four books . . . committed to the first
section of a project for which he has drawn up the plans, designed the framework
and vaults, sketched the connecting passageways and areas of shadow, following
the rules of a system that has already proven its value in his previous books and
won him his international reputation, he's now struck with boredom, or some
terrible misgiving. Everything comes to a halt, the plans go out the window . . .
he becomes lost, discouraged, destroys pages, abandons efforts . . . persistently
avoiding publication, and is exposed to the most jealous rumors of all kinds,
accusations of impotence, senility, his silence interpreted as an admission of error
or vacuity . . .[79] *empty - headedness*

Deleuze likewise remarks on this silence: "What happened during the
fairly long silence following *The History of Sexuality?* Perhaps Foucault
felt slightly uneasy about the book: had he not trapped himself within the
concept of power relations?"[80] Deleuze argues that the doubt and impasse
Foucault experienced is not because of his conception of power but rather
indicates the need for a theory of subjectification as a folding of force
upon itself, a folding of the outside.[81] This eight-year publication "gap" is
therefore both remarkably opaque and a remarkably productive crisis.
Foucault's silence exposes him to rumors, but it also allows for modifica-
tion and transformation.[82]

Both Miller and Deleuze have much to say about the centrality of the
concept of *se déprendre de soi-même,* the possibility of letting go of oneself, falling out of love with oneself, straying afield of oneself, and of
thinking otherwise. But for my purposes here, Guibert's narrator's conversations with Muzil reveal what a significant role the problem of the Name
plays in such a possibility. When Muzil hears of a projected "suicide hospital," he proposes instead the fantasy of a faked suicide hospital: "You'd
secretly slip behind the painting, and presto, you'd vanish, quite dead in
the eyes of the world, since no one would see you reappear on the other
side of the wall, in the alley, with no baggage, no name, no nothing, forced
to invent a new identity for yourself."[83] Guibert explains that "Muzil had
become obsessed with his own name. He wanted to obliterate it."[84] In a
passage that is strikingly reminiscent of the "Masked Philosopher" interview, the narrator recalls how

> I asked him to contribute an article on criticism to the newspaper I worked for,
> but he kept putting me off, at the same time trying to avoid hurting my feelings

by claiming he was unable to write because of excruciating headaches, so I finally suggested that he publish the piece under an assumed name. Two days later it arrived in the mail, a limpid and incisive text, along with this note: "What flash of insight told you that the problem isn't the head, but the name?" He proposed signing the article "Julien de l'Hôpital," and two or three years later, whenever I visited him in the hospital where he lay dying, I'd remember this somber nom de plume that never saw the light of day, because obviously the big daily newspaper I worked for had no use for an article on criticism by "Julien de l'Hôpital." A copy of it sat around for a long time in a secretary's files but had disappeared by the time Muzil asked for it back; I found the original at my place and gave him that, and Stéphane discovered at his death that he'd destroyed it, along with so many other texts, hurriedly, during the last few months before his collapse.[85]

Perhaps like Barthes's migraines in *Roland Barthes by Roland Barthes,* the headache is actually tied to a desire for opacity: "To have a (never very strong) headache is for me a way of rendering my body opaque."[86] In other words, to the pressure to write under his own name, Muzil responds, "Not tonight, I have a headache." As in "The Masked Philosopher," the critic's name and its necessity to the publishing industry represent a problem for Muzil/Foucault. This article, like diaries and photographs in Guibert's work, gets erased, only this time the force of destruction is clearly Muzil himself. At one point, Muzil asks the narrator to carry out the destruction of his manuscripts in the event of his death, and Hervé refuses, greatly disappointing Muzil.[87] Later, Hervé asks the same thing of Jules with regard to his own work, and notes the irony of this request when he couldn't agree to Muzil's.[88] In *Death and the Labyrinth,* Foucault recounts how "Kafka had entrusted his manuscripts to Max Brod to be destroyed after his death—to Max Brod, who had said he would never destroy them."[89] This is uncannily similar to the situation described by Guibert and reveals a striking prescience on Foucault's part.

We can see that Muzil's strategies are at different moments taken up and refused by Guibert. At one point, Hervé's doctor speaks to him as if to "remind me that my days were now numbered, that I shouldn't waste them writing under or about another name than my own."[90] This results in an ambivalent identification whereby Muzil's strategy is contrasted with Guibert's. But Muzil's thought *disturbs* Guibert's. I would suggest that not only systems of thought but also strategic possibilities both overlap and clash in this text. Guibert's putting into crisis of the forms of biography and autobiography is made possible by the critical possibilities envisioned by Foucault in his interviews. Thus, the narrator's conversations with Muzil are not anecdotes (descriptions of Foucault); they are inscriptions of Foucault into Guibert's work. This inscription of Foucault's person and thought into the work also therefore exceeds the dedication (*To the Friend . . .*).

Hervé explains that when Muzil gave him his copy of *Meditations*, he told him that "Marcus Aurelius had opened this work with a text praising his elders, different members of his family, his teachers, in which he thanked each person in particular, the dead first of all, for what they had taught him and the way they had changed his life for the better. Muzil, who was to die a few months later, remarked that he planned to write something similar soon about me—and I wondered how I could ever have managed to teach him anything."[91] This inversion of the typical hierarchy of mentor/mentee and older man/younger man is intimately tied to friendship, queer modes of life, and AIDS. Eve Kosofsky Sedgwick has described this other temporality in the following account from *Touching Feeling*:

> A more recent contingency, in the brutal foreshortening of so many queer life spans, has deroutinized the temporality of many of us in ways that only intensify this effect. I'm thinking, as I say this, of three very queer friendships I have. One of my friends is sixty; the other two are both thirty, and I, at forty-five, am exactly in the middle. . . . In a "normal" generational narrative, our identifications with each other would be aligned with an expectation that in another fifteen years, I'd be situated comparably to where my sixty-year-old friend is, while my thirty-year-old friends would be situated comparably to where I am. But we are all aware that the grounds of such friendship today are likely to differ from that model. . . . Specifically, living with advanced breast cancer, I have little chance of ever being the age my older friend is now. My friends who are thirty are equally unlikely ever to experience my present, middle age: one is living with an advanced cancer caused by massive environmental trauma . . . the other is living with HIV. The friend who is a very healthy sixty is much the likeliest of us to be living fifteen years from now. . . . [W]hat it means to identify with each other must also be very different. On this scene, an older person doesn't love a younger as someone who will someday be where she now is, or vice versa. No one is, so to speak, passing on the family name; there's a sense in which our life narratives will barely overlap. There's another sense in which they slide up more intimately alongside one another than can any lives that are moving forward according to the regular schedule of generations.[92]

Sedgwick's attention to the queerness of this intergenerational friendship has bearing on Hervé's relation to Muzil, and Guibert's relation to Foucault. Likewise, in the novel, the complex family of Jules, Berthe, their two children, and Hervé, which he believes to be united by AIDS, is also evidence of the complex temporality of illness Sedgwick describes. Family, however, becomes an obstacle to Hervé seeing Muzil in the hospital, where a doctor stops him: "He wasn't contesting the fact that I was one of Muzil's closest friends, but he claimed that blood relatives came first, so he refused to allow me to see Muzil again while he was still alive, and I wanted to spit in his face."[93] Hervé is only able to tell Muzil he loved him—waiting until the last minute—via a note. But Muzil's explanation of the text of praise in the *Meditations* in fact inspires Hervé to write such a text about Berthe: "I'd begun writing a text in praise of Berthe, something along the lines of what Muzil had sincerely or jokingly envisioned writing in my honor before his death, and every day I was terrified that Berthe would poke her nose into this manuscript, which I trustingly left lying on the desk."[94] We can sense Guibert's ambivalence in his restatement of Muzil's honorary gift as either sincere or joking (and we notice again the ambivalence of the public–private manuscript).

The inversions of mentor/mentee explained by Muzil via Marcus Aurelius are here given an affective dimension by Sedgwick, where the older does not love the younger friend as someone who will one day be where she is. Sedgwick's attention to this countergenerational temporality, in which life narratives are both nonoverlapping and more intimate than those with a "normal" trajectory, also helps us to comprehend the ambivalent identification of shared fate with Muzil experienced by Hervé. "Friendship as a Way of Life" is the queer concept Foucault uses to challenge routine, normal affective relations and restrictions. In a passage from this interview in which we might interpolate Foucault and Guibert, or Muzil and Hervé, without biographizing too much, Foucault explains:

> Between a man and a younger woman the marriage institution makes it easier: she accepts it and makes it work. But two men of noticeably different ages— what code would allow them to communicate? They face each other without terms or convenient words, with nothing to assure them about the meaning of

the movement that carries them towards each other. They have to invent, from A to Z, a relationship that is still formless, which is friendship: that is to say, the sum of everything through which they can give each other pleasure.[95]

Foucault explains that making ourselves infinitely more susceptible to pleasure, rather than working on liberating our desires, might be a way to escape the "two ready-made formulas of the pure sexual encounter and the lovers' fusion of identities."[96] Against what Sedgwick and Foucault repeatedly gloss as regular, scheduled, normal, codified, ready-made, formulaic, easy, convenient, reassuring, institutional, and preformed, friendship is defined as a creative force for inventing "from A to Z" a relationship that is still formless through which the partners can give each other pleasure.[97]

To Foucault's two reassuring ready-made formulas of the Romantic fusion of lovers' identities and the pure sexual encounter—two young men meeting in the street and having it off in fifteen minutes, which Foucault notes is a "neat image of homosexuality without any possibility of generating unease" since it actually corresponds to a reassuring canon of beauty and "cancels everything that can be uncomfortable in affection, tenderness, friendship, fidelity, camaraderie and companionship"[98]—I would like to add the oedipal patriarchal ready-made formula of father–son implicit in Sedgwick's discussion (the father–son bond is often not only desexualized but stripped of the possibility of pleasure). What if, rather than being a universal intrapsychic structure of desire that we are doomed to repeat, oedipal relationality was merely a sort of relational laziness, a lack of inventiveness and creativity? This would actually fit well with Foucault's and Sedgwick's emphasis on the innovative creativity of queer intergenerational friendship. I would simply note here that the late works of Roland Barthes (discussed in the next chapter) complicate Foucault's dismissiveness regarding the "trick" and the lovers' fusion of identities, since Barthes isolates precisely what is not reassuring about these two ways of relating. But Barthes is very much in agreement that affection is at this point the final transgression, much more so than sex, and that love is incompatible with proper sociability, institutions, and conventional narrative (this is a central claim in A Lover's Discourse).[99] Likewise, Foucault explains, "To imagine a sexual act that doesn't conform to law or nature is not what disturbs people. But that individuals are beginning to love one another—there's the problem. The institution is caught in a contradiction; affective intensities traverse it which at one and the same time keep it going and shake it up."[100] In another interview, Foucault explains that "the army, bureaucracy, administration, universities, schools, etc. . . . cannot function with such intense friendships. I think there can be seen a very strong attempt in all of these institutions to diminish, or minimize, the affectional relations," concluding that the appearance of homosexuality as a social/political/medical problem corresponds with the disappearance of friendship as an important social relation.[101] When the interviewer asks what specific institutions need to be established by gay people as alternatives to the nuclear family, Foucault simply suggests that "to use the model of family life, or the institutions of the family, for this purpose and this kind of friendship would be quite contradictory. But it is quite true that since some of the relationships in society are protected forms of family life, an effect of this is that the variations that are not protected are, at the same time, often much richer, more interesting and creative, than the others. But of course, they are much more fragile and vulnerable."[102] This typically antiprogrammatic statement agrees with Sedgwick's challenge to stop redeeming the family and to focus instead on the simultaneously vulnerable and richly creative forms of queer friendship across generations.[103] I take Hervé's relation to Muzil as a prime example of this inventiveness, which challenges the typical filial orders of generation, pedagogy, and love.

In Guibert's own tortured account of his amorous intergenerational relationship with a boy named Vincent in *Fou de Vincent,* he slips into a parental mode but then immediately recalls his dead friend Michel when trying to comfort the panicked sick Vincent: "Je me sens être mon père face à moi. J'essaye de faire revenir à toute allure, à sa place, Michel en moi, et sa sûreté, son sens de l'équité. L'ami mort parle par ma bouche pour réconforter Vincent, pour chasser la panique" ("It feels like I'm my father facing me. In his place, at top speed I try to bring back Michel in me, his assurance, his sense of equity. The dead friend speaks through my mouth in order to comfort Vincent, to drive away the panic").[104] The parallels with *To the Friend* are remarkable here, the same sense of *revenir* (revenant=ghost), the return of Michel/Muzil. And this intergenerational relationship hearkens back to the lessons of Foucault that are inscribed in Guibert's text, even as Muzil insists that it is Hervé who has taught him. All of this ambiguity lies in the dedication/title of what is in part a text of praise: *To the Friend Who Did Not Save My Life.*

The book itself might also be considered a bitter dedication to another friend, "Bill," who does not save the narrator's life, but who exerts an immense power over him by holding out the possibility of a "cure," a sort of antidote to the virus. At the end of the book he explains: "To 'save' my life, I've had to be transparent for Bill for eighteen months: to be prepared to report at any moment on one's plunging T4 count is worse than having to show what's in one's pants."[105] This passage reveals that having to be *transparent,* having to *report,* is more humiliating than simple sexual disclosure. Against this transparency, we find both Muzil's opacity (the "black diamond" of his biography) and Guibert's own strategy, which only appears to be making oneself transparent but might in fact be a hybrid form of opacity: the book that references another book, the diary, but which also distances itself from that book. Indeed, there are several "ignoble transcripts" at play here. Without privileging the end as a sort of "moral," it is important to see the way in which the narrator's "reports" on Muzil in the hospital are increasingly inverted in the rest of the text. Thus, the supposedly confessional journal form is used to express the difficult and ambivalent ethical necessity of betrayal, rather than simply importing the ill-fitting concept of confession to understand the "secrets" of Foucault's life (which is the case for James Miller). Foucault is undoubtedly an object of desire for all of these texts, but following Barthes's formulation about the amorous dedication, this figure *inscribes* something within those who desire him, bringing them to *catastrophe* but also into *crisis.* The AIDS crisis is not separable from this crisis of writing; it too is inscribed in Guibert's text, causing *narrative itself to experience a sort of vertigo* as Guibert writes about his friend's illness and his own. The form of Guibert's book recognizes the failure of the biographer's objectivity, but it does not therefore allow for a complete identification: even as he talks about shared fate, he juxtaposes his strategies with Muzil's. The work of fiction is the space of this ambivalence.

TWO

Matte Figures
Roland Barthes's Ethics of Meaning

He is troubled by any image of himself, suffers when he is named. He finds the perfection of a human relationship in this vacancy of the image: to abolish—in oneself, between oneself and others—adjectives; a relationship which adjectivizes is on the side of the image, on the side of domination, of death.

—Roland Barthes, "The Adjective," in *Roland Barthes by Roland Barthes*

I no longer need or desire to decipher him. . . . So I accede, fitfully, to a language without adjectives. I love the other, not according to his (accountable) qualities, but according to his existence. . . . The language in which the amorous subject then protests (against all the nimble languages of the world) is an obtuse language: every judgment is suspended, the terror of meaning is abolished.

—Roland Barthes, "Thus," in *A Lover's Discourse: Fragments*

IN HIS PREFACE TO RENAUD CAMUS'S 1979 novel of gay cruising, *Tricks,* Roland Barthes asserts the literary nature of the work in its "certain way of saying 'I.'" He then exemplifies the performative consequences of saying "I" one way rather than another when he addresses the "feats of discourse" that homosexuality continues to provoke: "Speaking of homosexuality permits those who 'aren't' to show how open, liberal, and modern they are, and those who 'are' to bear witness, to assure responsibility, to militate."[1] Barthes consistently rejected this responsibility to militate in the name of what he calls the politico-sexual,[2] and characterizes the pitfalls of identity politics thus:

To proclaim yourself something is always to speak at the behest of a vengeful Other, to enter into his discourse, to argue with him, to seek from him a scrap of identity: "You are . . ." "Yes, I am . . ." Ultimately, the attribute is of no importance; what society will not tolerate is that I should be . . . *nothing,* or, rather, more precisely, that the *something* I am should be openly expressed as provisional, revocable, insignificant, inessential, in a word irrelevant. Just say "I am," and you will be socially saved. To reject the social injunction can be accomplished by means of that form of silence which consists of saying things *simply.* . . . Renaud Camus's *Tricks* are simple. This means that they speak homosexuality, but never speak about it: at no moment do they invoke it (that is simplicity: never to invoke, not to let the Names into language—Names, the source of dispute, of arrogance, and of moralizing).[3]

Barthes's preface should be taken as an example of what he has called "affectionate criticism,"[4] and his treatment of Camus's narratives as "neutral . . . surfaces without shadows, without *ulterior motives*" proposes an approach to literature and sexuality that does not participate in "the game of interpretation" but figures a certain type of first-person opacity.[5] This opacity often constitutes a stumbling block for a mode of reading that sees "silence" about sexual identity as fully complicit with homophobia and the closet. Thus, D. A. Miller characterizes Barthes's relation to the act of gay self-nomination as "phobic" and argues that "silence, far from guarding a subject against these effects [prejudice, an unwanted identity, and so forth], would leave him all the more destitute of resources for resisting them. If Barthes's reticence has shielded anyone, it is his homophobic critics, who are spared having to show how deeply their attacks are motivated by a name he never claims."[6] Miller's gloss on the above passage fills in the responses of an unsympathetic Other: "Society continues to prefer the *sotto voce* stammering of homosexuality from which nothing in fact is more tolerated, more desired, than that it be *provisional* ('it's just a stage'), *revocable* ('keep your options open'), *insignificant* ('it doesn't really mean'), *inessential* ('are you sure?'), and, under the cumulative weight of all these attributes, expulsively *irrelevant*."[7] To the contrary, however, it is Miller's response, not Barthes's, that is on the side of homophobia. Barthes's "silence" is not a disavowal or a disowning; rather, it is a tactic by which he underscores precisely the vengeful Other in which he refuses to locate the meaning of his identity. (Barthes's reference to the

Other combines Althusser's theory of interpellation with Lacan's theory of alienation.)[8] Miller sees silence in much too limited a fashion as only complicit with homophobic intolerance, whereas Barthes seems to see "recognition of an identity" as the price of a tolerance that he views as intolerable. (In other words, Barthes adopts a certain manner of saying "I" in much the same way the narrator of Jean Cocteau's *The White Book* does when he declares: "I will not agree to be tolerated. This damages my love of love and of liberty.")[9] While Miller is correct to note that the Closet has never tolerated the Name, continually perpetuating the tradition of the *quod non nominandum*,[10] homophobia has also perpetuated the sad reverse discourse whereby homosexuality can only be tolerated if it is *essential, stereotyped,* and *irrevocably* cannot be helped, rather than a *provisional* or strategic choice ("Who would *choose* to be gay?"). Barthes explains: "If we find consistency insupportable, we cut ourselves off from an ethics of truth; we abandon the word, the proposition, the idea, once they *set* and assume a solid state, *stereotyped* (in Greek, *stereos* means *solid*)."[11] What alternative ethics are we faced with?

In his deliberation over the writing of *Bringing Out Roland Barthes,* Miller invokes a powerful term for Barthes and his readers, namely, "discretion": "However intimately Barthes's writing proved its connection with gay sexuality, the link was so discreet that it seemed to emerge only in the coy or hapless intermittences of what under the circumstances I could hardly pretend to reduce to just his repression. What might it mean for me, lifting the repression, to notice and articulate this link for him?"[12] Miller obviously sees his task as doing something *for* Barthes that Barthes cannot do for himself. But Miller acknowledges the risk of such a task: "Any knowledge I was able to produce of a 'gay' Roland Barthes couldn't help being a knowledge *between us* and *of us both,* fashioned within the practices and relations, real and phantasmatic, of gay community, and across the various inflections given to such community by, for example, nation and generation."[13] These questions of *inflection* might help us understand Miller's project, which is arguably much more about the concerns of a post-Stonewall American intellectual than about the supposedly coy and discreet Roland Barthes.[14] Indeed, the publication and packaging of Miller's *Bringing Out Roland Barthes* twinned with Barthes's posthumous and homoerotic work *Incidents* speaks volumes about both Miller's fantasy pairing with Barthes and the way in which his text and image vie with Barthes's own.[15] But all this Miller acknowledges as "the usual vicissitudes of adulation, aggression, ambivalence."[16]

In fact, there are moments in Miller's text when the joke is on him, and it is to his credit that he acknowledges as much. For instance, he explains that he had enjoyed the thought of going to Japan as an out gay man better equipped than the "pathetic" Barthes, but "was startled into fury when, rereading *Empire [of Signs]* just before my departure, the better to gauge the distance I had already traveled from its jurisdiction, I saw that Barthes, in writing of those impromptu drawings by means of which the inhabitants of Tokyo give directions to strangers, illustrated the phenomenon with a sketch of the same area of Shinjuku Ni-chome [the gay district] I had just committed to memory."[17] Miller's "startle" and subsequent "fury" here suggest something like, in John Whittier Treat's phrase, "great mirrors shattered," cracking from the pressure of Miller's ambivalent desire: both the desire *not* to identify with his image of Barthes and the desire for a gay reflection (despite differences of nation and generation).[18]

This is not an easy problem to resolve, but perhaps we get closer to what comes off as the misrecognition in Miller's taking it upon himself to "lift a repression" through his (obvious) identification with Barthes in this text, if we look at the disidentification performed in Leo Bersani's review of *Bringing Out Roland Barthes:* "By his tenderly uncompromising uncloseting of Barthes in works where homosexuality is at once absent and the key to intelligibility, Miller rescues Barthes from the dreary repetitiveness of hustlers and hangers-on. Like a good trainer in one of those gyms surely never frequented by the Proustian Barthes, Miller 'develops' Barthes' gay muscle."[19] Bersani here refers to the numerous insertions of Miller's gym body into the text, but despite his attribution to Miller of "tenderness" in seeking to overcome Barthes's undeveloped gay muscles, these textual acts reveal the incredible condescension and betrayal involved in his putative "rescue" of Barthes from himself.

It is worth continuing this consideration of Barthes's body (which, he insists, is a plural body).[20] Barthes proposes, in the caption to a final image in his text *Roland Barthes by Roland Barthes,* "To write the body. Neither the skin, nor the muscles, nor the bones, nor the nerves, but the rest: and awkward, fibrous, shaggy, raveled thing, a clown's coat."[21] In the succession of multiple grammatical negations, we here find more of the *negative theology* so notable in the above discussion of the *nothing . . . something* that I am. (Anyone who has taught Foucault, Barthes, or Derrida is familiar with guiding students through passages in which they must pass through a long list of "not this, or this" until they arrive at a positive statement.) Reducing "but the rest" to the question of gay muscle, Miller and Bersani wind up *closeting* Barthes's body just as much as Miller thinks Barthes does to himself by virtue of giving in to the homophobic will-to-invisibility that Miller describes. Thus, we might ask after the Proustian body of Barthes as it emerges in his most Proustian text, *Roland Barthes by Roland Barthes* (with its multiple anamneses, and its tour of photographs, beginning like the film version of Proust's *Time Regained*, Raoul Ruiz's *Le Temps retrouvé* [1999]).[22] But first, why is it a Proustian text?

Matte

By insisting that we consider the text *Roland Barthes*, with its splitting of the subject and personal pronouns "he," "you," and sometimes "I," as if spoken by a character in a novel, Barthes insists on the division between the author and the novelistic subject (the narrator) *even at his most autobiographical.*[23] After a list of italicized vignettes of anamnesis, Barthes writes: "These few anamneses are more or less *matte* (insignificant, exempt of meaning). The more one succeeds in making them *matte*, the better they escape the image-system."[24] This term "matte" comes to occupy the space I have been assigning to "opacity," but both should be taken as representing a certain *in-significance*, an exemption from meaning. Barthes somewhat ironically reflects: "Evidently he dreams of a world which would be exempt from meaning (as one is from military service)."[25] He specifies that this state is not an original, essential pre-meaning, but rather an exhausted, disappointed postmeaning. This also clarifies the sense in which he uses the words "inessential" and "insignificant," free from the tyranny of meaning.

Barthes explicitly links this question of relations that are matte, or opaque, to the question of his body: "My migraines are matte. To have a (never very strong) headache is for me a way of rendering my body opaque, stubborn, thick, *fallen*, which is to say, ultimately (back to the major theme) *neutral*."[26] I want to trace a series of these matte figures throughout the various fragments of Barthes's texts in the hopes of revealing this "theme" as it relates to an ethics of meaning and the problem of sexuality in Barthes's writing.

Barthes praises Camus's text for "speaking homosexuality but never speaking about it." This is a familiar objection raised by Barthes against speaking "about," "on," or "in the name of" something, separating the content or message expressed from its form of expression (i.e., militant speech, the scientific dissertation, the treatise, the lecture "on" a subject). Miller has ironically turned this critical strategy on Barthes's own text, claiming that "even when not spoken about in this writing, homosexuality does not fail to be spoken any the less."[27] But this notion of manifest versus latent content is overly indebted to a psychology of repression (a psychology of depth, a hermeneutics, a deciphering). The spatial and linguistic metaphor of the closet, so central to Miller's work, also seems to falter in the face of Barthes's own profusion of figures and metaphors. In a discussion of the neutral place of the "boîte," he imagines "the utopia of the third term, the drift far from the all-too-pure pair: *speaking/keeping silent*."[28] Barthes has a much more nuanced notion of "silence" that accommodates "speaking *simply*." Sexuality, speech, and writing are intricately related in Barthes's texts through a careful consideration of the problem of form.

In "F.B.," a text written in 1964 as a footnote to fragments by a young writer (who remains anonymous and does not seem to have published anything), Barthes practices an "affectionate criticism" that strikingly resembles his preface to *Tricks*. Barthes reveals how intimately he connects (homo)sexuality to the question of writing and the notion of a "matte" language in which meaning is fully "subjugated":

> Boy love forms a perfect circle outside of which nothing is left . . . it is only *writing* which traces that circle; the desire for boys is never, here, "culturalized," it has the naturalness of what is without cause and without effect, it is both without freedom and without fatality. This naturalness has major consequences for writing (unless, of course, it derives from writing): what is written does not appeal to *something else;* both soft and rich, writing is nonetheless *matte* . . . because there is no ellipsis in them, we can infer nothing from these texts.[29]

In this notion of "naturalness," it is not Nature that is invoked (indeed, "Nature has nothing particularly liberating about it",[30] but "naturalness" as a third term to the "Nature versus Nurture" debate alluded to (cause/effect, freedom/fatality).[31] The naturalness of writing is immanent (nothing is elided, nothing inferred, there is no appeal to *something else*), which corresponds with the immanent principle of the love of boys, and vice versa.[32] So we can see that the question of the desire for boys and the question of writing are one and the same: "This naturalness has major consequences for writing (unless, of course, it derives from writing)."

Barthes's discussion of F.B.'s "splinters of language" in fact allows him to develop a theory of the fragment and the "incident" that will be crucial to his own late style.[33] The fragment is differentiated from the maxim (another form notable for its brevity), which tends toward universality, essentialism, and arrogance.[34] The fragment is preferred for its resistance to any larger narrative logic, and Barthes orders his fragments using the system of the alphabet, an arbitrary system exempt from meaning (*A Lover's Discourse, The Pleasure of the Text,* and *Roland Barthes by Roland Barthes* are all ordered in this fashion.)[35]

In "F.B.," we also see the emergence of the concept of "not fragments but *incidents*."[36] In *Roland Barthes by Roland Barthes,* he notes that despite its fragmentary form, "even here, except in the *Anamneses,* whose value is precisely in this fact, nothing is reported without making it signify; one dares not leave the fact in a state of in-significance."[37] He conceives of the possibility of a converse book, which "would report a thousand 'incidents' but would refuse ever to draw a line of meaning from them; this would be, quite specifically, a book of haiku."[38] Of course, such a book was indeed published after Barthes's death, entitled *Incidents,* which recounts various encounters with boys and hustlers in both Morocco and Paris.[39] This book was received as a sort of "outing" and is undoubtedly the source of much of the rather condescending pity expressed by Miller and Bersani.[40] But in *Roland Barthes by Roland Barthes,* we can already see its potential in a fragment on projected books: "*Journal of Desire* (Desire's daily entries, in the field of reality) . . . *The Discourse of Homosexuality* (or: the discourses of homosexuality, or again: the discourse of homosexualities) . . . *Incidents* (mini-texts, one-liners, haiku, notations, puns, everything that falls, like a leaf), etc."[41] Though it was published after his death, Barthes in a sense wrote all three of these books in *Incidents*, which reflects on his relation to the country, his relation to Arab codes of (homo)sexual conduct ("Incidents"), and is the most extreme example of his preference for the short form.[42] In "Soirées de Paris," *Incidents* also features one of his experiments with the journal form (a form he links to Gide, as his *ur*-text: "The *Journal*, which I always particularly liked . . . that authenticity which outmaneuvers itself, twisting, until it is no longer authenticity").[43] In an essay published in *Tel Quel* entitled "Deliberation," Barthes reveals his doubts about the value of the journal:

> I guess I could diagnose this *diary disease:* an insoluble doubt as to the value of what one writes in it. . . . I note with discouragement the artifice of "sincerity," the artistic mediocrity of the "spontaneous"; worse still: I am disgusted and irritated to find a "pose" I certainly hadn't intended: in a journal situation, and precisely because it doesn't "work"—doesn't get transformed by the action of work—*I* is a *poseur*: a matter of effect, not of intention, the whole difficulty of literature is here.[44]

This conceptualization of literature as a set of "effects" rather than intentions, the most prominent of which is the "I," is a critique not only of the function of the author but also of the value placed on "expression" and "sincerity." Barthes explains modestly:

> I am not attempting any kind of analysis of the "Journal" genre (there are books on the subject), but only a personal deliberation, intended to afford a practical decision: should I keep a journal *with a view to publication?* Can I make the journal into a "work"? . . . [T]he aims traditionally attributed to the intimate Journal . . . no longer seem pertinent to me. They are all connected to the advantages and prestige of "sincerity" (to express yourself, to explain yourself, to judge yourself); but psychoanalysis, the Sartrean critique of bad faith, and the Marxist critique of ideologies have made "confession" a futility: sincerity is merely a second-degree Image-repertoire.[45]

Mingling Sartre and Lacan, Barthes alleges that sincerity is not an escape from the Imaginary/Image-repertoire but rather a second-degree form thereof (I am reminded of the claustrophobic mirror-confessional "I love you" at the end of Todd Haynes's film *Safe*).[46] Barthes's question of publication is taken up by François Wahl in his preface to the French edition of *Incidents* as a justification for publishing "Soirées de Paris," which could be mistaken for an intimate journal.[47] As in Barthes's lecture on Proust, "Longtemps, je me suis couché de bonne heure," in which he deliberates on the novel versus the essay, we should note the emphasis he places on the question of "what is to be done?" He stresses the "futility" and lack of "pertinence" of the prestige of sincerity and confession, following the critiques of psychoanalysis, existentialism, and Marxism, but we might ask: How has psychoanalysis contributed to the futility of confession? Is "psychoanalysis" mobilized here as a critique of confession, or one of its modalities? How might this connect with Foucault's critique of both confession *and* psychoanalysis? As Foucault explained (and Barthes no doubt knew well):

> The confession has spread its effects far and wide. It plays a part in justice, medicine, education, family relationships, and love relations, in the most ordinary affairs of everyday life, and in the most solemn rites; one confesses one's crimes, one's sins, one's thoughts and desires, one's illnesses and troubles; one goes about telling, with the greatest precision, whatever is most difficult to tell. One confesses in public and in private . . . one admits to oneself, in pleasure and in pain, things it would be impossible to tell anyone else, *the things people write books about.* One confesses—or is forced to confess.[48]

We can see that for Barthes, "expression" and the juridico-confessional mode of speech (to judge yourself) are not in opposition, but are implicated together in the genre of the journal.

Barthes argues that the journal form could only be redeemed through an extreme labor of writing, with its value lying in its *rhythmic* form. In "La vie posthume de Roland Barthes," Éric Marty elaborates an important critique of those (such as biographer Louis-Jean Calvet)[49] who have interpreted *Incidents,* in particular "Soirées de Paris," as a confessional "intimate journal" that reveals its author's secrets. Marty claims that they miss the literary dimension of the work (the careful use of italics, suspension points, etc.), its cruel sense of irony, and the fact that the subject of the journal is not the "moi" of Roland Barthes (the subject of introspection, self-knowledge), but rather the sole hero is time itself, the quotidian passage of "soirées."[50] Marty reveals the importance of this *transformation of work* for the journal, and the fact that in ending his journal on September 17, 1979, Barthes gives the work a posthumous tone already.[51]

Barthes also explains his distaste for "spontaneity" in his preface to *Tricks:*

> Take the spontaneous utterances, the spoken testimony then transcribed, as increasingly utilized by the press and by publishers. Whatever their "human" interest, something rings false in them (at least to my ears): perhaps, paradoxically, an excess of style (trying to sound "spontaneous," "lively," "spoken"). What happens, in fact, is a double impasse: the accurate transcription sounds made-up; for it to seem true, it has to become a text, to pass through the cultural artifices of writing.[52]

In his many transcribed and televised interviews, Barthes struggles with the already-said-in-writing. For Barthes, writing is the site of desire and pleasure, whereas speech partakes in the sphere of obligation. In participating in the "social game" of the interview, Barthes commonly repeats a set of misgivings, embarrassment of the biographical and the pedantic, wary of the need to explain himself or his writing.[53] In a relatively unsuccessful example of "praxis" in interrogating the structure of the interview, *Questions sans visage* (1977) features an anonymous interview between Barthes and Pierre Dumayet, each in separate but adjoining rooms with technologies for distorting their voices, and numbered questions picked at random.[54] The program attempts to critique the play of the name, the face, and the voice in the interview process, as the host gradually guesses that he is interviewing Roland Barthes from his vocabulary rather than from the usual markers of identity. The interview bears some resemblance to Foucault's "The Masked Philosopher," but the faceless anonymity is given over to an unmasking.[55]

Barthes consistently inverts the commonsensical attribution of impermanence and spontaneity to speech, compared with the monumental quality of writing. For him, speech is irreversible (one can only correct and retract by addition of another statement: by saying, "I expressed myself badly, rather . . ."), subject to the Imaginary, and the Law: "the Law appears *not in what is said but in the very fact of speech.*"[56] This argument about the juridical nature of speech is made both in his essay "Writers, Intellectuals, Teachers" and in his "Inaugural Lecture" at the Collège de France, in which he explains how

Jakobson has shown that a speech-system is defined less by what it permits us to say than by what it compels us to say. In French (I shall take obvious examples) I am obliged to posit myself first as subject before stating the action which will henceforth be no more than my attribute: what I do is merely the consequence and consecution of what I am. . . . But language—the performance of a language-system—is neither reactionary nor progressive; it is quite simply fascist; for fascism does not prevent speech, it compels speech.[57]

Like Foucault's preface to Gilles Deleuze and Félix Guattari's *Anti-Oedipus*, Barthes emphasizes the everyday reality of fascism, here inverting the assumption that fascism is simply repressive of speech, and like Foucault again, looking at what we are compelled to say.[58] Very few of Barthes's liberal commentators understand his equation of speech with fascism. Antoine Compagnon has asked, "Why does Barthes not see, why can he not see, or why does he not want to see the paradox of his pronouncement on the fascism of language . . . ? Where does this radical, essential, absolute suspicion regarding language, so contradictory with the freedom of his own wordplays and language-acts, originate? This question remains an enigma to me."[59] Barthes's critics seem to miss the gay specificity of this generalized suspicion. Regarding a similar problem for Foucault's critics, David Halperin explains that lesbians and gay men who, "far from having been the beneficiaries of liberal, humanist notions of freedom, truth, and rationality, have tended rather to be the targets of a new kind of terror carried out in their name," therefore have little cause to "feel deprived of a politics by Foucault's critique of the political economy of discourses."[60] Likewise, I don't find Barthes's suspicion enigmatic or shocking, but insist that it is a politico-theoretical rather than psycho-pathological suspicion (i.e., no enigma of origin).

Barthes looks for the structure of power and subjection at the level of the sentence itself. In an interview with *L'Express*, Barthes points out that "in the sixteenth century, Montaigne was still saying 'that am I,' and not 'I am that,' which was perfectly correct, since the subject is constituted by everything which happens to it and by everything it does. Because the subject is never itself until the end, as a product."[61] This fits with many of the lessons regarding the pronoun of the Imaginary, "I," in *Roland Barthes by Roland Barthes*, in which he sides with any theory that sees the subject as merely an effect of language.[62] As we see in the case of the journal "all the difficulty of literature is here," and in *Tricks,* that literature consists of "a certain way of saying 'I.'"[63] This may also explain the draw of the subject-effacing Japanese language for Barthes.[64]

In yet another extended deliberation on the problem of form (in this instance between the essay and the novel), Barthes reveals his indebtedness to Proust: "The Proustian oeuvre brings on stage (or into writing) an 'I' (the Narrator); but his 'I,' one may say, is not quite a self (subject and object of traditional autobiography): 'I' is not the one who remembers, confides, confesses, he is the one who discourses; the person this 'I' brings on stage is a writing self whose links with the self of civil life are uncertain, displaced."[65] Likewise, therefore, *Roland Barthes by Roland Barthes* is not an autobiography, a series of remembrances, confidences, or confessions, but rather brings into writing a subject, a narrator "R.B.," who is never "hampered, validated, justified by the representation of an individual with a private life and a civil status."[66] Barthes clarifies the difference between a novel and a biography in an interview upon the publication of *Roland Barthes by Roland Barthes.* The interviewer remarks, "You were saying that every biography is fictive, novelistic, a novel that doesn't dare speak its name. Isn't *Roland Barthes,* which is a biography, also a novel?" to which he responds, "It's a novel, but not a biography. The detour is not the same. . . . I put myself on stage as a character in a novel, but one without a name, in a way, someone who wouldn't have any adventures suitable for a novel."[67] Reversing the interpretation of Barthes's work as a biography that dares not speak its name (or the name of homosexuality), Barthes insists that "any biography is a novel which dares not speak its name."[68]

The Empty Sign

All of which leads to the epigraph to *Roland Barthes by Roland Barthes,* later explained in one of the fragments: "All of this must be considered as if spoken by a character in a novel—or rather by several characters . . . the image-repertoire is taken over by several masks (*personae*), distributed according to the depth of the stage (and yet no one—*personne,* as we say in French—is behind them)."[69] This figure of the masked subject on stage

("I advance pointing to my mask")[70] is a favorite one throughout Barthes's writing, which considers language itself as theater. But it is in reference to another form of theater, Japanese Bunraku puppet theater—which Barthes reads as the antithesis of anthropomorphic and metaphysical Western theater—that we find a figure that seems to resonate best with Barthes's critique of meaning. In "Lesson in Writing," Barthes discusses the master who controls the Bunraku puppet:

> As for the master, it has already been said that his head is left uncovered, smooth and bare, without make-up, this conferring on him a *civic* (and not theatrical) appearance; his face is offered to the spectator for reading, but what is so carefully and so preciously given to be read is that there is nothing to be read—here we find that exemption from meaning which does indeed illumine so many works of the East and which we are scarcely able to comprehend, since for us to attack meaning is to conceal or oppose it, never to absent it.[71]

This figure is therefore crucial as an alternative to a figure like that of "the closet" that is so important to *Bringing Out Roland Barthes,* in which Miller imagines only the possibility of meaning *opposed* or *concealed* but never meaning *exempted,* or *absented.* In an interview with Raymond Bellour, Barthes clarifies that in Japan he found what he refers to as an ethic of the *empty sign:* "Japan offers the example of a civilization where the articulation of signs is extremely delicate, sophisticated, where nothing is left to the nonsign; but this semantic level, expressed in the extraordinary finesse with which the signifier is treated, in a way means nothing, says nothing: it doesn't refer to any ultimate signified, and thus for me it expresses the utopia of a world both strictly semantic and strictly atheistic."[72] He explains that in a career in which he has dedicated himself to the study of signs and signification, it is only natural that he would develop an ethics with regard to semantics. He elaborates this ethics in his two most *novelesque* tracings of amorous figures: *Empire of Signs* and *A Lover's Discourse.*[73]

Empire of Signs and the above-quoted comments might appear to invoke a rather traditional Orientalist attitude toward the East, part of a colonialist fantasy that seems irreconcilable with ethics. In "Roland Barthes Abroad," Dalia Kandiyoti has argued that Barthes's *Empire of Signs* unfolds a "poetics of liquidation" whereby in his text

he will leave aside the "vast regions of darkness (capitalist Japan, American accul-
turation, technological development)" and occupy himself with flashes of light,
the rupture of the symbolic, with a Zen-like "exemption from meaning." The
Orient is a space of liquidation—of meaning, intelligibility, the signified. One of
the most fundamental satisfactions of travel in Japan is the loss of meaning, the
unintelligibility that not knowing a language affords. . . . The search for a happy
alterity, unadulterated by the oppressive weight of Western meaning systems, an
"us" as opposed to "them" discourse, falls back into a quest for authenticity and
results in an erasure of *métissage* that represses all (historical) mediation.[74]

Though Barthes is clearly criticizing Western meaning systems through the
example of works of the East—such as Western theater and puppetry as
metaphysical metaphors versus Bunraku theater-as-writing—I would
argue that Barthes views the exemption of meaning as a formal project,
rather than an essential quality. He asserts that he is not "lovingly gazing
toward an Oriental essence," but rather that "Japan has afforded him a
situation of writing. The situation is the very one in which a certain disturbance of the person occurs, a subversion of earlier readings, a shock of
meaning lacerated, extenuated to the point of its irreplaceable void, without the object's ever ceasing to be significant, desirable."[75] Yet the problem
is that this situation aptly describes the situation of Orientalist writing
(shock, disturbance, subversion, desire).[76]

However, this is less a timeless contradiction of traditional essences or
search for authenticity and more a proposal of differences in semiotic and
aesthetic work. Zen Buddhism and haiku are considered as formal operations and techniques for wearing-out or arresting meaning, but are not a
priori essentially lacking in significance. Barthes's attempt to "illumine the
works of the East" through concepts of loss of meaning (Barthes's understanding of *satori*) and exemption from meaning is not to argue that "The
Orient" simply has nothing to say—though Barthes's phrasing invites this
(mis)apprehension—it is rather to emphasize the signifier at the expense
of an ultimate theistic signified.

Again we meet with the problem of opacity, its negative and positive
valuations. In an early section entitled "Without Words," which sets the
stage for his fantasy and real relation to Japan as a white European who
does not know the language, Barthes argues: "Now it happens that in
this country (Japan) the empire of signifiers is so immense, so in excess

of speech, that the exchange of signs remains of a fascinating richness, mobility, and subtlety, despite the opacity of the language, sometimes even as a consequence of that opacity."[77] This positive value attributed to the term opacity—where first it is a hindrance but ends as a positive consequence—is actually rare for Barthes (who as I have said prefers the term "matte"). In *Roland Barthes by Roland Barthes*, for instance, he titles a section "Opacity and Transparence," in which he lays out the following tactic:

1. The social division produces an opacity (obvious paradox: where there is an extreme of social division, the situation seems opaque, massive).
2. Against this opacity, the subject reacts, opposing it in whatever way he can.
3. However, if he is himself a subject of language, his combat cannot have a direct political outcome, for this would be to return to the opacity of the stereotypes. Hence this combat assumes the movement of an apocalypse: he participates to the utmost, he exasperates a whole set of values, and at the same time he lives utopianly—it might be said he *breathes*—the final transparence of social relations.[78]

The opacity of social relations and stereotype are precisely those things for which Kandiyoti faults Barthes: the liquidation of historical mediation and the political realities of difference in his utopian relation to Japan in an attempt to exasperate Western values. However, authenticity is not what is being sought here. Barthes's opposition between a negatively valenced opacity and a positively valued transparence might seem to contradict my own project and use of these terms, but this evaluation is complicated by Barthes's much more frequent rejection of the illusion of the "transparence" of communication. In the previous passage on the opacity of the Japanese language, this desire for linguistic transparence is revealed as an ideological assertion that "*there is no communication except in speech.*"[79] Instead, Barthes emphasizes the richness and subtlety of signification whereby the body acts and shows itself in the modern urban life of Tokyo as part of a "pure—but subtly discontinuous—erotic project."[80] This project is potentially therefore both ethical and amorous.[81]

Ironically—by contrast—*A Lover's Discourse* describes the mania of signification and interpretation suffered by the amorous subject, in which *everything means something*. Some have read the text as rather coyly using

the generic male pronoun to discuss both the lover and the beloved—
though it links Barthes to the homoerotic philosophy of Plato.[82] However,
in *Reading Boyishly: Roland Barthes, J. M. Barrie, Jacques Henri Lartigue, Marcel Proust, and D. W. Winnicott,* Carol Mavor reads Barthes's
text and intertexts (Werther and Winnicott) as thoroughly queer: "Queerly,
boyishly, Barthes wears his love for Werther and his love for his mother
on his sleeve. . . . Barthes comes out in *A Lover's Discourse* as a queer man
whose relationship with his lover mirrors the crisis of the infant who,
without transitional objects, believes that the breast is still under his magic
control."[83] Thus, Mavor reads the maternal love in *A Lover's Discourse*
and *Camera Lucida* as queerly gendered, rather than genderless or sexless.
But must we consider *A Lover's Discourse* as a "coming out"?

Despite Barthes's characterization of the lover as in the "crucible of
meaning" while obsessing about the other, in *A Lover's Discourse* he also
proposes the possibility of a unique ethical relation to the other: "It is
not true that the more you love, the better you understand; all that the
action of love obtains from me is merely this wisdom: that the other is not
to be known; his opacity is not the screen around a secret, but, instead, a
kind of evidence in which the game of reality and appearance is done
away with."[84] This passage indicates the possibility of love as a non-
epistemological ethics *against* interpretation. And it is here that Barthes
gives us the most pronounced definition of opacity.

In *Roland Barthes by Roland Barthes,* we also find that a "matte"
quality in human relationships defines Barthes's own ethics of meaning
(again in relation to a certain Orientalism). He recalls, "In Morocco, they
evidently had no image of me; my efforts, as a good European, to be *this*
or *that* received no reply: neither *this* nor *that* was returned in the form of
a fine adjective; it never occurred to them to *gloss* me, they unwittingly
refused to feed and flatter my image-repertoire. Initially, this matte quality
of human relationships had something exhausting about it, but gradually
it came to seem a triumph of civilization or the truly dialectical form of
erotic discourse."[85] Therefore, he imagines "the perfection of a human
relationship in this vacancy of the image: to abolish—in oneself, between
oneself and others—*adjectives.*"[86] Thus, for Barthes, an ethical approach
to the sign (an ethic of the empty sign) implies an ethical approach to

human relationships, in the hopes of escaping what he calls the image-system (or the traps of the Imaginary, the image-repertoire).

Barthes's ethical approach to meaning is always tactical, and depends on the situation. In an interview with Guy Scarpetta, Barthes admits that "nonmeaning is immediately recuperated by meaning (as the meaning of nonmeaning). . . . Meaning cannot be attacked head-on."[87] He explains to Pierre Boncenne: "Given this framework, we encounter an ethical question: Should one struggle or not? Should one struggle to wear out meaning, destroy it, transmute it . . . or should one turn away from this struggle? I think that the answers to these questions can only be tactical ones, and that they will depend on the way one judges our current historical situation and the combat at hand."[88] In "Writers, Intellectuals, Teachers," Barthes argues that a criticism that applies itself to meaning is more historically correct: "Ideological criticism is today precisely condemned to operations of theft: the signified, exemption of which is the materialist task par excellence, is more easily 'lifted' in the *illusion* of meaning than in its destruction."[89] This consideration of tactics with regard to the exemption of meaning suggests a rejection of deciphering/interpretation, but not its foreclosure in a subjective dismissal. Yet historically, Barthes realizes that trickery, cheating, and theft with regard to meaning is a less utopian (and petit bourgeois) way to confront ideology. He suggests an immanent and materialist tactic with regard to the war of meanings, rather than a flight into transcendence. But Barthes also prefers a notion of tactics (and ethics) with regard to meaning over a strategic (or moralistic) attack on meaning: "Like a watchful cook, he makes sure that language does not thicken, that it doesn't *stick*. This movement, one of pure form, accounts for the progressions and regressions of the work: it is a pure language tactic, which is deployed *in the air*, without any strategic horizon."[90] Against a militaristic strategy, he proposes the Neutral as "the second term of a new paradigm, of which violence (combat, victory, theater, arrogance) is the primary term."[91]

The paradigm of meaning and the paradigm of sex are intimately linked. Barthes cites the example of Arab countries with a French colonial population where "'homosexuality, a transgressive practice, then immediately reproduces within itself . . . the purest paradigm imaginable, that of *active/passive*, of *possessor/possessed, buggerer/buggeree. . . .*' In such countries then, the alternative is pure, systematic; it knows no neutral or complex term."[92] Thus, in the 1971 article that he is citing (an interview with Guy Scarpetta entitled "Digressions"), Barthes argues that "what is difficult is not to liberate sexuality according to a more or less libertarian plan but to disengage it from meaning, including transgression as meaning."[93] So we see that like Foucault, Barthes does not advocate a liberation of sexuality according to a liberationist project. Rather, he proposes a tactical *disengaging* of sexuality from meaning. The metaphor of "the closet" is in some ways condemned to a notion of "liberation" *of* sexual meaning, the meaning *of* sexuality, rather than the possibility that one might "release it from meaning."[94] Marty points out that for Barthes, homosexuality was not a state but rather a desire, a potential for happiness, and thus Barthes made of his homosexuality a *non-savoir*, a non-knowledge, and it is only those who interpret his homosexuality as a form of knowledge "about" him who have posthumously transformed him into a petit-bourgeois oedipal homosexual.[95] Barthes argues in *Roland Barthes* for a *pluralism* in which "sex will be taken into no typology (there will be, for example, only *homosexualities*, whose plural will baffle any constituted, centered discourse, to the point where it seems to him virtually pointless to talk about it)."[96] Also critical of the taxonomy of perversions, Foucault makes a similar argument when he asserts that homosexuality is not a form of desire but something desirable.[97]

In his interview with Raymond Bellour, in which Bellour seems to criticize Barthes for his utopian and literary notion of political liberation ("with a view to later or never," "you shut yourself up within the Empire of Signs"),[98] Barthes responds: "I do not think that *to await* is *to shut oneself up*. It should be noted that, in our culture, closure is always presented as shameful; we still practice a romantic mythology, an alpine mythology of vastness, openness, totality, stirring inspiration. But counterclosure is not necessarily an opening, it's more likely to be freedom from the tyranny of the center."[99] Here Barthes performs an important critique of the mythology of "openness" in opposition to "closure," which is also at work in the metaphor of "the closet." Barthes provides a different spatial metaphor, citing the example of a Japanese dwelling, noting that "it can be emptied-out, un-furnished, de-centered, dis-oriented, dis-originated."[100] So while Barthes rejects the notion that his utopianism is a form of "shutting oneself away," he nonetheless provides a spatial metaphor that is "free from the tyranny of the center." The Japanese dwelling, therefore, is another example of his ethic of the empty sign, *emptied-out, dis-originated.* Instead of this Japanophile metaphorics, we could also find an alternative spatial metaphor in Barthes's discussion of the most French paradox of a monument: the Eiffel Tower. Barthes again questions the mythic value accorded to enclosure: "The Tower is a paradoxical object: one cannot be shut up within it since what defines the Tower is its longilineal form and its open structure. How can you be enclosed within emptiness, how can you visit a line? . . . What becomes of the great exploratory function of the *inside* when it is applied to this empty and depthless monument which might be said to consist entirely of an exterior substance?"[101] How, therefore, do we approach an empty sign? What becomes of the *explanatory* function of the "inside," the enclosure, indeed of the closet, when applied to Roland Barthes?

Unlike the closet, which conceals meaning, Barthes imagines a sexuality and an identity that is equally *in-essential* and *in-significant,* in which the tyranny of meaning is abolished. "To abolish—in oneself, between oneself and others—adjectives"; this ethical relation is personal and social, and figures an erotic discourse in which the other is no longer "glossed," but is rather the subject of a matte relationality.[102]

Neutral

Rejecting rumors that Roland Barthes had "let himself die" after being hit by a van near the Collège de France in 1980, Foucault described watching him teach a week before the accident: "I thought, He's in his element, he's acquired the distinguished bearing of a man who is mature, serene, completely developed. I remember thinking, He'll live to be ninety years old; he is one of those men whose most important work will be written between the ages of sixty and ninety."[103]

In 1977, accepting the chair of literary semiology at the Collège, for which Foucault recommended him, Barthes voiced his hope to renew "each of the years it is given me to teach here" the manner of "presenting a discourse without imposing it," thus acknowledging the inevitability of power in discourse, but finding the means of loosening, baffling, lightening this power.[104] At the origin of every course, Barthes located a fantasy, and in his 1978 course at the Collège it was the Neutral, or rather "The Desire for Neutral." The Neutral is that which "baffles" the paradigm (paradigmatic meaning depends on a binary opposition of terms: A/B, For/Against, or, in the case of the Neuter, Masculine/Feminine). The Neutral suggests the possibility of a "suspension" of the arrogant conflicts of meaning.[105]

One of the "figures" of the Neutral is "Silence." In a subsection entitled "To Outplay Speech," Barthes considers silence as a tactic to outplay the "oppressions, intimidations, the dangers of speaking."[106] Yet he notes that silence quickly becomes a sign: "Here, we reencounter a process that struck me as early as *Writing Degree Zero* and has obsessed me ever since: what is produced so as not to be a sign is very quickly recuperated as a sign. That's what happens to silence: one would like to reply to dogmatism (heavy system of signs) with something that outplays signs: silence. But silence itself takes on the form of an image . . . fatality of the sign: it is stronger than the individual."[107] Miller's understanding of how Barthes's silence "signifies" the closet is a good example (and Miller clearly believes that homophobic discourse is stronger than the individual, and cannot be outplayed by silence). An early twenty-first-century example would be the way in which silence about sexual orientation (in celebrity interviews or on social networking websites, paragons of the image-repertoire) more often than not functions as a sign of homosexuality. While it would seem that the "heavy system of signs" known as heteronormativity would encourage a "straight until proven otherwise" assumption, the recent dogmatic obligation of "outness" for both gay and straight people in these social arenas means that "what is produced so as not to be a sign is very quickly recuperated as a sign."

Barthes explains that while silence was initially used as a "weapon assumed to outplay the paradigms (the conflicts) of speech," it then "congeals itself into a sign (which is to say, is caught up in a paradigm)."[108] Thus, "the Neutral, meant to parry paradigms, will—paradoxically—end up trying to outplay silence (as sign, as system)."[109] Again, we can see Barthes's sensitivity to tactics. He cites a passage from Blanchot's *The Infinite Conversation* on a problem of behavior framed by Kafka:

> "Kafka wondered at what moment and how many times, when eight people are seated within the horizon of a conversation, it is appropriate to speak if one does not want to be considered silent": a familiar anxiety, I believe, for most of us: I have to say something, no matter what, etc. otherwise they'll think I'm bored (which is, in any case, the truth, etc.). . . . → how many repetitions are required for a sign either to be constituted—or to outplay the opposing sign ("I am not silent")? → the Neutral would be defined not by permanent silence—which, being systematic, dogmatic, would become the signifier of an affirmation ("I am systematically taciturn")—but by the minimal expenditure of a speech act meant to neutralize silence as a sign?[110]

Opacity likewise appears to be caught up in a paradigm, but I am defining it as a tactic to outplay (neutralize) both obligatory confessional speech and closeted silence.

In the course, he also revisits and recasts his by then well-known objections to the objectifying powers of the adjective. We get the sense that once again Barthes does not want to be dogmatic, but considers a tactical situation: "Suppress the adjective? First of all, this is not 'easy' (to say the least!), and then, in the end, it would suppose an ethics of 'purity' ('truth'/'absoluteness')."[111] He urges his auditors, "Don't bleach language, savor it instead. Stroke it gently or even groom it, but don't 'purify' it," and at least recognize that there is "a time for the adjective. Perhaps the Neutral is that: to accept the predicate as nothing more than a moment: a time."[112] Thus the subject of the course, like the journal, becomes time (the session or "séance" is like the soirées in "Soirées de Paris").

However, he is particularly aware of the bad images of the Neutral: "Except for certain philosophers and for Blanchot, which is to say everywhere in the *doxa*, the Neutral has a bad press: the images of the Neutral are depreciative. Each bad image is locked into a bad adjective (once again the negative role of the adjective)."[113] He goes on to list several of these bad adjectives: Thankless, Shirking, Muffled, Limp, Indifferent, Vile. Under "Shirking," Barthes explains that the subject "in the Neutral" is said to be fleeing his or her responsibilities, and indeed, the *doxa* "lives comfortably within the paradigm (the conflictual opposition)" and believes that the only way to respond is to contest it.[114] However, he notes that it does not imagine "that there could be another response: to slip, to drift, to escape," due to the "defamatory mark that rests on a logical sophism: not to oppose, means to be complicit."[115] I have already discussed the ways in which the queer subject's attempt to drift is perceived as an attempt to flee or slip into "the closet," and how this is seen as complicity with homophobia. Yet one could also argue that the *doxa* lives quite comfortably with the conflictual opposition represented by the closet (though "the closet" would be a doxa or Myth on the Left, as Barthes puts it in his early *Mythologies*).[116]

The scrambling, baffling, even scandalous aspect of the Neutral is clearly its appeal for Barthes, who nonetheless acknowledges all the "bad images" of the Neutral as *failure* or *impotence*. Rather than uselessly protest against this "virile" denigration of the Neutral (as nonvirile), what can be done is to propose a third term: "to drift by displacing the paradigm. → For 'virility,' or for lack of virility, I would be tempted to substitute vitality. There is a vitality of the Neutral: the Neutral plays on the razor's edge: in the will-to-live but outside of the will-to-possess" or what Barthes, citing a poem by Pasolini, calls "a desperate vitality."[117] This move of sidestepping the opposition is a repeated gesture of the Neutral in Barthes's course.

Barthes is also obliquely responding to his homophobic critics when he discusses "the deprecating adjective." Though he uses a universalizing tone, the passage instead speaks directly to Barthes's specific situation (as identified by Miller):

> I (like everyone) sometimes hear myself qualified (as a writer) with intentionally depreciative adjectives: accusation of "preciousness," of "theoretical coquetry," of muffling, etc. The aggression (the unpleasantness) doesn't only arise from the (depreciative) intention but from this: 1. The adjective that comes from outside me upsets the Neutral in which I find my quietude. . . . 2. The adjectival interpellation throws me back like a ball (a stake) into the vertigo of reciprocal images: by adjectivizing me as "precious," the other puts himself in a paradigm, he adjectivizes himself as "plain," "direct," "frank," "virile"; and to this paradigm (I-bad/he-good) there responds the symmetrical and reversed paradigm.[118]

Echoing this awareness of the power of "adjectivizing," Barthes also addressed his "image" in a colloquium at Cerisy-la-Salle dedicated to him in 1978:

> Here is how I become an image (a "French fried") under the offensive of a quite minor language-system: the dandiacal and "impertinent" Parisianism apropos of *A Lover's Discourse*: "Delicious essayist, favorite of intelligent adolescents, collector of avant-gardes, Roland Barthes offers us memories which are anything but, in the tone of the most brilliant salon conversation, but with a touch of narrow pedantry apropos of 'ravishment.' Recognizable, among others, Nietzsche, Freud, Flaubert." Nothing for it, I must pass through the Image; the image is a kind of social military service: I cannot get myself exempted from it; I cannot get myself discharged, cannot desert, etc.[119]

Barthes here laments that he cannot be a "draft dodger" when it comes to the military service of the image. For another example of Barthes's bad image in reviews, consider this remark about Barthes's *S/Z* by Gore Vidal: "He has a passion, incidentally, for lizardlike dodges from the direct statement."[120] Note how this confirms Barthes's diagnosis of how the other posits himself as "direct" in the paradigm that is established.

However, in a later text (from 1981, a year after Barthes's death), Vidal is more generous toward him and his preface to *Tricks*: "For a time, Barthes was much admired in American academe. But then, a few years ago, Barthes began to write about his same-sexual activities; he is now mentioned a bit less than he was in the days before he came out, as they say. Barthes notes that Camus's book is a 'text that belongs to literature.' It is not pornographic. It is also not a Homosexual Novel in that there are no deep, anguished chats about homosexuality. In fact, the subject is never mentioned; it just is."[121] After quoting the same passage with which I began this chapter about the feats of discourse provoked by homosexuality whereby "everyone gets busy whipping it up," Vidal writes, "You can say that again! And Barthes does. But with a nice variation. He makes the point that you are never allowed *not* to be categorized. But then, 'say "I am" and you will be socially saved.' Hence the passion for the either/or."[122] While Vidal and Miller each explain Barthes's fate among homophobic critics, Vidal seems to contradict Miller's view of Barthes's closetedness, or at least its periodization.

In his sociology of the French academy, *Homo Academicus*, Pierre Bourdieu cannot resist painting a portrait of Barthes as a theoretical dandy, butterfly, or flotsam:

> Roland Barthes represents the peak of the class of essayists, who, having nothing to oppose to the forces of the field, are condemned, in order to exist, or subsist, to float with the tides of the external or internal forces which wrack the milieu, notably through journalism. He calls to mind the image of a Théophile Gautier whom a contemporary described as "a spirit floating on every breeze, quivering at every touch, able to absorb every impression and to retransmit it in turn, but needing to be set in motion by a neighboring spirit, always eager to borrow a watchword, which so many others would then come to seek from him."[123]

Bourdieu suggests that "Barthes gives instantaneous expression to all the changes in the forces of the field while appearing to anticipate them, and in this respect it is sufficient to follow his itinerary, and his successive enthusiasms, to discover all the tensions which were applied to the point of least resistance of the field, where what is called fashion continually flowers."[124] While Miller would draw attention to this critical use of homosexual connotation—flowery, fashionable, enthusiastic, but passive—what strikes me is the way Bourdieu's otherwise very useful depersonalizing concept of the "field" and force relations deprives Barthes of any potential resistance (especially to the forces of journalism) and misconstrues the collaborative disposition and generosity so palpable in Barthes's work and courses.

In contrast with Bourdieu's classification of Barthes as a fashionable essayist floating outside of the professional milieu, Régis Debray classifies Barthes among a class of professionals who are by their very nature disengaged. Debray diagnoses "a characteristic semiological personality—ironical, uninvolved, non-violent, skeptical, relativistic, or of sunny disposition—whose traits alone bespeak professional competence and *habitus*," which he contrasts with the butch "psychological profile of the mediologist," that is, Debray himself, which "is perhaps less contemplative, closer to collective action. . . . At the least he loved once upon a time the battlefields."[125] This is yet another example of the paradigm of virility and nonvirility.

In his course on the Neutral, Barthes does not mention all the deprecating adjectives used to qualify his writing as a way of defending his image. Instead, for him it is an example of the lure of the image-system.

The opposition of values (precious/frank, coquettish/virile) is also a perfect example of the paradigm at work: "Formally both value paradigms have entered some kind of deal, 'work' like a turnstile . . . vertigo without respite, because the turning excludes respite, suspension, the Neutral. I am caught in the weariness of the paradigm."[126] Rather than react against this homophobic trap of the "deprecating adjective" with the "courage" Miller seems to want from Barthes, "Weariness" instead becomes one of the figures of the Neutral. Indeed, throughout the course one can hear Barthes's complaints against the demands made on him in his state of mourning his mother's recent death: solicitations of opinions, interviews, and so forth. At several points Barthes begins to describe an "ethology of the Intellectuals":[127] what he identifies as a French taste for debates and the way reviews of books have been replaced by interviews.[128] He laments "the terrorism of the question: journalist: a kind of cop who likes you, who wants the best for you," finding in every question the germ of a *double-bind* situation, and given Eve Kosofsky Sedgwick's analysis of homophobic double binds it is no surprise that Barthes claims: "In this sense, every question is indiscreet, it is—however sublime its contents—inquiry about the sexuality of the other → = what is your sexuality."[129] But Barthes's desire for the Neutral as "a right to be silent—a possibility of keeping silent" need not be viewed as a symptom of the closet; rather, it marks a very *queer* desire "to give imprecise answers to precise questions: this imprecision of the answer, even if it is perceived as a weakness, is an indirect way of demystifying the question . . . every question can be read as a situation of question, of power, of inquisition."[130] Barthes thus encourages us to demystify the situation of the question: What is your sexuality?

Barthes's diagnosis of the interview situation will also serve us well as we turn to Andy Warhol. Warhol likewise sought out the possibilities of silence and managed to demystify the interview situation by giving imprecise answers to aggressive questions. Wayne Koestenbaum has argued, "A journalist's hostile, unknowing questions can be acts of discursive violence. As if imitating Wilde's 1895 trial, Warhol torqued the witness stand, through irony and camp, into a tea party, and taught us how to circumvent intimidation by mesmerizing the bully," and this aptly describes a tactic that fits both Warhol and Barthes well.[131]

THREE

"What Do You Have to Say for Yourself?"
Warhol's Opacity

I've been called "Complex, naive, subtle and sophisticated—" all in one article! They were just being mean. Those are contradictory statements but I'm not full of contradictions, I just don't have very strong opinions on anything.

—Andy Warhol in an interview with Gretchen Berg

I am not contradictory, I am dispersed.

—Roland Barthes, *Roland Barthes by Roland Barthes*

THE QUESTION "WHO IS ANDY WARHOL?" is often put in terms of an enigma: "What does Andy Warhol want?"[1] Warhol is often portrayed as mute, nonverbal, instinctual, passive, autistic, apolitical (if not right wing), noncommittal, lacking intention, monosyllabic, and opaque.[2] Often this characterization seems to authorize others to speak for him, to find commentary or meaning where there seemed to be simply "no comment," to argue that the Warhol persona has managed to effectively obscure his work and his intentions. Indeed, when one reads interviews with Warhol like "Andy Warhol: My True Story" with Gretchen Berg, one gets plenty of statements like "there was no reason for doing it at all, just a surface reason," "I'm not more intelligent than I appear," and finally, "I'm very passive. I accept things. I'm just watching, observing the world."[3] This seems to authorize accounts such as Stephen Koch's characterization of Warhol as "The Tycoon of Passivity," where "as always, he kept silent."[4]

How should we approach Warhol's "opacity"? The biographical impulse dominates books about Warhol, whether Victor Bockris's *Warhol: The Biography* or the large numbers of "tell-alls" by the superstars and affiliates (it also sets the narrative structure of the films on Warhol: Kim Evans's *Andy Warhol* [1987] and Chuck Workman's *Superstar: The Life and Times of Andy Warhol* [1990]).[5] Often a certain pathos and psychologism, propped up by biographical information, fills in the gaps in Warhol's story, even in art historical accounts. As an illustration of this biographical-psychologizing tendency, a few of the comments on the jackets of several Warhol volumes will suffice:

> [*Andy Warhol: The Biography*, by Victor Bockris:] One of Bockris's finest achievements is to apply the gloss of Warhol's homosexuality to his life story, without sententiousness or false speculation. Thus, the man who said "I want to be a machine" emerges as a normal human, perplexed and anguished by the nature of love, and finding in art some solace for the pain he felt . . .
>
> [*Holy Terror: Andy Warhol Close Up*, by Bob Colacello:] Using his skills as a reporter, Colacello chronicles the amazing saga of the public Warhol and delves into the secret heart of the private Andy in a portrayal both frank and compassionate—from his insecurity about his physical appearance, his intimate relationships, his hypochondria, his wistful loneliness, his apparent personal cruelty, and his voyeurism to his shopping and collecting fetishes.
>
> [*Andy Warhol, Poetry, and Gossip in the 1960s*, by Reva Wolf:] Andy Warhol is remembered as the artist who said that he wanted to be a machine and that no one need ever look further than the surface when evaluating him or his art. Arguing against this carefully crafted pop image, Reva Wolf shows that Warhol was in fact deeply emotionally engaged with the people around him and that this was reflected in his art.

What I take issue with is the tendency toward "humanizing" Warhol in these accounts—which often hinge on the shift from Andrew Warhola to Andy Warhol, and almost obsessively denounce the famous "machine" statement.[6] There seems to be an attempt to hang on to humanist conceptions of an essential self at all costs in the face of Warhol's consistent undermining of such a model of subjectivity.

If we are to follow the somewhat psychologizing reading of Warhol's nonverbal style as indicating, as he seems to suggest, shyness (Sam Green told Warhol: "Now *please* don't do your monosyllabic shy act and ruin everything"),[7] then we would need a careful consideration of the productivity of shyness.[8] Eve Kosofsky Sedgwick has discussed the link between Warhol and the queer performativity of the affect shame in "Queer Performativity: Warhol's Shyness/Warhol's Whiteness": "It seems clear enough that Warhol can be described as a hero of certain modern possibilities for embodying the transformations of 'queer' shyness and for amplifying its heuristic power to expose and to generate meaning. Warhol's career offers seemingly endless ways of exploring the relation of queer shame/shyness to celebrity; to consumer culture; to prosopopoeia, the face and the portrait."[9] This impressive inventory offers great potential for thinking about Warhol's shyness (and how shame is always related to exhibitionism).[10] It also provides us with a way of thinking about Warhol's queerness that is itself productive. This does not necessarily involve generating or exposing a straightforward meaning. Rather, Warhol's shyness and queerness produce useful *tactics* in relation to artistic practice, the interview, and publication. Simon Watney has asserted that against the "obliterative homophobia" of contemporary Pop Art criticism, Warhol "represented a public face of queerness. He was transparently queer."[11] While also focusing on the public aspect of Warhol's persona, I am interested in looking not at Warhol's transparent queerness, but rather his *queer opacity.*

I am thus also suspicious of a reading of Warhol's "silence" that would collapse it into a matter of the closet. While it is certainly true that negotiating the epistemology of the closet in midcentury American society was a rather tortured operation (with a series of double binds relating to the binary public/private), I prefer to maintain an emphasis on Warhol's opacity as a specific discursive tactic not *immediately* linked to questions of invisibility *or* disclosure. To reiterate David Van Leer's argument: "The sexual character of language is rarely direct, and post-Stonewall criticism has occasionally stigmatized such writing as 'closeted.' But just as invisibility does not impede all forms of speech, so the refusal to identify one's personal interests can facilitate other kinds of gay statements."[12] Van Leer explains that his analysis focuses "on language itself, turning from the visible to the verbal, from homosexual narratives to homosexual dictions, rhythms, rhetorics."[13] This will also be my approach to Warhol.[14]

It is both heartening and ironic that in my consideration of what, if anything, Warhol has to say for himself, I find that others have already said *almost* what I want to say (often going to press as I was working on this project): specifically Wayne Koestenbaum's biography *Andy Warhol* and his afterword to *I'll Be Your Mirror: The Selected Andy Warhol Interviews*

1962–1987, Gavin Butt's *Between You and Me: Queer Disclosures in the New York Art World, 1948–1963*, and Kelly M. Cresap's *Pop Trickster Fool: Warhol Performs Naivete*. Like the earlier edited volume *Pop Out: Queer Warhol*, my hope is that such queer intellectual solidarity does not obviate my "own" distinctly nonpsychological, nonbiographical approach to Warhol's opacity.[15]

What I propose is that we read *with* rather than *against* Warhol's discursive tactics, that we view his persona as a significant "work" in itself,[16] that we *take his word* regarding his desire to be a machine or that if we want to know who Andy Warhol is we should look at the surface ("If you want to know all about Andy Warhol, just look at the surface of my paintings and films and me, and there I am. There's nothing behind it."),[17] and thus not reduce his opacity to a transparency, a comforting reflection with which we can identify, or a depth psychology. For me, Warhol's queer opacity is an attempt to baffle, stymie, or sabotage particular functions of truth, individuality, and authenticity.

I want to look specifically at the written and filmed interviews with Warhol, since the interview is a discursive situation that plays a significant role in the production of authenticity, authority, and truth. Likewise the autobiography, the diary, and the "philosophy." (We are promised on the jacket of *The Philosophy of Andy Warhol*: "At last the private Andy Warhol talks . . . about himself.")[18] How does Warhol use/abuse the medium of the interview, or the book? He is not always or even often "silent"; rather, he plays at and plays with the idea of making a statement. He is very aware of the limitations of these formats (interrogation, bad press, coerced statements/judgments) but also the possibilities for what the interview and the memoir have to offer as opportunities for "voice portraits."

For all his supposed ineloquence, Warhol does have a very characteristic style of speech and writing and was obviously very skilled at manipulating discursive situations, though often not by making a statement in terms of a conventional, intentional "I," or as a singular author. Often he authorizes others to speak for him, in translation—Pat Hackett as interpreter, "redactor," or even ghostwriter—by proxy, or as literal stand-ins. Therefore, I would like to begin with Warhol's observations regarding the format of the interview itself, and go on to look at these specific tactics for negotiating (and undermining) situations in which one is asked to "speak for/as oneself." This will also involve a consideration of Warhol's investment in particular recording and communication technologies, and what we might consider as Warhol's significant interventions in other genres than the interview, namely, the novel, the philosophy, the diary, and the memoir.

The Interview

Warhol's interviews exist in film, television, audiotape, and written formats. It is worth considering the general assumptions implicit in the interview format before looking at how Warhol disrupts the situation. In his authoritative *American Journalism, a History: 1690–1960*, Frank Luther Mott suggests that "perhaps the first formal interview with a famous man was [Horace] Greeley's story of his talk with Brigham Young in the *Tribune* August 20, 1859," noting that this type of interview with a famous public figure was taken up by other papers and was adopted slowly in England and France from the American model. But he also points out that "the interview, with its intimate details of the behavior and words of the great, was frequently criticized as unwarranted invasion of privacy."[19] In his discussion in "The Rise of the Independent Press 1872–1892," he explains that "interviewing—the formal question-and-answer technique applied to men of all degrees of importance—continued to receive the condemnation of the censorious. This was because questions were often flippant and the replies ill considered. Interviewing, said the *Nation*, 'makes fools of great men.'"[20] We should keep this in mind when it comes to Warhol, who Cresap says often "played the fool,"[21] but who also managed to make a travesty of the interview itself, as Koestenbaum has argued: "A journalist's hostile, unknowing questions can be acts of discursive violence. As if imitating Wilde's 1895 trial, Warhol torqued the witness stand."[22]

Following Mott's history, Brian Winston also makes the connection between Jeremy Bentham's early nineteenth-century legal reforms regarding witness testimony and the rise of the interview in journalism, which, he argues, was then adopted by documentary cinema: "Despite the interview's basic artificiality and unnaturalness as a mode of discourse, it becomes, after *Housing Problems* [1935], a staple of the Griersonian documentary."[23] In a discussion of Jennie Livingston's Harlem drag ball documentary *Paris Is Burning* (1990), Ann Cvetkovich argues that the format of the documentary implicitly assumes that "the camera has the power of surveillance, enabling it to investigate and expose the truth of its subjects. . . . The interview format, for example, draws upon realist and empiricist epistemologies that assume that truth can be obtained from the testimony of subjects speaking in their own voices."[24] bell hooks has faulted Livingston for using a rather standard talking-heads ethnography form, but the participants often seem to relate ironically to the format itself.[25] The epistemological framework is constantly undermined in the game that the quizzical participants are playing with the documentary format itself. As a queer filmmaker, Livingston herself acknowledges a potential critique of her own documentary—for the way in which it explains the drag ball subculture's terminology and strategies to outsiders—by including as the final intertitle "PIG LATIN," demonstrating a simultaneously exclusive *and* inclusive mode of speech.

The interview also often concerns the "private life" or biography of the interviewed subject. Roland Barthes, in a biographical interview for *Tel Quel* with Jean Thibaudeau, prefaces his responses with a caution: "Of course it was a game, which neither Jean Thibaudeau nor myself, deriving from a theoretical space in which biography is not taken so seriously, were taken in by. . . . [A]ny biography is a novel which dares not speak its name."[26] Toward the end of the interview, after Barthes has answered all the biographical questions, Thibaudeau asks, in keeping with the "game" they are playing, "What is this 'interview'? What is the 'posterity' to which, in its televisual guise, it would appear to be destined?" To which Barthes responds: "I would like to use your question to put the interview on trial," referring not to this interview but to the everyday spoken interview, which Barthes criticizes for its assumption that speech is thought in its purest state:

> During the interview the author *acts as if* he is thinking. (I am questioning an
> institution, not the performances; I don't deny that some interviews are well

thought out, and in some circumstances useful. Moreover, to systematically refuse interviews would be to play another role, that of the secretive, wild, unsociable thinker.) In relation to writing . . . the interview seems even more vain, to the point of being absurd. Its practice supposes that the writer, having *written* (a text, a book), still has something to *say*: what? (264–65)

While Barthes does not reject the interview outright, he plays "games" with the assumptions of identity that go with the interview and the biography. Warhol displays a similar tactic—not of straightforward refusal, but of a disruption of the assumptions of the interview—yet with slightly different goals, occasionally trying to maintain a certain "mystery," but often inverting the epistemological operations of knowledge about him.[27] In the interview with Gretchen Berg, he explains, with characteristically contradictory logic and (false?) naïveté regarding his image: "I'd prefer to remain a mystery, I never like to give my background and, anyway, I make it all up different every time I'm asked. It's not just that it's part of my image not to tell everything, it's just that I forget what I said the day before and I have to make it all up all over again. I don't think I have an image, anyway, favorable or unfavorable."[28] But in *The Philosophy of Andy Warhol,* Warhol reveals some of the advantages of such a tactic: "People used to say that I tried to 'put on' the media when I would give one autobiography to one newspaper and another autobiography to another newspaper. I used to like to give different information to different magazines because it was like putting a tracer on where people get their information."[29] This fantasy of omniscience (the "tracer") nonetheless refutes the notion of total control over one's image. Warhol believes that most articles are "preordained"—in general, authors know what they're going to say about you before they ever interview you, and it is hard to tell who will be kind and who will be mean—but he then explains: "When somebody writes a really mean article, I always just let it go because who are you to say it isn't the truth?"[30]

In general, Warhol is very skeptical about the truth or the "real you." Jonas Mekas quotes an interview with Warhol that reveals some of the problems faced by journalists who wish to render Warhol's opacity more legible: "'I've been thinking about it,' conceded Warhol. 'I'm trying to decide whether I should pretend to be real or fake it. . . . You see,' said

Warhol, craning his head absently, 'to pretend something real, I'd have to fake it. Then people would think I'm doing it real.'"[31] Note the journalistic insertion of Warhol's body into his speech, rendering neither one the less opaque for it ("craning his head absently"). This pinpoints the problem of Warhol's opacity for those who wish to describe him, a certain aggressivity in the relation between the journalist and Warhol himself: "Almost every journalist never wants to know what you really think—they just want the answers that fit the questions that fit the story they want to write, and their idea usually is that you shouldn't let your own personality butt in on the article they're writing about you or else they'll really hate you for sure for giving them extra work, because the more answers you give, the more answers they have to twist to fit their story."[32] Warhol recounts in *POPism: The Warhol '60s* how before the tape recorder reached a dominant status in the medium of the transcribed interview, interviews were primarily a matter of jotting notes and writing a story that was far more impressionistic anyway: "In those days practically no one tape recorded news interviews; they took notes instead. I liked that better because when it got written up, it would always be different from what I'd actually said."[33] Rather than complain about the fact that he is not allowed to express himself, or that what he says gets distorted, Warhol rejects the notion of his "own voice" altogether: "Interviews are like sitting in those Ford machines at the World's Fair that toured you around while someone spoke a commentary; I always feel that my words are coming from behind me, not from me. The interviewer should just tell me the words he wants me to say and I'll repeat them after him. I think that would be so great because I'm so empty I just can't think of anything to say."[34] In one of the best examples of Warhol's peculiar interview tactics on film, Warhol tells the interviewer, who sits perpendicular to him—resembling an analyst to an analysand—that he would rather the interviewer just told him what to say.[35] The interviewer responds by reasserting that he is there to ask Warhol questions, but Warhol insists that he should give him the *answers* too, which he will then repeat back verbatim. This "naughty child" game of obstinacy and verbal repetition constitutes one of Warhol's techniques for managing the situation of the interview.

Yet in Warhol's discussion of his words coming from behind him, we might also find more than a slight resemblance to Michel Foucault's inaugural lecture at the Collège de France, in which Foucault imagines slipping imperceptibly into a discourse already begun, "enveloped in words, borne away beyond all possible beginnings."[36] As Foucault intends to convey in his inaugural lecture, discourse precedes the individual speaking subject, who never really "begins" but rather *takes place*, or, as Foucault explains in "The Thought of the Outside," represents a grammatical *fold* in the "continuous streaming of language."[37] Maurice Blanchot's *The One Who Was Standing apart from Me* indicates just such an experience of the "outside."[38] Foucault argues that its anonymous *he* and *I* are linked by a "constant questioning . . . and by the uninterrupted discourse manifesting the impossibility of responding."[39] However, a neutral space of language is cleared by this withdrawal, this "hollowness that is perhaps nothing more than the inexorable erosion of the person who speaks."[40] Blanchot describes such an erosion of the speaking subject in terms that echo Warhol's peculiar relationship to words:

> To say that I understand these words would not be to explain to myself the dangerous peculiarity of my relations with them. . . . But they don't need that understanding in order to be uttered, they do not speak, they are not interior, they are, on the contrary, without intimacy, being altogether outside, and what they designate engages me in this "outside" of all speech, apparently more secret and more interior than the speech of the innermost heart, but, here, the outside is empty, the secret is without depth, what is repeated is the emptiness of repetition, it doesn't speak and yet it has always been said already.[41]

Not only Warhol's speech, but also Warhol's artwork is just such an experience of the outside: Warhol can ask other people what he should paint because "Pop comes from the outside."[42] The secret is without depth, what is repeated is the emptiness of repetition: "I want it to be *exactly* the same. Because the more you look at the same exact thing, the more the meaning goes away, and the better and emptier you feel."[43] Foucault has commented that in Warhol's painting, "concentrating on this boundless monotony, we find the sudden illumination of multiplicity itself—with nothing at its center, at its highest point, or beyond it."[44] As in Blanchot, the outside and the innermost center are therefore empty. This illumination is "a flickering of light that travels even faster than the eyes and successively lights up the moving labels and the captive snapshots that refer to each other to eternity, without ever saying anything."[45] This repetition is empty; as in Blanchot, it "doesn't speak and yet it has always been said already."

The Magic 8 Ball

Another of Warhol's tactics for negotiating the interview has been called his "monosyllabic" style.[46] There exists, in fact, a CD tribute to this famous style that consists only of Warhol saying "uh . . . yes," "uh . . . no" alternately.[47] This pleasure in the binary of affirmation/denial sometimes gives way to "uh . . . I don't know" or "I haven't really thought about it." But, in general, Warhol tends to prefer a simple yes or no answer, which is often not what the interviewer might have been expecting. A long phone interview with Jordan Crandall from 1986 features a funny instance of this technique: "JC: Do you like interviews? AW: Yes. JC: Yes? AW: No. JC: No? AW: No. JC: Yes and no? AW: Yes."[48] The minimal response often collapses the interviewer's question into a statement. One excellent example of this style on film can be seen in an interview (featured in Evans's *Andy Warhol*) in which a smirking Warhol, standing next to Ivan Karp in front of Brillo boxes, is asked by a female reporter the following questions:

> Q. Do you think that people don't understand your work?
> A. Uh . . . no.
> Q. Andy, do you think that Pop Art has sort of reached the point where it's becoming repetitious now?
> A. Uh . . . yes.
> Q. Do you think it should break away from being Pop Art?
> A. Uh . . . no.
> Q. Are you just going to carry on?
> A. Uh . . . yes.

Due simply to the ironic juxtaposition, a coherent though seemingly contradictory insistence on Pop art is nonetheless affirmed. This affirmation of the boring, the repetitive, and the "populism" of Pop are steady features of Warhol's oeuvre. But this monosyllabic style also displaces Warhol from a position of assertion (as intentional free statement) and puts him in a position that resembles a Magic 8 Ball (Yes, No, Try Again Later).

In a session on the problem of "The Answer" in Barthes's course on the Neutral, his description of interviews is particularly relevant to Warhol, despite the irony of their respective differences (the "logothete" Barthes was skilled with language but disliked journalism; Warhol was allegedly poor with language but aspired to break into journalism). Barthes describes how the situation of power in interviews "implies that one knows how to reply to big dissertation questions (what is writing? nature? health? etc.), that one should be interested in the question, that one should accept the way the question is asked," and considers "the multiplication of interviews, the arrogance, the intimidation of the demand" as an "index of the current ascension of journalism as power."[49] He discusses H. P. Grice's normative rules governing contributions to good conversation ("make your contribution as informative and not more informative than is required," "do not say what you believe to be false" or "that about which you lack evidence," "be relevant," "be perspicuous").[50] Given this situation, he considers what he calls "beside-the-point answers": tactical departures, flights, silences, forgettings, deviations, and incongruities. He considers these "a subfield of the Neutral since they baffle the arrogant request for a good reply."[51] In what way, then, did Warhol try to baffle journalistic arrogance?

In John Wilcock's article "L.A. Weekend with Warhol," he contrasts a "failed" Warhol interview conducted by NBC with a "perceptive" interview by Richard Whitehall for *Cinema Magazine*:

> The contrast between the two interviews pointed up once again how people carry preconceived ideas to new situations and find in Warhol almost exactly what they are looking for. The extent to which they are "put on" seems to be in exact ratio to how much they believe in (or are scared by) such a concept. This writer having studied the Warhol mystique rather closely for about three years has come to the tentative conclusion—all conclusions are tentative around Andy—that the silver-haired genius is the nearest thing to being neutral that is attainable by any human being. And in that lies his uniqueness. There are people, of course, who deplore such a concept on "moralistic" grounds: How dare he not show emotions? How dare he like and accept EVERYTHING? etc. etc. But such quibbles

are irrelevant. Why waste time on debating the rights or wrongs of something that merely IS?"[52]

As Barthes noted in his course, the Neutral thus presents a kind of scandal for those who expect a good debate ("how dare he?"). But the Neutral also succeeds in baffling the moralistic demands of the interviewer.

Wayne Koestenbaum, in his sensitive Warhol biography, puts forward a simultaneously psychological and pragmatic reading of Warhol's tactics in interviews:

> Andy had perfected his asinine persona, the mute and inexpressive face that, Billy Name told me, Andy developed in response to media stupidity. Reporters wanted to make a joke of Warhol, who was wary of words, and who may also have been terrified—paralyzed—by interviewers. So he responded with evasions, stammerings. . . . He considered interviews to be collaborative art pieces; his job was not to convey truth but to perform. Avoiding direct response and concocting an affectless persona were credible ways of "coming out" to the media, which would hardly have tolerated him explicitly stating his intention to elevate homoerotic desire above every representational or expressive task.[53]

Koestenbaum's psychological approach is less interesting to me than his acute attention to the problem of what was strategically effective, which brings us back to Foucault's definition of strategy as employed in three ways:

> First, to designate the means employed to attain a certain end. . . . Second, to designate the way in which a partner in a certain game acts with regard to what he thinks should be the action of others and what he considers others think to be his own. . . . Third, to designate the procedures used in a situation of confrontation to deprive the opponent of his means of combat and to reduce him to giving up the struggle.[54]

The question of "coming out" is complicated by such sensitivity to strategy, and our sense of resistance is equally complicated when we consider Warhol's response is not a direct response. It is perhaps more accurate to talk about tactics rather than strategy. Following Michel de Certeau's definition of "tactics" as a means of making do with a situation that one does not properly "own," we can think of Warhol's interviews as precisely tactical. Certeau suggests,

The space of a tactic is the space of the other. Thus it must play on and with a terrain imposed on it and organized by the law of a foreign power. . . . This nowhere gives a tactic mobility, to be sure, but a mobility that must accept the chance offerings of the moment, and seize on the wing the possibilities that offer themselves at any given moment. . . . It poaches in them. It creates surprises in them. It can be where it is least expected. It is a guileful ruse.[55]

I would argue that Warhol's "ruses" are a matter of poaching in the space of the other, that is, the space of the interview as defined by the interviewer's questions (the law of a foreign power). In Koestenbaum's afterword to the collection of Warhol's interviews published in *I'll Be Your Mirror*, he isolates a series of these ruses (the roles of martyr, dummy, comedian, and fool), insisting that "when Warhol's responses to questions sound inane, they interrogate our discourses of inanity."[56] Warhol's tactics can act like a mirror, showing the inanity of the interviewer's questions.[57] They also suggest the possibility of thinking about stupidity itself. In Barthes's "Deliberation," he includes a journal entry considering this possibility: "For some years, a unique project, apparently: to explore my own stupidity, or better still: to *utter* it, to make it the object of my books. In this way I have already uttered my 'egoist' stupidity and my 'lover's' stupidity. There remains a third kind, which I shall someday have to get on paper: political stupidity."[58] I would suggest that Warhol's interviews (along with *The Andy Warhol Diaries*) might be productively read along these lines.

Koestenbaum is right to note Warhol's evasion of direct response in favor of stammering. Like Herman Melville's Bartleby, Warhol's linguistic formulas are confounding and devastating, leaving nothing in their wake. Gilles Deleuze has made an argument about Melville's characters that might well be applied to Warhol: "Angels or saintly hypochondriacs, almost stupid. . . . Petrified by nature, they prefer . . . no will at all, a nothingness of the will rather than a will to nothingness (hypochondriachal 'negativism'). They can only survive by becoming stone, by denying the will and sanctifying themselves in this suspension."[59] Certainly, these adjectives have all been applied biographically to Warhol as saintly-hypochondriac-stupid-nothingness. But this question of a nothingness of the will, as opposed to a will to nothingness, is an important distinction to consider in terms of Warhol's linguistic formula for interviews.

How should we read Warhol's tendency toward negation? Consider this famous response:

Q. Do you think pop art is—?
A. No.
Q. What?
A. No.
Q. Do you think pop art is?
A. No. No, I don't.[60]

Several readings might be made of this set of responses. Is Warhol refusing to answer the question altogether? Is he arguing that Pop art simply "isn't" art, or that more radically that it "isn't" at all (in some existential sense)? Certainly, his preemption works well to derail the question. Thus, like Foucault's or Deleuze's readings of survival strategies, the goal is to subsist in a suspension, or—judo-like—deprive the opponent of the means of combat and force them to give up the struggle.

The monosyllabic style of response is certainly Warhol at his most "machine-like" and distills the interview into a yes–no "questionnaire." But to move further away from the idea of intention or the simplicity of firsthand interpretations of his work by the artist himself, Warhol also deploys a strategy that we might call a tactic of "deferral" or "proxy." Koestenbaum's reading of Warhol's interview tactics as a kind of collaborative performance is a very useful way of conceptualizing the scenario and Warhol's approach to it.

Deferral/Proxy

Deferral is a useful term in its double sense of "putting off" and "deferring to" someone better equipped to handle something. This latter person might be thought of as Warhol's "proxy" respondent. We find this in several interviews, where Warhol authorizes another to respond with a simple turn marked by "isn't that it?" "is that true?" or "what do you think?" This also explains the importance of the famous "entourage" and the intellectual patrons and advocates of Warhol being on hand at all times. Among the entourage, Candy Darling, Brigid Polk (Brigid Berlin), Edie Sedgwick, and Warhol's assistant Gerard Malanga were often called upon to give statements to the press about Warhol and his projects.[61] Among the intelligentsia and art world, spokespeople were Ivan Karp, Henry Geldzahler, and Emile de Antonio (each consecutively or simultaneously playing a role of agent, friend, and champion of the cause of Pop).[62] In an interview tape-recorded by Billy Klüver, Geldzahler tries to get Warhol to talk: "How can you interview an artist who can't talk? (Laughs) It's completely ridiculous." Warhol then asks "Can you be silent for a week? I mean a minute?" Geldzahler insists: "Talk something!" "No! What am I to say?" is Warhol's response. Geldzahler ends up saying far more than Warhol on the recording (which was turned into an LP record and book).[63]

One excellent example of deferral/proxy can be found in de Antonio's film *Painters Painting* (1973), which features both "De" and Brigid with Andy Warhol on a couch facing a mirror.[64] Warhol is wonderfully evasive in his interview segment, but not in the sense of concealing the truth. Rather, he will default to De or Brigid and attribute the authorship of what are supposed to be his work and ideas to them. He claims that making art commercially was De's idea—"De said so. . . . Isn't it true?"—to which De responds, "Not entirely, Andy." Warhol then recites that "all people are the same" and that he wants to "be a machine," to which De says, "That isn't true," and Andy asks, "Is it true Brigid?" Brigid and Andy seem to enjoy teasing and imitating each other and giggling about how drying one's hair is a work of art, and it becomes increasingly clear that the issue of whether Brigid does Andy's work has been answered but also does not seem to matter to either of them. They can't seem to take the interview seriously (and the fact that all of this is filmed in a mirror only acts as a further irony). What is at stake here is both funny and important. It is funny in that it is a queer feminized sphere that interrupts the interview's serious intent in favor of "girl talk" such as gossip, name-dropping, hairstyling, and laughter. It is important in the sense that it shows what Warhol's displacement of authorial intent and the priority of the self looks like in practice (the practice of the silk screen and mass production being the major artistic mode employed—with Warhol's assistants Gerard Malanga and Ronnie Cutrone). *POPism* addresses rumors (that Warhol himself started) regarding how "I don't even do my own paintings, Brigid Polk does them for me": in order to appease collectors, "I had to make a public retraction."[65]

It could easily be argued that a preoccupation with Warhol's singular authorial intent lags far behind the sorts of collaborative work that was being attempted across several disciplines and media in the 1960s (Fluxus, for example), but here we are faced with one of the problems of art historical prejudices. The *signature, that guarantee of authorship,* when reconfigured as the *brand name* "Warhol," unsettles certain questions of individual *production,* but need not abolish the question of Warhol's *productivity* beyond such a preoccupation.

Impersonation

Warhol's tactics for questioning authorship, identity, and property had multiple permutations. Reva Wolf addresses the question of forged artworks, forged signatures, and impersonation in her chapter "Artistic Appropriation and the Image of the Poet as Thief": "Warhol developed myriad activities as the 1960s moved forward: Allen Midgette appeared at lectures as if he were Warhol, Warhol claimed that his friend Brigid Polk (Brigid Berlin) made his paintings, and so on. On one occasion, at a midnight film screening, Warhol reportedly introduced Malanga as 'Andy Warhol,' and Malanga then signed autographs for Warhol."[66] Edie Sedgwick was another partner-in-crime in several such situations. The reporter Mel Juffe is quoted in *POPism* as pointing out that "one of your favorite jokes at the time was shoving different people forward and saying they were you."[67] These "pranks" are not without their consequences; as Warhol explains in *POPism,* the colleges to which Allen Midgette was sent as Warhol's stand-in were not happy when they discovered the stunt:

> These antistar identity games were something we were doing anyway, as a matter of course. It wasn't until about four months later that somebody at one of the colleges happened to see a picture of me in the *Voice* and compared it to the one he'd taken of Allen on the podium and we had to give them their money back. . . . But the whole situation got even more absurd. Like, once I was on the phone with an official from one of the other colleges on that tour, telling him how really sorry I was when suddenly he turned paranoid and said: "How can I even be sure this is really you on the phone *now?*" After a pause while I gave that some thought, I had to admit, "I don't know."[68]

It is worth noting that Warhol's desire to challenge star identity (with anti-star identity games) contradicts the orthodox view of Warhol's allegedly uncritical obsession with stardom. Warhol admits that these "no-fault put-ons" were not allowed when contracts were being signed, and "what we thought of as a joke was what some people would call 'fraud'"; regarding Brigid Polk doing his paintings for him, he acknowledged that "the wrong flip remark in the press can cause just as many problems as a broken contract."[69]

But despite the legal issues, this tactic was obviously crucial for Warhol. In one of the funniest passages from *POPism*, Warhol simultaneously asserts his artistic "hand" and exhibits an incredible humor and candor about his image: "One afternoon as I was silkscreening some Jackie canvases, I watched Lou answer the phone, then hand it over to Silver George, who identified himself: 'Yes, this is Andy Warhol.' That was fine with me. Everybody at the Factory did that. . . . Anyway, it was more fun to let other people take the calls for me, and I'd sometimes read interviews with me (supposedly) that I'd never given at all, that had been done over the phone."[70] Silver George displays great relish in his "objective" description: "I have a slightly faggy air, and I do little artistic movements."[71] But Warhol remarks that "it didn't matter, I was 99 percent passive in those days, so I just let Silver George go on describing me—whatever he said couldn't be worse than the way a lot of journalists described me anyway. . . . When Silver George hung up, he said they were really thrilled because they heard I never talked and here I'd just said more to them than anyone they'd ever interviewed. They also said how surprised they were that I could be so objective about myself."[72] This game of impersonation is one in which Silver George and Warhol both seem to take pleasure, Warhol's "passivity" also providing a space to undermine the presumptions of the interview and objectivity while facilitating collaboration. David Bailey's 1973 documentary *Warhol* contains further examples of Warhol allowing others to impersonate him, including Tony Zanetta made up as Warhol reading famous Warhol interview quotations, and a "ventriloquist" interview where a friend answers Bailey's interview questions while Warhol just moves his lips.[73]

The sort of objectivity remarked upon by the phone interviewer above also appears in a passage from *Philosophy* written and recorded collaboratively by Bob Colacello, Warhol, Brigid Polk, and Pat Hackett, which features a phone call between Andy as "A" and Brigid as "B":

> "I have to look into the mirror for some clues. Nothing is missing. It's all there. The affectless gaze. The diffracted grace . . ."
>
> "What?"
>
> "The bored languor, the wasted pallor . . ."
>
> "The what?"
>
> "The chic freakishness, the basically passive astonishment, the enthralling secret knowledge . . ."
>
> "WHAT??"
>
> "The chintzy joy, the revelatory tropisms, the chalky, puckish mask, the slightly Slavic look . . ."
>
> "Slightly . . ."
>
> "The childlike, gum-chewing naïveté, the glamour rooted in despair, the self-admiring carelessness, the perfected otherness, the wispiness, the shadowy, voyeuristic, vaguely sinister aura, the pale, soft-spoken magical presence, the skin and bones . . ."
>
> . . .
>
> "It's all there B. Nothing is missing. I'm everything my scrapbook says I am."[74]

This demonstrates an intense awareness on Warhol's part of the image he claimed he didn't have in the interview with Gretchen Berg. These "objective" descriptions of Warhol are remarkably reappropriated through his publication of them in his books (which can be thought of as contributions to Warhol's "image"). The "image-repertoire" that so vexed Roland Barthes is here pushed to its limit (the imaginary—the set of masks—is invoked repeatedly, but in a phone conversation that importantly gives only the voice, not the face).[75] Sedgwick has read these passages as revealing the "holographic space of Warhol's hunger to own the rage of other people to describe him—to describe him as if impersonally, not to say sadistically. The effect of this shy exhibitionism is, among other things, deeply queer."[76] Sedgwick's analysis questions too neat an opposition between these *queer affects*—shyness and exhibitionism—and identifies their proximity as an intensely *queer effect*.

We can find perhaps the best examples of this sadistic rage to describe Warhol in Nat Finkelstein and David Dalton's book of ranting and photography, *Andy Warhol: The Factory Years 1964–1967*, and Stephen Koch's *Stargazer: The Life, World, and Films of Andy Warhol*.[77] Both of these texts are remarkable in the degree of *ressentiment* and disavowal they express when describing Warhol and the activities/personages of the Factory. Despite his sometimes acute awareness of Warhol's opacity, it is Koch who desperately tries to "capture" Warhol's presence, and he gives us the phrase "A childlike gum-chewing naïveté."[78] He also enacts a disavowal of the 1960s that appears in many of the testimonies ("recovery narratives") of the surviving superstars in *Superstar: The Life and Times of Andy Warhol.* It seems that when these texts reflect on the "Times," they need to make sober(ing) denouncements, in Koch's "The End of the Other World," for instance, of "those unreproduceable parties of the 1960s, irresistible and grotesque," or assessments like "as the 1960s began to fall apart . . . the precious Aquarian Age of Innocence turned out to be another self-flattering lie. Perhaps, if people had looked carefully enough in the mirror, they would have seen that."[79] These are all rather boring and traditional denunciations of narcissism—its supposed nonproductiveness[80]—and that truly Victorian sin: vanity.[81]

Koch's rhetorical style is reminiscent of Susan Sontag's notorious "Notes on 'Camp,'" which shares this problematic concern for "objectivity": "I am strongly drawn to Camp, and almost as strongly offended by it. That is why I want to talk about it, and why I can. For no one who wholeheartedly shares in a given sensibility can analyze it; he can only, whatever his intentions, exhibit it. To name a sensibility, to draw its contours and recount its history, requires a deep sympathy modified by revulsion."[82] This revulsion is what D. A. Miller and others have identified as Sontag's phobic de-homosexualization of camp.[83] The major problem with the objectivist standpoint is that in dissecting the sensibility of camp, Sontag is aware that "to talk about Camp is therefore to betray it."[84] As in the case of Sontag, we should be aware of the intense homophobia in much of what constitutes the "urbanity" of those writing about Warhol's world.

But the responsibility we are supposed to gain in the 1980s accounts of the '60s represents nothing other than a disavowal. (This disavowal is quite in line with the more general Reaganite revisionism about the social upheavals of the 1960s.) What is remarkable, then, is that Warhol refuses to moralize in his reflection on *"The Warhol Sixties,"* and actually embraces Koch's book with his quotation from it and his statement quoted on the back cover: *"Stargazer* is to die over!" What is brilliant about this endorsement is its phrasing, whereby the conventional phrase "to die for"—in all its camp flavor—is reconfigured as "to die over" which in fact accentuates the way in which Warhol is treated as a corpse by all of these historical documents (as Barthes puts it, "a relationship which adjectivizes is on the side of the image, on the side of domination, of death").[85] But I would argue that what is remarkable about Warhol's reaction to those who attempt "to describe him as if impersonally" is his productive manipulation of the im-personal (im-personation). This is quite close to what Barthes finds in "Figures of the Neutral": the possibility of "the vacancy of the 'person,' if not annulled at least rendered irretrievable."[86]

"That was the way he really talked?"

Another major tactic employed by Warhol relates to the problem of "articulateness," which is a major preoccupation of *POPism*. Certainly, figures such as Emile de Antonio, Sam Green, Ivan Karp, and Paul Morrissey were much better at making statements to the press, art world "types," and college audiences, and they could articulate Warhol's project "better" than him, which Warhol authorizes through these tactics of proxy and deferral. However, one can also sometimes sense a disavowal of intellectualism throughout much of *POPism*, especially regarding Susan Sontag and Jonas Mekas, perhaps the best examples of "defenders" of underground work, rallying around the figure of Jack Smith, but also somewhat expropriating his work. Warhol exacts some revenge in describing Sontag: "David told me that he'd heard that she didn't think too much of my painting—'I hear she suspects your sincerity,' he said. Well, that was no surprise, since a lot of dazzling intellects felt that way."[87] In the chapter on 1967, Warhol suggests that the Pop style where "you didn't talk, you just did outrageous things . . . was all played out—everyone was ready for some articulation, and Paul was nothing if not articulate."[88] Warhol's concern for "articulateness" actually speaks to a broader matter of sensitivity to speech itself within *POPism*. Ivan Karp was "so good with words," and

Warhol parenthetically remarks, "(As I said, that was the way he really talked)."[89]

Much of *POPism*'s role as memoir has to do with capturing the style and sound of people's speech. There is great attention paid to the unique "grain of the voice" itself:

> [VIVA:] She talked constantly, and she had the most tiresome voice I'd ever heard—it was incredible to me that one woman's voice could convey so much tedium. . . . [T]hat weary voice of hers, the dreariest, driest voice in the world.[90]
>
> [TAYLOR MEAD:] He had a slow, easy, if-anyone-happens-to-care delivery.[91]
>
> [LOU REED:] Lou's voice was dry and flat, and he had droll timing.[92]
>
> [NICO:] [S]he had this very strange way of speaking. People described her voice as everything from eery, to bland and smooth, to slow and hollow, to a "wind in the drainpipe," to an "IBM computer with a Garbo accent."[93]
>
> [SUSAN BOTTOMLY (INTERNATIONAL VELVET):] Susan Bottomly's voice was the strangest thing to hear coming out of this girl. Everybody went around doing Susan Bottomly imitations. It was a monotone, but not at all like Nico's: Susan's was a low-pitched American monotone. What she was like was a very beautiful, sexy cow.[94]
>
> [JACKIE CURTIS:] [T]he creepiest part of a sex change has nothing to do with appearance—*it's the voice*. In Jackie's case, he did what most men do when they want to sound like a woman—he dropped his voice to a whisper. However, the thing was, whispery voices never made the drag queens sound more femme—they only made them sound more desperate.[95]
>
> [EMILE "DE" DE ANTONIO:] He spoke beautifully, in a deep, easy voice with every comma and period falling into place.[96]
>
> [WARHOL HIMSELF:] I reacted my usual way—modest noises came out of my mouth, the sounds you make when you're embarrassed but saying thank you.[97]

Barthes has discussed the issue of the voice in various texts (most notably his discussion of "The Grain of the Voice" in musical recordings),[98] but nowhere as poignantly than in *Roland Barthes by Roland Barthes* in a fragment entitled "*Sa voix*," which I will quote in full for its remarkable resonance with Warhol:

> *Sa voix* ~ his voice
> (No one's in particular. Yes, in particular! It's always someone's voice.)
> I try, little by little, to *render* his voice. I make an adjectival approach: agile, fragile, youthful, somewhat broken? No, not quite; rather: *overcultivated*, having

a faint British flavor. And how about this: clipped? Yes, if I expatiate: he revealed in this clipped quality not the torsion (the grimace) of a body controlling and thereby affirming itself but on the contrary the exhausting collapse of the subject without language, presenting the threat of aphasia under which he struggles: contrary to the first, this was a voice *without rhetoric* (though not without tenderness). For all these voices, the right metaphor would have to be invented, the one which, once encountered, would possess you forever; but I fail to find any such thing, so great is the gap between the words which come to me from the culture and this strange being (can it be no more than a matter of sounds?) which I fleetingly recall at my ear.

Such impotence has a reason: the voice is always *already* dead, and it is by a kind of desperate denial that we recall it: living; this irremediable loss we give the name of *inflection:* inflection is the voice insofar as it is always past, silenced.

Whereby we may understand what *description* is: it strives to render what is strictly mortal in the object by feigning (illusion by reversal) to suppose it, to desire it *living:* "as if alive" means "apparently dead." The adjective is the instrument of this illusion; whatever it says, by its descriptive quality alone, the adjective is funereal.[99]

This melancholic struggling to describe the mortal object of the voice is a work of *rendering* and *conjuring*.[100] This is the primary occupation of *POPism* as a memoir (or a history) in my opinion, and its elegiac character need not only be found in the final postscript (those depressing postscripts to so many descriptions of queer "underground" scenes in the '60s and '70s, such as John Waters's *Shock Value*).[101] It has built into it the difficulty of inventing the right metaphor that "once encountered, would possess you forever" for capturing "this strange being": the voice.

Victor Bockris has made a convincing argument about "Andy Warhol the writer," claiming that in his writing, "Warhol was most interested in depicting what I call 'voice portraits.'"[102] When Bockris met Warhol at *Interview* magazine, Warhol's advice was to go into the interview with no questions and no preconceptions, "with as empty a mind as possible": "This way, the interviewer will get the most accurate and revealing image of the subject via the topics he or she chooses to discuss, as well as the grammar, syntax, and vocabulary used. If a tape is transcribed very accurately, with each 'uhm,' 'err' and 'but' included, what is redacted is a voice portrait."[103] This can be found in the interviews Warhol did for *Interview* between 1974 and 1982, as well as in Warhol's taped "novel" of twenty-four hours with Ondine on amphetamines, *a: a novel*.[104] Bockris explains that a number of inconsistencies occurred in the process of having the tapes transcribed by a number of people (including Moe Tucker and a group of high school girls), including censorship, misspelling, brackets that open but never close, and so forth. But Warhol decided to embrace the manuscript exactly as it was, and Bockris argues that "in preserving the manuscript's shattered state Warhol was actually presenting the precise aura of the conversations. Because as we know, people don't actually speak in sentences."[105] In a discussion of the work of transcribing speech into writing in the interview format, Barthes insists that there is "no language without a body," and sees speech as "wrestling with language out in the open" with "all those *buts* and *therefores* in our public speech, all those repetitions and explicit denials. . . . Writing is often sparing of them, venturing into asyndeton—that cutting figure which would be unbearable to the voice, as unbearable as a castration."[106]

Warhol explained the reason for keeping the spelling mistakes: "I wanted to do a 'bad book' the way I'd done 'bad movies' and 'bad art,' because when you do something exactly wrong, you always turn up something."[107] What Warhol manages to turn up is a portrait of Ondine's style of speaking, with his viciousness, his wit, his pleasure in renaming (Warhol's nickname was "Drella": a portmanteau of Dracula/Cinderella), playing with rhythms and rhymes in language. One of the most playful passages features Taxine (Edie) commenting on Ondine's style of speaking:

> o [ONDINE]—Well, we could even, we could make up a game that would be even better. Games are so . . .
> t [TAXINE/EDIE]—Well, you know.
> o—The only way to talk is to talk in games, it's just fabulous.
> t—Ondine has games that no one understands.
> o—It's wonderful (*Laughter*).[108]

Language has often been compared to a game of chess, with each move determining the next set of moves (this figure appears in Saussure, Wittgenstein, and Lyotard); would it be too facetious to argue that the most mobile chess piece is the queen? This ludic and performative quality, but also crucially strategic or tactical element of discourse, is part of what I find in Warhol's discursive tactics, although the opacity of Warhol's speech differs somewhat from the opacity of Ondine's "camping" in *a: a novel*.

The opacity of Ondine's speech in *a: a novel* might be called "chatter," if we remove this term from its pejorative associations. Eleanor Kaufman has indicated how *chatter* might be understood as distinguishable from both meaningful speech and silence (both of which are at issue in any reading of Warhol), and be affirmed and elevated in a consideration of form (as opposed to the content of speech). She explains, "Chatter is in this manner elevated as a form in its own right—a form that, as such, far surpasses anything that the content of the chatter might disclose."[109] Kaufman argues that chatter might indicate a refusal to separate meaningful speech from empty speech, and indeed to separate speech from silence.[110] Warhol's spoken silence and Ondine's chatter together form *a: a novel*, and like the works that Kaufman studies in her *Delirium of Praise*, it becomes impossible to distinguish between the two voices. Both in a sense say "nothing," but this way of saying nothing ends up affirming the *form* of chatter and the durational, recorded novel itself. The very form of the recorded novel refuses another heavily charged opposition, that between speech (as "presence") and writing. It is clear that Warhol's novel cannot be added to the history of the repression of writing in philosophy as described by Jacques Derrida. This is due to the simple fact that speech is not accorded a privileged position vis-à-vis "presence" or "truth" in Warhol's text, which blurs the line between speech and writing (possibly creating a third term, what Barthes has called "the written" in "From Speech to Writing").[111]

The inclusion of the parenthetical description of sounds *(Opera) (Sigh) (Laughter) (voices) (Ondine makes a funny sound) (Drella laughs subtly) (Someone says something)* adds another purely sonic layer and imposes a certain level of "stage direction" to what sometimes reads like a script. Like in the film *Madonna: Truth or Dare* (1991), the recording apparatus (tape/camera) is sometimes addressed directly or drawn attention to, and sometimes not.[112] Also, like Madonna's commissioning Alek Keshishian to film her on tour with supposedly "all access," for which she is criticized by Warren Beatty (in a rather disingenuous denunciation of publicity from a major actor, who invokes a model of "public/private" "on/off-camera" that has mutated by the time Madonna makes use of the publicity machine),[113] another Old Hollywood type criticizes Warhol for his use of the tape recorder:

> I [IRVING DU BALL/LESTER PERSKY]—Ondine, if you ever throw the side he's pointing at, this is the most passive put-on I've ever seen; as a result of having this, Drella doesn't have to participate in life.
>
> T—Oh is that why he's saying . . .
>
> I—Why he has to participate . . . no, it's amazing, he holds this to all of us.
>
> O—no, that's, my dear, this is, he's holding it only to me darling, he's holding holding it o-only to me and he's participates far more than he would without it. (*Pause*)
>
> I—How do you know when you run out of tape?[114]

What is at stake in this confrontation (and Ondine makes it clear that his "darling" is meant to be "catty") is the question of Warhol's investment in recording apparatuses. Koch, following Geldzahler, suggests that the tape recorder and the telephone act as "baffles" that Warhol can use as a form of evasion or self-protection, but I believe there is more to it than that psychologism can account for.[115]

For the Record

In *The Philosophy of Andy Warhol,* Warhol explains the role played by the tape recorder:

> The acquisition of my tape recorder really finished whatever emotional life I might have had, but I was glad to see it go. Nothing was ever a problem again, because a problem just meant a good tape, and when a problem transforms itself into a good tape it's not a problem anymore. An interesting problem was an interesting tape. Everyone knew that and performed for the tape. You couldn't tell which problems were real and which problems were exaggerated for the tape. Better yet, the people telling you the problems couldn't decided any more if they were really having the problems or if they were just performing.[116]

Warhol referred to his tape recorder as his "wife." It was with him at all times and is featured prominently in *The Philosophy of Andy Warhol.* In a dialogue with one of the many friends and associates who are each referred to only as "B" in *Philosophy*—whose appended subtitle is *(From*

A to B and Back Again) — "B" describes a situation in which Queen Soraya makes "A" shut "her" (his "wife") off: "I heard her tell you to and then somebody said you looked so sad sitting next to Soraya, and I said, 'Oh it's just because she made him turn off his tape. A likes everybody except people who make him turn off his tape. It's like saying come to dinner but don't bring your wife.'"[117] This friend understands that for Warhol the question "Are you having a good time?" really means "Is your wife having a good time?" This level of mediation is often referred to as Warhol's passive voyeurism (a rather muddy psychological category given Laura Mulvey's conceptualization of voyeurism as active and sadistic).[118] It parodies intersubjectivity even as it points to an emergent subjectivity with quite a different relationship to affect and enjoyment that can only be referred to as the affect of the machine, the "magnetophone" as one French journalist referred to it, a term Andy found so "great."[119] This level of technological mediation, which causes people to perform for the machine, is also a major part of the Factory "Screen Tests" described in *POPism,* where whoever stopped by was placed in front of the camera that Warhol or his assistant would set up and just walk away from, letting the film reel run for its few minutes' duration.[120]

One statement in *Philosophy* makes it clear how much Warhol identified with the tape recording apparatus: "My mind is like a tape recorder with one button — Erase."[121] This is a truly hallucinatory, impossible figure that loops the tape recorder into its own erasure. Recording and playback technology disembodies the voice all the time, as in the Ford machines where "someone spoke a commentary." But the other major communication technology that Warhol relies on is the telephone, the device that plays a major role in the Factory (with the only "rules" of the Factory pertaining to answering the phone so as to not give away whether the person asked for is there or not),[122] and in many of the above instances of Warhol's interview and impersonation strategies. But the telephone also plays a major role in the sorts of pleasurable improvised conversation Warhol engaged in with his various friends: "You should have contact with your closest friends through the most intimate and exclusive of all media — the telephone."[123] Christopher Isherwood characterized *POPism* as "as absorbing as the best telephone gossip, funny yet full of insights," and this fits the general tone of both *POPism* and *Philosophy* (since *Philosophy* begins with just such a phone conversation).[124]

Pat Hackett explains the inception of *The Andy Warhol Diaries* as follows: "In the fall of 1976 Andy and I established a weekday morning routine of talking to each other on the phone. Ostensibly still for the purpose of getting down on record everything he had done and every place he had gone the day and night before and logging cash business expenses he had incurred in the process, this account of daily activity came to have the larger function of letting Andy examine life. In a word, it was a diary."[125] Rather than following this movement from the quotidian and material to the personal and the reflective, I would like to stay at the level of the material concern of the *Diaries*. Indeed, what is so striking to the reader is the meticulous accounting of every expense, including cabs and phone calls. While these indicate a fear of a tax audit, they also might be considered for how they function within a larger strategy of opacity, whereby the search for a hidden depth is confounded by a material opacity in the form of *Merz* or receipts.[126] (I am reminded of a scene in Pedro Almodóvar's *All About My Mother* [1999] when the transsexual prostitute La Agrado presents her authentic "life story" as a series of receipts for her cosmetic surgery.)[127] We can look at the *Andy Warhol Diaries* as yet another ironic deployment of a literary form that is traditionally linked to confessional, revelation, and authenticity.[128]

Thus, like Victor Bockris, I am arguing that "Andy Warhol the writer" transforms the formats he employs, often subverting some of the assumptions that generally go along with them. By founding *Interview* magazine,[129] Warhol directly intervenes in the format that he undermined the most, and it is worth asking why *Interview* is somewhat of a "bad object" for most art historical accounts of Warhol's oeuvre.[130] Part of it has to do with suspicion of Warhol's proximity to conservative figures like Nancy Reagan, but both Bockris and Colacello have emphasized the significance of Warhol's unique approach to the possibilities that the interview opens up. While it might be argued that the interview is still a search for authenticity (the "unmediated" voice portrait), it is clear that Warhol refuses the interview's role as interrogation (the production of authority and truth). The *Diary* is insistently material; though it is not without reflection and gossip, I see it as functioning like the famous "time capsules" in which Warhol kept his mail, in preserving the material traces of daily life. The *memoir* is used partially to correct history and manage his reputation (to wash his hands of the ruination of the superstars), but is most productive in its attention to the voice itself, to ways of speaking. *Philosophy* uses the decidedly queer tradition of the *aphorism* to construct a nonsystematic set of statements (sometimes poetic, other times like punchlines, sometimes banal, other times acute). And while the *novel* is an unrelentingly "bad book," it renders the polyvocality and density of speech unlike novelistic dialogue. What inheres in these experiments with various forms is a resistance to the assumptions of authenticity, disclosure, and transparency. They represent tactics of opacity that demand that we read them differently, without a desire for a "hidden depth." We must instead look at what happens on the surface of these texts. Finally, there in that most investigative and authenticating of formats—the interview—we insistently encounter Warhol's opacity and his discursive tactics of deferral, proxy, impersonation, and in-authenticity. Are these merely forms of evasion? I would maintain instead that what opens up is a space for a different mode of discourse whose concern is not for the truth. Thus, what emerges is not simply "silence" but rather different modes of speaking that displace the question of speaking for or as oneself.

FOUR

Unseen Warhol/Seeing Barthes

Another opposition destroyed is that of inner/outer. Consider the Western
theater of the last few centuries. Its function is essentially to reveal what
is reputed to be secret . . . while concealing the very artifice of the process
of revelation. . . . With Bunraku, the sources of theater are exposed in
their void. What is expelled from the stage is hysteria, that is theater itself,
and what is put in its place is the action necessary for the production of
the spectacle—work is substituted for interiority.

—Roland Barthes, "Lesson in Writing"

IN THE PREVIOUS CHAPTER, I wanted to move away from the customary
emphasis on Warhol's visual art and toward an extended examination of
his discursive strategies of opacity. In the next two chapters I will be moving back from the verbal to the visual aspects of Warhol's persona, but via
the detour of writing. I begin with Barthes's writing on photography,
specifically a portrait of Warhol. This chapter thus extends the themes of
portraiture and autoportraiture found in the earlier chapters on Foucault
and Barthes. In the next chapter, I will discuss a posthumous portrait of
Warhol and his Time Capsules: the documentary *Andy Warhol: The Complete Picture.*[1] While I will treat the static portrait and the cinematic portrait separately, both chapters look at tactics for thwarting the viewer's
desire for the "unseen" and the "complete picture."

Studium/Punctum

Roland Barthes's *Camera Lucida: Reflections on Photography* advances a
theory of photography with a now-famous distinction between the *Studium,*

what a photo is "about," its social and historical meaning, and the *Punctum*, that aspect or detail of a photo that "pricks" the viewer individually and uncannily. In this manner, Barthes considers a series of photographs, including a portrait of Andy Warhol by Duane Michals (*Andy Warhol*, 1958) that is not reproduced in Barthes's text (figure 1). Barthes expands his theory of the *punctum* by way of this picture:

> There is another . . . expansion of the *punctum:* when, paradoxically, while remaining a "detail," it fills the whole picture. Duane Michals has photographed Andy Warhol: a provocative portrait, since Warhol hides his face behind both hands. I have no desire to comment intellectually on this game of hide-and-seek (which belongs to the *Studium*); since for me, Warhol hides nothing; he offers his hands to be read, quite openly; and the *punctum* is not the gesture but the slightly repellent substance of those spatulate nails, at once soft and hard-edged.[2]

This "game of hide-and-seek" links up with Michel Foucault's theory of "games of truth," in particular where the "truth" of the subject is sought in that person's sexuality, the secret truth of his or her identity. In the interview "The End of the Monarchy of Sex," Foucault diagnoses "this great 'sexography' that makes us decipher sex as the universal secret."[3] Hidden/revealed is the paradigmatic opposition within confessional discourse, and this also constitutes the mechanism of "the closet." Eve Kosofsky Sedgwick has pointed to the Proustian logic whereby *"the spectacle of the closet"* is effectively presented as *"the truth of the homosexual."*[4] Critics have debated whether Warhol and Barthes were "open" about being gay. D. A. Miller read Barthes as "closeted" in his book *Bringing Out Roland Barthes,* but it is perhaps more accurate to say that both Barthes and Warhol *have been* closeted, rather than that they *were* closeted.

Both Warhol and Barthes propose an alternative to the notion of an identity "hidden behind" the surface. Both question the role that the face plays in these games of identity, as both true marker of identity and mask. Let us return to Barthes's description of the master who controls the Bunraku puppet:

> As for the master, it has already been said that his head is left uncovered, smooth and bare, without make-up, this conferring on him a *civic* (and not theatrical) appearance; his face is offered to the spectator for reading, but what is so carefully and so preciously given to be read is that there is nothing to be read—here

Figure 1. *Andy Warhol*, 1958. Photograph by Duane Michals. Copyright Duane Michals; courtesy Pace/MacGill Gallery, New York.

we find that exemption from meaning which does indeed illumine so many works of the East and which we are scarcely able to comprehend, since for us to attack meaning is to conceal or oppose it, never to absent it.[5]

Barthes's reading of the Warhol portrait echoes his reading of the Bunraku puppet-master whose face is "given to be read" in the same way that Warhol offers his hands "openly" to be read. Warhol's famous aphorism from an interview with Gretchen Berg—"If you want to know all about Andy Warhol, just look at the surface of my paintings and films and me, and there I am. There's nothing behind it."—is likewise echoed by Barthes's assertion in *Roland Barthes by Roland Barthes* that there is nothing behind his mask, "personne" behind his "personae."[6] Thus, the alternative to "concealed" identity that both Barthes and Warhol seem to be proposing is rather an "absenting."

This is indeed "provocative," as Barthes notes, because such an absent subject is open to the critiques of Miller and Leo Bersani, who find in this practice a collusion with homophobia, what Bersani calls "The Gay Absence."[7] But "gay absence" is not necessarily Warhol's aim (as difficult as it may be to ascertain an ultimate goal for Warhol). Steven Shaviro has insisted that Warhol hides nothing behind his surfaces, there is no "depth, denial, or struggle" to decipher or uncover.[8] On a similar note, in an essay on Warhol entitled "That Old Thing, Art . . . ," Barthes explains that "the Pop artist does not stand *behind* his work, and he himself has no depth: he is merely the surface of his pictures: no signified, no intention, anywhere."[9] Rather, as in Barthes's reading of Bunraku, Warhol substitutes work for interiority.

The editors of *Pop Out: Queer Warhol* explain that they wish to recover Pop's "queer context and content" against the "de-gaying" of Warhol in much criticism of Pop Art.[10] This also adequately describes the work performed by Simon Watney's piece in the collection, "Queer Andy." Watney begins with an anecdote about getting busted during a screening of *Lonesome Cowboys* in order to specify the seductive, and illicit, queer context and content of the film and of Warhol's work. This strategy of recovery and specification works against what Watney calls a "virtual cliff-face of denial and displacement" in critical work on Warhol, which tends to stress technical matters and the "banality" or "arbitrariness" (thus inconsequentiality) of his subject matter. Against the "obliterative homophobia" of contemporary Pop Art criticism, Watney wishes to argue that Warhol "represented a public face of queerness. He was transparently queer."[11]

I share Watney's desire to locate Warhol's life within a history of homophobia and forms of resistance to it, along with his wish to examine Warhol's "curious, quintessentially queer combination of intense shyness and dandyism."[12] Certainly, the repoliticization of dandyism and camp is a crucial task in an arena of criticism that uses these two words "dandyism" and "camp" in Susan Sontag's sense as depoliticized and depoliticizing.[13] However, the downside of a gay response to Sontag and others' de-gaying and depoliticization of camp and dandyism is the recourse to essential notions of gayness or queerness. What does it mean to say that Warhol exhibited behaviors or attitudes that are "quintessentially queer" or "transparently queer"? Watney's discussion of childhood and shame, as well as what he calls precocious genius and precocious queerness, runs the risk of privileging the biographical in a specific explanatory way (as does almost every Warhol documentary and biography).

Though it goes against chronological order, I would like to argue that Watney is far more careful and critical regarding the issue of biography in his earlier piece entitled "The Warhol Effect."[14] Watney discusses the "afterlife" of Andy Warhol in the form of an auction of his seemingly indiscriminate collections. He indicates that "biographies have already been announced, to satisfy that curiosity which seeks to 'know' the artist, in the mainstream tradition of art critical and art historical humanism, and invariably finds the artist as the unique and irreducible source of his or her work."[15] This art historical humanism and *curiosity* is perhaps best exemplified by the book from which I have lifted my chapter title: John O'Connor and Benjamin Liu's *Unseen Warhol*, but almost every Warhol biography exploits the idea of a hidden or secret Warhol *behind* the public persona (e.g., Victor Bockris and Bob Colacello).[16]

In contrast, Watney argues that "Warhol constantly aspired to detach himself from a traditional authorial role, to dissolve himself into an inviolable persona."[17] He goes on to explain that there is no necessary connection between the star's persona and person. Watney argues that Warhol's portraits exemplify his "disinterest in any appeals to psychological or biographical notions of 'depth' or 'insight'" but rather reveal the sitter's position within a larger system of public representations or personas. He claims that "no artist has ever undermined notions of Self more thoroughly and insistently than Warhol."[18] Inspired by Foucault, Watney proposes that Warhol established a "poetics of the provisional" that makes one's life into a work of art, and that this is more productive than measuring Warhol against "the criteria of predetermined models of artistic value which his own work quietly invalidates."[19] He argues that "Warhol is now safely indistinguishable from what survives as the ongoing critical intelligence and sensibility of the Warhol effect."[20]

Despite Robert Hughes's dismissiveness and homophobia, I actually think there is some merit in his observation that Warhol is not a likable popular artist: "Warhol's public character . . . has been the opposite: an abnormal figure (silent, withdrawn, eminently visible but opaque, and a bit malevolent)."[21] The merit lies in this peculiar phrase, "eminently visible but opaque," in the sense that Warhol's opacity refuses the search for depth in the form of intentionality, authenticity, psychology, and so forth.

This seems to me to have specific advantages against a desire to represent Warhol as being recognizably and transparently queer, insofar as such a desire seeks a clear form of identification. I do not believe that Simon Watney is guilty of such a procedure, because of his emphasis on a queer poetics of the provisional, but we might read this as a provisional poetics of "queer," thus insisting that the word's meaning not be decided in advance, where Watney's phrasing "Queer Andy" becomes simply substitutable for "Gay Andy."

What I have been calling "queer opacity" is a refusal of the quintessentiality of queerness.[22] This is how I propose that we might read such Warhol aphorisms as: "I never fall apart because I never fall together."[23] This model of subjectivity, with an emphasis on fragmentary or provisional identity, is also very dear to Roland Barthes, in particular in *Roland Barthes by Roland Barthes* where he asserts, "I am not contradictory, I am dispersed."[24] Indeed, shifting, drifting, cruising, and dispersal are crucial to Barthes's queer subjectivity. He even refers to himself in his "Inaugural Lecture" at the Collège de France as "a patently impure fellow" and "a fellow of doubtful nature."[25]

Echoing this notion of dispersed identity, *Camera Lucida* also features reflections on Barthes's "own" image in the form of the photographic portrait:

> What I want, in short, is that my (mobile) image, buffeted among a thousand shifting photographs, altering with situation and age, should always coincide with my (profound) "self"; but it is the contrary that must be said: "myself" never coincides with my image; for it is the image which is heavy, motionless, stubborn (which is why society sustains it), and "myself" which is light, divided, dispersed . . . if only Photography could give me a neutral, anatomic body, a body which signifies nothing! Alas, I am doomed by (well-meaning) Photography always to have an expression: my body never finds its zero degree, no one can give it to me (perhaps only my mother? For it is not indifference which erases the weight of the image—the Photomat always turns you into a criminal type, wanted by the police—but love, extreme love).[26]

Warhol, on the other hand, sought out this Photomatic indifference, as illustrated by his early experiments with Photomat portraits (*Ethel Scull Thirty-Six Times*, 1963) and self-portraits (*Self-portrait*, 1964), and in his use of criminal mug shots (*The Thirteen Most Wanted Men*, 1964–65).

Warhol was well aware of how much society sustains the image, the stubborn image: the portrait. The identity photo is central to the functioning of society; your face is who you are. Barthes is right to argue that the Photomat always turns you into a criminal type; Warhol's mug shots simply confirm it.[27]

Barthes and Warhol each deal differently with the problem of the portrait. A "failed" publicity photo seems to have been chosen for the dust jacket of the U.S. English translation of *Camera Lucida*. In it, Barthes is looking down and making an awkward, indeterminable expression. Within the text, he explains the portrait situation in terms that aptly fit Barthes's author photos: "I decide to 'let drift' over my lips and in my eyes a faint smile which I mean to be 'indefinable,' in which I might suggest, along with the qualities of my nature, my amused consciousness of the whole photographic ritual."[28]

Warhol highlighted the social rituals of photography: the society portrait, the artist's self-portrait, the screen test. Warhol's late camouflage self-portrait silk screens (1986) highlight a strategic game of "hide-and-seek" with the public. He seems to be both concealing and revealing himself. By comparison, it is well known that Warhol was quite unkind in his desire to "reveal" the secret masculinity of his transsexual and drag queen superstars (Jackie Curtis, Candy Darling, and Mario Montez), but perhaps this was to draw attention to the widespread social fascination with the revelation of queer secrets, what Eve Kosofsky Sedgwick has called "knowingness."[29] In their essay on Divine (the drag star of John Waters's films), Sedgwick and Michael Moon discuss Marjorie Garber's *Vested Interests: Cross-dressing and Cultural Anxiety,*[30] which, they note, "demonstrates very valuably that the relished, taboo omnipresence in our culture of cross-dressing and trans-gender coding may well constitute the very possibility of gender coding at all. What this work does not consider—or at least does not take responsibility for enunciating—is that the rabid frenzies of public deniability are an inextricable part of the same epistemological system as the sophisticated pleasures of public knowingness—pleasures which such work itself richly indulges."[31] I would, however, like to give credit to Marjorie Garber for recognizing that drag might better be discussed in terms of its queer opacity than in terms of epistemology. Garber cites Severo Sarduy's essay "Writing/Transvestism," finding in it "the directive to look *at* rather than through the transvestite once again," and noting that "Sarduy does not need to disarticulate his fictive transvestites from their homosexuality in order to do so. He does not read or write transvestism as a figure for something else[;] . . . for Sarduy, what that face expresses, and what transvestism expresses, is *itself*."[32] Garber also draws attention to Warhol's own appearance in drag, citing Marcel Duchamp's feminine alter ego "Rrose Selavy," in a collaborative series of photographs by Christopher Makos, "Altered Images" (1981).[33]

Douglas Crimp has discussed Warhol's *Screen Test #2* (1965),[34] where Mario Montez, in drag, is asked by Ronald Tavel to show his penis, and Crimp comes to a remarkable conclusion:

> So I'll return, in closing, to the shaming of Mario Montez in *Screen Test #2*. As I mentioned before, I wanted, in my earlier essay on *Blow Job* to contest the cliché of Warhol's filmic vision as voyeuristic. I argued there that formal features in Warhol's films—different formal features in different films, of course—worked to foreclose a knowingness about the people represented in them. Warhol found the means to make the people of his world visible to us without making them objects of our knowledge.[35]

This precarious mode of vision-without-knowingness is part of a queer ethical project, one that I believe Duane Michals's portrait of Warhol accomplishes in its foreclosure of the function of the face-as-identity in favor of the opaque visibility of Warhol's hands. Unlike the camouflage self-portraits, the game of hide-and-seek will be rejected by those who read the portrait. There is one notable exception: Richard Meyer has argued that in the Duane Michals portrait of 1958, "Warhol retreats from representation, covering his face as though unworthy of the camera's attention. It is almost as if desirable masculinity has itself displaced Warhol from the visual field, demanding that he remain off-frame, wanting but not *wanted*."[36] This understanding of Warhol's psychology (closely linked to the earlier question of shame) has also been applied biographically to Barthes's "self-image."[37] But I differ in my reading of the framing and the visual field of Michals's portrait, since the both luminous and tactile *quality* of the image need not foreclose desire for—or pleasure in—this image. The image is clearly worthy of the camera's attention, and ours (Silver George impersonating

Warhol: "I have very nice hands . . . very expressive . . . I keep them in repose or touching each other").[38] Michals's photography is simply too aestheticizing to be read as an allegory of ugliness, even as Barthes reads its substance as "slightly repellent . . . at once soft and hard-edged."[39]

Symposium

Duane Michals forms a common reference point within an intergenerational network of admirers in what might problematically be called postwar *gay writing* in France: Michel Foucault, Roland Barthes, Renaud Camus, and Hervé Guibert. I would like to clarify how they might be considered a network, establishing a particular milieu. First, to borrow from Eleanor Kaufman's work, these writers have expressed a kind of "delirium of praise" for one another in various prefaces, intertextual references, and published love letters.[40] A brief list would include Barthes's untranslated "Fragments pour H.," which Guibert published without permission in his *L'Autre Journal,* but which Barthes referred to rather enigmatically in his Collège de France course on the Neutral;[41] Guibert's novelesque treatment of Barthes's *A Lover's Discourse: Fragments* in his also untranslated *Fou de Vincent;*[42] Barthes's preface for Renaud Camus's *Tricks* (which itself alludes to Barthes and photography);[43] and Foucault and Barthes's expressed affection and solidarity at the Collège de France.[44] Each author has also either prefaced or discussed Michals's photography as it was exhibited in France.[45] Each of them uses Michals in advancing his own theory of photography and its relation to death and reality. Taken together, they form a symposium on photography and queer desire.

The conversation "begins" with the publication in 1980 (shortly before his death) of Barthes's reflections on photography, *La chambre claire* (*Camera Lucida*), followed in 1981 by Guibert's book on phantom photography, *L'Image fantôme* (*Ghost Image,* in which Guibert transfers into narrative photos that are unreproducible, or that failed, or that haunt him), followed by Foucault's preface to the catalogue for a Paris exposition on Duane Michals in 1982, entitled "La Pensée, l'émotion," followed by Renaud Camus's preface to a book on Duane Michals, which he entitles "L'ombre d'un double," published in 1997.[46] Each critic sees photography as essentially connected to death, but only Barthes and Camus see the photograph as a sort of "proof" of reality, proof that something actually once existed before a camera even though the photograph only speaks of its death. Guibert and Foucault use the notion of "trick" photography—of which Michals's is a shining example—to argue that photographs need not represent reality, and in fact offer no clear proof of reality (Guibert especially deals with the fact of retouched photographs).[47] Instead, photographs offer the viewer an "experience"—and Foucault mentions the work of a certain "H.G." as doing the same thing for him.[48]

The role that homosexuality plays in each is also quite varied. Barthes is at his most lyrical when discussing the body of a "boy with his arm outstretched" in a Mapplethorpe photograph: "The photographer has caught the boy's hand (the boy is Mapplethorpe himself, I believe) at just the right degree of openness, the right density of abandonment: a few millimeters more or less and the divined body would no longer have been offered with benevolence (the pornographic body shows itself, it does not give itself, there is no generosity in it)."[49] Guibert is also frustrated with the pornographic image, its stereotype of desire (a very Barthesian objection).[50] Ralph Sarkonak has revealed the ways in which Hervé Guibert's *Ghost Image* can be read as an attempt to outdo Barthes:

> For example, Guibert does not hide his homosexuality: . . . "It's not that I want to dissimulate it, or that I want to boast about it arrogantly. But it's the least I can do in the way of sincerity. How can you speak about photography without speaking of desire? If I mask my desire, if I deprive it of its gender, if I leave it undefined, as others have done more or less cleverly, I would feel as if I were weakening my stories, making them flabby." It would be hard to be more direct without naming Barthes outright. We remember the coquettish way he played with the topic of homosexuality in *Roland Barthes by Roland Barthes* as well as the kind of genderless love he describes in *A Lover's Discourse* where the third-person masculine pronoun used to refer to the beloved could be interpreted as a neutral "one"-type pronoun in French.[51]

Ironically, Guibert goes on to uncannily echo Barthes: "It's not even a matter of courage (I'm not a militant), it has to do with the truth of writing. I don't know how to put it more simply."[52] All of the vocabulary of the supposedly coquettish *Roland Barthes by Roland Barthes* is here: the refusal of courage, the refusal of militancy, the favoring of the truth of writing as it is praised in Barthes's preface to Camus's *Tricks*, in terms of "putting it simply." As Sarkonak demonstrates, the rivalry expressed by Guibert toward his older sometime-mentor is nonetheless voiced in Barthesian terms. I am uneasy with the oedipal logic of this desire to outdo Barthes in terms of gay specificity, which finds its echo in Miller's own occasionally condescending tone in *Bringing Out Roland Barthes*. It is important that these texts were written *after* Barthes's death. Thus, what Miller calls the *inflection of generation* is not something that can be dissolved in the harmony of gay "community." (Let us recall Barthes's definition: "Inflection is the voice insofar as it is always past, silenced.")[53] Likewise, it is disappointing to see the way in which Guibert, Miller, and Leo Bersani have recourse to the metaphor of "flabbiness" to typify Barthes; as previously noted, Bersani praises Miller for the way in which he "'develops' Barthes's gay muscle." At one point, Miller claims that Barthes's late style and last writing is "like a body that necessity has compelled to abandon the gym . . . uncaring on the question of how it looks."[54] Pierre Saint-Amand is right to criticize this opposition between the "Hard and Soft": "In his presentation of Miller's text, Bersani allows himself to be seduced by the same athletic prejudice, forgetting, moreover, the critique he himself had formulated concerning 'psychic tumescence.' He too falls into the trap of supervirilization."[55] Saint-Amand demonstrates how far removed this is from Barthes's own "Gay Erotics," which he brings out in a reading of the earlier mentioned Mapplethorpe photograph.

The vexed relation between Guibert and Barthes is further illustrated by a faux pas Guibert made in requesting to take an admittedly trite photographic portrait of Barthes with his mother: a request in a letter that arrives either before or shortly after the moment of her actual death and that Barthes does not receive in his grief.[56] This grief over the loss of his mother becomes the subject of the second part of Barthes's *Camera Lucida*. Guibert's fascination with photography's proximity to death also explains his interest in Michals's photography. Guibert in fact collaborated with him on the publication in 1981 of Michals's *Changements*, a project of photographs and texts about aging and death, including a series in which Michals stages his own death. The text for the book was created by Guibert after an interview in Paris in November of 1978, and several letters.[57] But Guibert also cites Michals's photograph *The Captive Child* as one of his personal favorites in *Ghost Image,* in a list of photos with a common thread of death and the love of boys.[58]

Camus's preface is remarkable for its biographical tone, in which he compares the similar Eastern European immigrant backgrounds of Michals and Warhol (and a name change for the latter).[59] Camus does a thematic reading of Michals's photography in terms of *doubling:* mirrors, reflections, taste for binary oppositions (spirit/matter, appearance/reality, youth/ old age, artist/model, life/death), superimposition, transparent presences, phantom silhouettes, double exposures, effacement, and dissimulated faces. He cites Michals's portrait *Andy Warhol* from 1958 as an example of this last theme.[60] He claims that the occurrence of homosexuality in the work, namely in Michals's *Homage to Cavafy,* is "serene" and "triumphally assumed."[61]

Foucault is the most embarrassed about the indiscretion of writing on photography, of narrating it.[62] However, his recounting of a Michals photo from *Homage to Cavafy*—of two nearly identical men, one lighting the other's cigarette—is the most remarkable for the way in which it empties homosexuality of meaning. Foucault explains (and here I'm translating) that between these two men's bodily gestures it is difficult to imagine a greater proximity, a communication more affirmed, and more readable by the habitual "décrypteurs" of desire. But he points out that the text written below the photograph (common to much of Michals's work) reads: "just to light his cigarette was a great pleasure." Foucault claims that this text makes all the reciprocity and complementarity of the photo disappear, dislocated into a singular pleasure of which the other is necessarily ignorant.[63] This effectively short-circuits the "decryption" of desire that Foucault elsewhere argued has so marked our understanding of sexuality, especially homosexuality. Rather than being "serene" or "triumphally assumed," desire is replaced by the pleasure of one in the ignorance of the other, which Foucault suggests is perhaps similar to the thought of this photo that expresses a pleasure that we cannot know, of which we are "lightly/slightly ignorant" (a clumsy translation of "légère").

So, schematically: for Barthes photography signifies both death and proof of reality; for Guibert photography is haunted by death and doubt, that is, falsifiable reality, but also speaks the truth of desire; for Camus photography is obsessed with death and doubling; and for Foucault photography is closer to thought or experience than to any necessity of objectivity, proof, or reality, and it in fact says less about homosexual desire than we think. In between these accounts, Michals (himself a desired object for each critic) allows them each to grapple with the role of queer desire in photography. Guibert writes a chapter of *Ghost Image* entitled "Diffraction" in which he and T. (a.k.a. "Jules")[64] reflect on a remarkably queer form of desire in admiring another person's reflection in the glass of the windows of the *métro*.[65] This desire is diffracted (once again we find the reflective and doubling theme brought out by Camus), deniable (it is easy to claim you weren't looking at anything but simply staring into space), and secret, which for Guibert makes it valuable. The gaze filtered through its reflection loses some of its brutality and gains in impunity, complicity, and perversity: "We alone can intercept the gaze that we exchange indirectly . . . the consent in our gaze is our secret alone, a mirage suspended in air that will soon disappear."[66] Regarding secrecy, Guibert concludes *Ghost Image* with a fictional dialogue that echoes the end of *Roland Barthes by Roland Barthes:*

> "I feel completely empty now that I've told you this story. It's my secret. Do you understand?"
> "And now?"
> "I don't want to have to ask you not to repeat it."
> "Yes, but now your secret has also become my secret. It's part of me, and I'll treat it as I do all my secrets—I'll get rid of it when the time comes. Then it will become someone else's secret."
> "You're right. Secrets have to circulate . . ."[67]

While Guibert exploits the secret, in a quite Foucauldian way and vis-à-vis Foucault himself in *To the Friend Who Did Not Save My Life,* Foucault is remarkable for his rejection of this convoluted reading of desire in favor of a discussion of pleasure, especially in the case of photography.

I would like to argue that the same is true for Barthes. In Barthes's view, the body in photography is "given" rather than secretly stolen (and that is what makes the Mapplethorpe photo *desirable*). Despite Guibert's oblique attack on Barthes for masking his desire, as we have seen Barthes is much more interested in texts that "speak homosexuality but never speak about it," such as Camus's neutral narratives that "do not participate in the game of interpretation" but are instead "surfaces without shadows, *without ulterior motives*."[68] In Barthes and in Warhol, there is nothing behind the mask, what is "given to be read" is the surface, and we may in fact be confronted with an absence of meaning (though not necessarily pleasure). In Michals's portrait, Warhol offers his hands to be read, quite openly. Following Barthes, the *studium* of the photo could be read as Warhol's secrecy, his hiding, his masking of his face and perhaps his desire, but the *punctum* is not this gesture but the surface of Warhol's nails. This overwhelming quality of the detail Barthes calls the *punctum* also overpowers the entirety of his reading: "This brings the Photograph (certain photographs) close to the Haiku. For the notation of a haiku, too, is undevelopable: everything is given, without provoking the desire for or even the possibility of a rhetorical expansion."[69] Barthes also likens Camus's *Tricks* to a series of haikus: "If it weren't for their extent and their subject, these *Tricks* might be haikus; for the haiku combines an asceticism of form (which cuts short the desire to interpret) and a hedonism so serene that all we can say about pleasure is that *it is there* (which is also the contrary of Interpretation)."[70] This rejection of interpretation is what marks Barthes's reading of the Michals portrait of Warhol, and what frustrates most attempts to interpret Warhol. But as in Foucault's short-circuiting of the habitual decryption of desire in Michals's photography, we find here a short-circuiting of that most culturally vexed yet habitual notion that queer desire is something to be decrypted and unmasked, revealed from being concealed, to find ulterior motives and hidden truths. What is given to be read "quite openly" in the photograph is not the face, that marker of true identity, but the hands, the surface: "And there I am. There's nothing behind it." Both Barthes and Warhol experiment with the surface, and with "face value," but I would suggest that taking Warhol *at face value* may mean not privileging the value of his face.

Barthes wants "to change systems: no longer to unmask, no longer to interpret," imagining "the abolition of the manifest and the latent, of the appearance and the hidden."[71] But how do we accomplish this? To conclude, we must return to the problem of reading, whether it is reading a photographic or written text. Are we left with nothing if we abandon de-coding, unmasking, hermeneutics that seeks the secret truth?[72] In a short talk called "On Reading," Barthes argues that reading *perverts* structure: "Reading is the gesture of the body (for of course one reads with one's body) which by one and the same movement posits and perverts its order: an interior supplement of perversion."[73] Sedgwick has similarly charted the queer work of becoming a *perverse reader*.[74] Barthes asserts that here we can glimpse the paradox of the reader: "It is commonly admitted that to read is to decode[,] . . . but by accumulating decodings (since reading is by rights infinite), by removing the safety catch of meaning" a reversal occurs and the reader finally "does not decode, he *overcodes;* he does not decipher, he produces, he accumulates languages, he lets himself be infi-nitely and tirelessly traversed by them: he is that traversal."[75] The reader's traversal of and by language therefore moves from deciphering to a kind of production, and this accumulation of discursive strategies in all their productivity is precisely the method of my perverse reading of opacity.

opacity as being read, i.e. production.

FIVE

Andy Warhol Up-Tight
Warhol's Effects

My mind is like a tape recorder with one button—Erase.

—Andy Warhol, *The Philosophy of Andy Warhol (From A to B and Back Again)*

It is as if the label "Andy Warhol" would signify, not a person, in the sense of a human subject, but storage: boxes, reels, spools, Polaroids, all labelled "Andy Warhol."

—Peter Wollen, *Raiding the Ice Box: Reflections on Twentieth-Century Culture*

THE POTENTIAL OF THE "ARCHIVE" as a technology of memory has gained increasing attention within queer studies, in part because questions of "cultural memory" get invested with particular urgency in the age of AIDS. The archive seems to offer some resistance to the "obliterative homophobia" of much official history. In *An Archive of Feelings: Trauma, Sexuality, and Lesbian Public Cultures,* Ann Cvetkovich explains that "in insisting on the value of apparently marginal or ephemeral materials, the collectors of gay and lesbian archives propose that affects—associated with nostalgia, personal memory, fantasy, and trauma—make a document significant."[1] She goes on to argue that such an "archive of feelings" is both material and immaterial, and lives not only in institutions but also in cultural genres, such as documentary film and forms of performance. Such an approach to ephemera, performance, and the archive (both "actually existing" archives, and those created by cultural history and criticism) marks a turn to what Eve Kosofsky Sedgwick has termed "reparative reading." She describes the desire of a *reparative impulse* as "additive and accretive. Its fear, a realistic one, is that the culture surrounding it is inadequate or inimical to its nurture; it wants to assemble and confer plenitude on an object that will then have resources to offer to an inchoate self," citing *camp* as such a practice of "'over'-attachment to fragmentary, marginal, waste or leftover products . . . the disorienting juxtapositions of present with past, and popular with high culture."[2] Rather than prescribe (or proscribe) what should or should not be archived, my aim is to consider how this work is already under way in art practice and history, by looking at a particular case study: the Archives of the Andy Warhol Museum in Pittsburgh.

Time Capsules

Two chapters of Andy Warhol's *The Philosophy of Andy Warhol (From A to B and Back Again)* forecast the ambivalent role played by the Warhol Museum archives. In the chapter titled "Time," Warhol projects into the time after his death:

> At the end of my time, when I die, I don't want to leave any leftovers. And I don't want to be a leftover. I was watching TV this week and I saw a lady go into a ray machine and disappear. That was wonderful, because matter is energy and she just dispersed. That could be a really American invention, the best American invention—to be able to disappear. . .
>
> The worst thing that could happen to you after the end of your time would be to be embalmed and laid up in a pyramid. I'm repulsed when I think about the Egyptians taking each organ and embalming it separately in its own receptacle. I want my machinery to disappear.
>
> Still, I do really like the idea of people turning into sand or something, so the machinery keeps working after you die. I guess disappearing would be shirking work that your machinery still had left to do. Since I believe in work, I guess I shouldn't think about disappearing when I die.[3]

Warhol's famous desire to be a machine is here split into two types of machine: an American disappearance machine, versus a kind of machinery that continues to "work" after you die. Warhol's anxiety about leaving leftovers is particularly ironic given what happened after his death. The documentary *Andy Warhol: The Complete Picture* (2002) explains how

Warhol's death threw the art world into confusion: "His house, jam-packed with artworks, antiques, and untold mountains of *junk,* was immediately declared off limits[;] . . . his studio, also overflowing with unfinished paintings, artworks, antiques, and yet more junk was similarly barricaded against scavengers, friends, and even his family." The narrator explains that after his death, Warhol's estate was estimated to be worth $600 million, and "much of Warhol's massive collection of the precious and the everyday" is now housed at the Andy Warhol Museum, opened in his hometown of Pittsburgh in 1994. Over shots of the museum's archives, filled with identical cardboard boxes arranged on Spacesaver shelves, the voiceover continues enumerating "a legacy of hundreds of thousands of things, including six hundred Time Capsules and four thousand audio tapes. . . . Fifteen years after his death the archaeological dig prompted by all this evidence of a life left behind is still uncovering clues about elusive Andy Warhol, the Citizen Kane of the art world."

The origin of these Time Capsules is explained in Warhol's *Philosophy* in the chapter "Atmosphere": "I just drop everything into the same-size brown cardboard boxes that have a color patch on the side for the month of the year. I really hate nostalgia, though, so deep down I hope they all get lost and I never have to look at them again . . . but my other outlook is that I really do want to save things so they can be used again someday."[4] Again, we can note the ambivalent attitude toward Warhol's "leftovers": preservation (nostalgia) versus disappearance (amnesia). The *Citizen Kane* reference is of course entirely appropriate, and while the documentary explains that Warhol's Time Capsules—full of all the "detritus" of a working month at Warhol's Factory—are preserved at the archive (and are still being catalogued), Warhol's collectibles took ten days to auction off (in what must have resembled the final scene of Welles's film).[5] The documentary—simultaneously about the archive and a biographical portrait of Warhol (complete with a conventional oedipalizing account of his "sensitive" artistic childhood)—also thus models itself on the enigmatic riddle-solving structure of *Citizen Kane.* The narrator quotes Truman Capote's famous characterization of Warhol as a "sphinx without a secret" (or riddle) but also quickly undermines it with "but to believe that is to believe all this adds up to nothing." With some irony, then, the documentary seeks out the "real Andy Warhol hiding behind the genuine fakes" through interviews with friends, associates, and experts.

Warhol Museum archivist John Smith makes a similar statement about the Time Capsules that perhaps best characterizes the "hermeneutics of suspicion" with which critics approach the alleged enigma of Warhol's persona:

> The writer Truman Capote once referred to Warhol as a "Sphinx without a riddle." And indeed, Warhol spent his career constructing his famously enigmatic, disengaged, and dispassionate public persona. In THE Philosophy of Andy Warhol, he wrote that, "I'd prefer to remain a mystery. I never give my background, and anyway, I make it all up different every time I'm asked." With the discovery and dissemination of the Time Capsules, we have perhaps not only found the riddles that eluded Capote, but many of the answers that Warhol tried to suppress as well.[6]

It is hard to determine if this is a kind of posthumous revenge of truth (like James Miller's approach to Michel Foucault in The Passion of Michel Foucault), or a game of truth set in motion by Warhol but eagerly played by critics and researchers.[7]

Perhaps the best intervention in the crisis caused by the auctioning of Warhol's "junk" can be found in Simon Watney's "The Warhol Effect" where he cites the Observer headline "Warhol: A $35m Junk Hype." Watney explains that "precisely because of its sickening snobbery, the Observer draws attention to the conflicting traditions concerning artistic identity which operate in the contemporary marketplace. For in one sense, Warhol simply cannot be reconciled to the type of heroic originating Fine Artist required as the price of admission to the Fine Arts tradition. . . . We should not underestimate the significance of this carte-blanche refusal of post-Renaissance aesthetic hierarchies, and the professional identities which they established."[8] The Warhol documentary also closes with this auction of his seemingly indiscriminate collections, interviewing the buyer of his massive cookie-jar collection, and following his flea-market shopping partner Stuart Pivar, who questions Warhol's ability to evaluate worth.[9]

Since I agree with Watney's claim about the ongoing critical intelligence of "The Warhol Effect," when I visited the Archives of the Andy Warhol Museum doing research, I went not in search of the key to solve the

Warhol riddle (the "Rosebud" that would finally enable a proper biographical narrative to be written), but looking only for this surface "effect" of
Warhol's persona, in Warhol's literal "effects" kept safe in the Time Capsules.[10] As I communicated in the last two chapters, my conviction is that
Warhol's persona is in fact his greatest "work," and rather than undercut-
ting its machinery, I wanted to see how it continues to work after his death
as a technology of cultural memory. As Watney points out, "Strangely, at
first, we recognize that Warhol's death has in no way constituted an inter-
ruption of his career, at any level of commentary."[11] Who, then, stands to
inherit Warhol's effects?[12]

A Queer Reading

Andy Warhol: The Complete Picture explains Warhol's existence—highlighting his shyness and yet desire for fame—through an oedipal scenario
whereby the family (the ethnic group and the hometown) are given privileged possession of Warhol's life. Those who pose a threat to the family are
variously characterized in the film as "transvestites, street hustlers, junk-
ies, and rebellious society girls," and this reveals the privileged "knowingness" with which queer worlds are called upon only then to be dismissed
in heteronormative cultural discourse. One of the critical authorities in
the Warhol documentary, Stephen Koch, has been criticized by Douglas
Crimp for precisely this condescending, arch *knowingness* regarding the
alleged "hustler" of Warhol's film *Blow Job*.[13] Crimp characterizes Koch's
approach as "a knowledge that is presumptive, knowing; a knowledge of
the other for the self; a making of the other into an object for the subject."[14] How to avoid this "knowing" treatment of Warhol's and his world?

A "queer" reading of the story of Warhol's world and his self-invention
in New York City would instead emphasize the tensions surrounding
"metrosexuality." Perhaps the clearest account of this story can be found
in Didier Eribon's *Insult and the Making of the Gay Self* in the chapters
"The Flight to the City" and "The City and Conservative Discourse." Eribon explains that "the city represents an aspiration to freedom and self-
realization" but that "the cities mentioned above as symbols of a freedom
that was either lived or dreamed of (Berlin, Paris, Amsterdam, London,

San Francisco, New York . . .) have thus at the same time, and in symmetrical fashion, represented everything the guardians of social and moral order—the apostles of religion, familialism, and oppression of women and homosexuals—held (and continue to hold) in horror."[15] This is an apt description of attempts to make New York City more "family friendly" by making it less publicly queer.[16]

A queer reading of Warhol's construction of a personality for himself outside of Pittsburgh and *apart from the family* (even while living with his mother: i.e., "family without familialism")[17] would thus emphasize the discontinuities rather than the narrative continuities of Warhol's life.[18] A great deal of authority is given to Warhol's family and older brothers in biographical documentaries, as if Andrew Warhola was who Warhol "really" was, thus getting the story "straight" in both senses. This ironic problem of the family and their claim on Warhol also informs Stanislaw Mucha's documentary *Absolut Warhola,* which seeks Warhol's Ruthenian family origins in the towns of Medzilaborce and Miková, Slovakia.[19] To his credit, Mucha's interviews productively exploit the tensions between the extended family and the legend, revealing how the subject of Warhol's unnamable, impossible homosexuality haunts the narrative of the family tree, and the debates surrounding the Warhol Museum of Modern Art in Medzilaborce. Mucha's documentary presents its search for Andrew Warhola's origins as a failed quest almost from the outset (they can't find the town: geography as ontological metaphor) but expresses less regret about this fact than *The Complete Picture*'s quest for the real Andy Warhol.

One of the best examples of how to queer the *Citizen Kane* story is Todd Haynes's *Velvet Goldmine* (1998), not just in Haynes's cinematic quotation of the framing, interview scenes, and narrative structure of Welles's film, but in Haynes's insistence that the construction of the celebrity's persona and story is finally up to the "queer reader" of the evidence (who cannot distance himself from his own desire for the object he is investigating).[20] Haynes could be seen as following a suggestion in Roland Barthes's *A Lover's Discourse:* "Instead of trying to define the other ('What is he?') I turn to myself: 'What do I want, wanting to know you?' What could happen if I decided to define you as a force and not as a person? And If I were to situate myself as another force confronting yours? This would happen: my other would be defined solely by the suffering or the pleasure he affords me."[21] This displacement of the question of the person in favor of a Nietzschean theory of force seems more productive for a consideration of the detective–journalist's desire, and the suffering and pleasure surrounding "camp" celebrities.

Haynes's Bowie-esque Maxwell Demon and Andy Warhol's camp Wildean epigrams both delight and frustrate the eager knowingness of the press, and their opacity is part and parcel of the work of being a celebrity. In their brilliant discussion of Divine, Eve Sedgwick and Michael Moon explain, "In our attention to Divine we are especially interested in the part played in the process of her self-creation by celebrity itself . . . as an ontological status that *dis*articulates the intersections among the person, the artist, the fictional character, and the commodity."[22] They go on to ask: "What can a celebrity body be if not opaque? And yet what if the whole point of celebrity is the spectacle of people forced to tell transparent lies in public? We have already mentioned what we take to be a central chord in our culture of 'knowingness.' . . . The economics of knowingness helps us ask new questions about the transparent lies that constitute celebrity, as well."[23] But of course I am actually interested in staying at the level of Warhol's opacity to see what it might show us about the celebrity persona *as an effect.*

Warhol's role as publisher of *Interview* magazine also reveals a desire to intervene in the way fame is constructed. As Ingrid Sischy, editor-in-chief of *Interview,* suggests in the *Complete Picture* documentary, Warhol imagined an "alternative media vehicle that maybe would treat fame in a different way." The Andy Warhol Museum Archives house the entire back catalogue of *Interview* magazine, and in all the interviews which I consulted that were "conducted" by Warhol between 1974 and 1982, it was clear that Warhol consistently undermined the usual techniques of getting the stars to talk about their "inner" selves.[24] What we get is simply the surface effects of the celebrity interview: what they are wearing, what they order at the restaurant, and so forth. The politics involved in Warhol's publishing enterprise at *Interview* have been a subject of debate, especially in the "Discussion" section of *The Work of Andy Warhol*: in the 1970s and '80s, was Warhol capitulating to conservatism, consumerism, and cynicism? The panelists do not come to a conclusion, but Nan Rosenthal makes an important intervention regarding whether Warhol can be considered a social critic: "I would like to hear this question discussed without any reference to intentionality. Do these works have an effect sustaining social criticism, rather than did Andy Warhol intend them that way."[25] One of the effects of the unique approach to the interview in *Interview* magazine is an undermining of the distinction between "public" and "private," which has been so important to the Star System (and full of so many double binds for gay men such as Warhol). In *Roland Barthes by Roland Barthes,* in a section on *le privé* (private life), Barthes explains how relative is the concept of the private:

> It is certainly when I divulge my *private life* that I expose myself most: not by the risk of "scandal," but because then I present my image-system in its strongest consistency; and the image-system, one's imaginary life, is the very thing over which others have an advantage: which is protected by no reversal, no dislocation. Yet "private life" changes according to the *Doxa* one addresses: if it is a *Doxa* of the right (bourgeois, petit bourgeois: institutions, laws, press), it is the sexual private life which exposes most. But if it is a *Doxa* of the left, the sexual exposition transgresses nothing: here "private life" is trivial actions, the traces of bourgeois ideology confessed by the subject: confronting this *Doxa*, I am less exposed in declaring a perversion than in uttering a taste [that thus becomes *unspeakable*] . . . contradicting what can be said, what is expected that you would say, but which precisely—the very voice of the image-system—you would like to be able to say *immediately* (without mediation).[26]

This passage is particularly illuminating regarding the treatment of Warhol or Barthes as "closeted" gay men, who each may have thought of his "private life" as not just his sex life depending on which *Doxa* he was addressing. The question of mediation also opens up new approaches to reading *Interview,* like Warhol's collection of clippings, as a kind of extended consideration of the "image-system" and its relation to speech.

Gretchen Berg has said that she "began to think of her interactions with Warhol as 'mediations' rather than as interviews."[27] "Mediation" should be thought of here in its multiple senses: to intervene, to bring about, to form a connecting link, to be a means of conveying. In his *Media Manifestos,* Régis Debray emphasizes the *means* of "archiving traces and putting them into circulation . . . [since] symbolic productions of a society at a given

instant *t* cannot be explained independently of the technologies of memory
in use at the same instant"; in other words, "mediations at once technological, cultural, and social."[28] As discussed in chapter 3, all of this is effected
through the technological mediation of the tape recorder, with which Warhol strongly identified as a "recording" machine—referring to his Sony tape
recorder as his "wife."[29] In an interview with Bernardo Bertolucci for the
December 1977 issue of *Interview,* Warhol explains: "I don't know. When
Watergate happened I didn't know whether Nixon copied me or whether
I copied Nixon. I had to stop taping for a while," to which Bertolucci
responds, "Yes, but at least it's shown. It's not secret."[30] What is most
important about Warhol, then, is that the technology is *foregrounded.*

The Warhol Archives include thousands of Warhol's taped conversations, which can still be listened to in the form of cassette tape copies[31]—
a precarious technology with decay-effects built into it, posing classic problems for the archive.[32] Commenting on Warhol's constant taping, Peter
Krapp explains: "In fact, keeping more mnesic representations inevitably
entails the contamination of memory with forgetting: a pure remembrance
would be nothing but forgetting, detail but no difference, images without
categories. If forgetting and memory are not opposites, then we might say
that Warhol tried to gain a hold in the moment through the forgetting of
forgetting."[33] This aptly describes the way the Warhol tape archives undermine the binary oppositions of memory and forgetting, the moment and
the monument, speech and writing, life and death. As Krapp notes, "when
the *Andy Warhol Diaries* came out after his death, consisting of carefully
edited transcriptions of tapes by Pat Hackett, it could be said that his wife
[Sony] had written his memoirs while he was still alive."[34]

Warhol's opaque persona ("I want to be a machine")[35] works together
with the machinery of the press, and continues to work long after he is dead
in the form of the archive. "Since I believe in work, I guess I shouldn't
think about disappearing when I die," Warhol suggests. The fantasy of a
machinery that would keep working, or would work without him, almost
materialized in 1980 in the form of an animatronic robot Andy Warhol
that Lewis Allen attempted to produce for a "No-Man" show featuring
Warhol's famous aphorisms, and which Warhol hoped might replace him
on talk shows and publicity junkets (this can also be seen in the *Complete*

Picture documentary, and is mentioned in the *Andy Warhol Diaries*).[36] But Warhol's image was itself largely prosthetic: wigs, corsets, and so forth are all carefully preserved in the archives and displayed within the *Complete Picture* documentary by Assistant Archivist Matt Wrbican, who explains that Warhol began to think of his two-tone wigs formally as themselves works of art, and was planning to do a framed edition of forty of his wigs. (Wrbican plays a crucial role in the documentary, and he was also crucial in helping me with my own research. It often felt as if those who come to the archive do so out of a self-consciously fetishist relation to Warhol.)

Fittingly, a similar android-portrait was conceived in 2005 in honor of Philip K. Dick, science fiction author of *Do Androids Dream of Electric Sheep?*[37] According to a press release, "The conversational dialogue of the robot will be similar to the synthetic post-mortem interview with PKD written by Erik Davis."[38] Warhol also suggested the possibility of a "ghost interview" during an interview with David Bourdon: "Let's get a ghost to do our interview. Then we won't have to do any more thinking."[39] Both Dick and Warhol are obvious candidates for such postmortem interviews and android-portraits, in part because they explored the potential of the "posthuman" in their works (literalizing Foucault's controversial consideration of "the end of man" in *The Order of Things*).[40] Thus the "No-Man" shows put on by the robots known as "Andy Warhol" and "PKD-A" mean that they continue to work as linguistic machines after the deaths of their authors.

In Freud's "The Uncanny," he references Ernst Jentsch's observation that uncanny impressions arise out of an ambiguity between human and automaton (like the doll Olympia in E. T. A. Hoffmann's *The Sandman,* or the androids in Ridley Scott's 1982 film *Blade Runner,* based on Philip K. Dick's novel).[41] Yet Freud quickly dismisses this as mere intellectual uncertainty (lacking the hallmark of the castration complex and repetition compulsion that Freud sees as characteristic of the uncanny). However, Warhol's attitude toward machines and the double is remarkable for its lack of "robophobia." This is reflected in his machine-like silk screening at the Factory, which is notable for the lack of concern it shows for the loss of the "aura" of the original in the age of mechanical reproduction (a clear source of the paranoia about "replicants" in *Blade Runner*).[42] In

"That Old Thing, Art . . . ," Barthes reads these silkscreen prints as disturbing the classical value of the person, but as evidence nonetheless of "the double" finally rendered benign: "Repetition disturbs the person (that classical entity) in another fashion: by multiplying the same image, Pop Art rediscovers the theme of the Double, of the Doppelgänger; this is a mythic theme (the Shadow, the Man or the Woman without a Shadow); but in the productions of Pop Art, the double is harmless—has lost all the maleficent or moral power, neither threatens nor haunts: the Double is a Copy, not a Shadow: *beside,* not *behind:* a flat, insignificant, hence irreligious Double."[43] Richard Meyer likewise locates a homoerotic fantasy in "Warhol's Clones" with his doubled Elvises reflecting a queer pleasure in duplication and sameness that is also visible in the masculine gay "clone" style that became dominant in 1970s urban gay life.[44]

Lacking the homophobic paranoia usually associated with the trope of the double—as seen for instance in the film adaptations of Patricia Highsmith's psychological thrillers, Alfred Hitchcock's *Strangers on a Train* (1951) or Anthony Minghella's *The Talented Mr. Ripley*—the "Andy Warhol robot" is therefore yet another example of the double rendered benign or homoerotic: the erotics of the same.[45] (This is also visible in Chris Cunningham's "roboerotic" music video for Björk's "All Is Full of Love," in which a Björk robot and its double copulate with the assistance of several machines.)[46] Warhol and his robot thus qualify as a canny example of the uncanny double that Freud links to a primary narcissism and wish for immortality rejected by a later more self-critical ego.[47] But this might explain why others find robots, clones, Warhol, and his image "uncanny": they make no effort to conceal the work of narcissistic doubling, and they reproduce artificially.

The immortal or "timeless" quality to Warhol's persona also often invites the comparison to the great mythic figure of the undead: the vampire. Warhol was nicknamed "Drella" to capture his hybrid persona as both Dracula and Cinderella, and the *Complete Picture* documentary makes much of this comparison: Paul Morrissey's 1973 Warhol-produced *Blood for Dracula* (1974)[48] is read allegorically as "about" the new business-driven Warhol of the 1970s ("a pale, weak, ineffectual, Eastern European count poisoning himself on the blood of degenerate aristocratic whores . . .

who or what could have been on Morrissey's mind?"); the renaissance
of Warhol's interest in painting in the 1980s is read as follows: "In characteristic vampire style, Andy fed on the blood of his young admirers
[Haring, Basquiat, Scharf] only too happy to let them take a bite out of
him in return."[49]

The Empty Closet

But what if we were to be more generous and read this intergenerational
collaboration as revealing a queer temporality not tied to the proper order
of "generations" based on the heterosexual family? As Judith Halberstam
has explained, "Reproductive time and family time are, above all, heteronormative time/space constructs . . . [but] all kinds of people, especially in
postmodernity, will and do opt to live outside of reproductive and familial
time as well as on the edges of logics of labor and production."[50] While
Warhol's emphasis on production and capital accumulation obviously
excludes him from the latter point, those who were a part of his world
do fit in with the type of risky "queer subjects" Halberstam describes as
living outside both of these logics.

This is where we might consider the fate of what at first appears "un-
archivable," namely those parties, happenings, and apartments ("nests")
that were themselves works of art (often created under the influence of
amphetamines), which, although completely ephemeral, are obliquely
archived in Warhol's *POPism: The Warhol '60s, Chelsea Girls* (1966), and
Billy Name's photographs of the "Silver" Factory.[51] This gives us a second
sense of the "leftovers" of Warhol's archive proper (not to be confused
with the commonplace idea that Warhol "used up" talented but dysfunc-
tional people). In *POPism,* Warhol remembers a Judson dancer named
Freddy Herko who committed suicide by "dancing" out of a window: "The
people I loved were the ones like Freddy, the leftovers of show business,
turned down at auditions all over town. They couldn't do something more
than once, but their one time was better than anyone else's. They had star
quality but no star ego—they didn't know how to push themselves. They
were too gifted to lead 'regular lives,' but they were also too unsure of themselves to ever become real professionals."[52] Warhol's pop-psychology may

seem banal here, but it does in fact reflect Warhol's Pop-psychology based entirely on the concept of "work" as distinguished from amphetamine-driven "busywork" (concentration on minutiae: notebook drawings, tinfoil, mirrors, feathers, glitter).[53] This is the fate of "decoration": window decoration (where Warhol got his start) and set decoration ("Tom's apartment looked like a stage set").[54] It is likewise the fate of parties, happenings, and much performance art. It also describes the contrasting "legacy" of Jack Smith, whose *Flaming Creatures* (1963) Warhol obviously admired, but whose performances have only begun to receive the kind of canonization or preservation that Warhol's estate has enjoyed.[55]

This tension between the preservation and disappearance of Warhol's "leftovers," which is so perfectly framed in *Philosophy,* thus begs the question of the relation of these problems of Space, "Atmosphere," and Time to queer subjectivity. In *Andy Warhol: The Complete Picture,* performance studies scholar Peggy Phelan suggests that in Warhol's art "there was a theatricality in the disappearance" and that in drawing attention to his removal of himself, his absenting of himself, Warhol kept the desire for his appearances going. This dynamic comes close to the metaphoric space and temporality of "the closet" so thoroughly dissected by Sedgwick in *Epistemology of the Closet* and carefully applied to Warhol by Jonathan D. Katz.[56] The closet is literalized in the passages about emptying out space from Warhol's *Philosophy:*

> I believe that everyone should live in one big empty space. . . . I like the Japanese way of rolling everything up and locking it away in cupboards. But I wouldn't even have the cupboards, because that's hypocritical. But if you can't go all the way and you really feel you need a closet, then your closet should be a totally separate piece of space so you don't use it as a crutch too much. If you live in New York, your closet should be, at the very least, in New Jersey.[57]

The Time Capsules are thus alluded to in the *Philosophy* using terms that are central to readings of Warhol: disappearance, work, hiding and enclosure; but these terms also easily connote the metaphor of the closet. I have been suggesting that this is both a fitting and a limited approach to Warhol. The "storage space" described above can be thought of as keeping "skeletons in the closet" or as the repository of the Time Capsules, but in literalizing the "closet" I think Warhol points us away from a reading of his desire for disappearance or absenting as simply a desire for the closet.

Instead of revealing the machinations of the closet, Warhol's apparently enigmatic disappearances and leftovers force us to acknowledge that the "work" of producing Warhol's queer persona is ongoing. Rather than looking for the real Warhol hidden beneath the surface (the hidden fears and intentions that others are so happy to provide Warhol with after-the-fact), we can look to the archives of the Andy Warhol Museum for the surface effects that Warhol's collection of "effects" continue to produce long after his death. Such work demonstrates how cultural memory is both constructed and deconstructed, troubling distinctions between public and private, the canon and the archive, memory and forgetting. The documentary *Andy Warhol: The Complete Picture* does not in fact complete the story (though it does signal the importance of the museum and its archive), and it ironically concludes with a response from a filmed Warhol interview where Warhol is at his most opaque: "oh, that won't last very long."

Coda: Warhol as Brand

To illustrate the extent to which the work of producing "Warhol" is ongoing, I would like to briefly elaborate on some of the other endeavors of the Andy Warhol Museum and the fate of Warhol as a "brand" in the twenty-first century.

In 1997, the Warhol Museum organized an exhibition on Warhol's connections to the world of fashion. The accompanying publication, *The Warhol Look: Glamour, Style, Fashion,* argues, "Today's merging of art and fashion is in large measure the legacy of Andy Warhol. This book, which accompanies a major exhibition opening at the Whitney Museum of American Art in New York, shows the decisive impact of his work on fashion and glamour and how the 'Warhol style' influenced contemporary art."[58] In her *New York Times* article "The Selling of Saint Andy," Ruth La Ferla also notes the large amount of references to Warhol in twenty-first-century fashion and attempts to catalogue the fate of Warhol as a commercial brand.[59] She begins by quoting an advertisement that Warhol placed in the *Village Voice* in 1968: "I'll endorse with my name any of the following: clothing, AC-DC, cigarettes, small tapes, sound equipment, ROCK 'N' ROLL RECORDS, anything, film and film equipment, Food, Helium, Whips, MONEY!! love and kisses ANDY WARHOL. EL5-9941." Like Jorge Luis Borges's fictional Chinese encyclopedia, cited by Foucault in *The Order of Things*,[60] it is fascinating to note Warhol's clever placement of an all-encompassing category—"anything"—in the midst of the specific items. La Ferla points out that Warhol was not being coy, and hoped to erode the line between art and commerce. Indeed, Warhol's signature on the Factory assembly-line silk-screening process and his role as producer of Paul Morrissey's *Andy Warhol Presents* . . . films were early experiments with the Warhol name-as-brand and endorsement (in fact, it is quite common now for film directors to present other directors' work: for instance "David Lynch presents," "Peter Jackson presents," and "Quentin Tarantino presents"). But La Ferla points out that

> even the seer in Warhol could not have envisioned the degree to which he has become commercialized. In time for the holiday season, nearly 20 years after his death in February 1987, the marketing of Andy Warhol is in full flood. . . . Warhol's mercantile essence, both high and low, is distilled in carpets and coffee mugs, calendars and greeting cards, T-shirts, tote bags and a style of Levi's wax-coated jeans called Warhol Factory X, for $185. To judge by all the merchandise, Warhol is being positioned as the next Hello Kitty. . . . It is "the fulfillment of Andy's fantasy about business art" said Jeffrey Deitch, the art dealer and former Warhol associate. "I think he would have been amazed to see what has developed." Warhol-inspired wares are being sold in stores like Macy's and Nordstrom and in youth-oriented chains like Urban Outfitters and high-end fashion boutiques like Fred Segal in Los Angeles.[61]

The article suggests that perhaps some of this is due to a degree of nostalgia for New York City's more rebellious past, but both *The Warhol Look* exhibition and the flood of merchandise catalogued by the *Times* article suggest that Warhol still seems "of the moment."

In fact, it is possible to argue that both aspects are true, given that the "moment" we are speaking of is the "perpetual present" of postmodernity. Fredric Jameson has famously characterized postmodernism as the logic of late capitalism, and argued that postmodern art has lost a sense of historicity, but is in fact hopelessly nostalgic, condemned to endless recycling and quotation, that is, pastiche. In his essay "Postmodernism and

Consumer Society," he identifies Warhol as one of the prime suspects of a kind of blank parody, or irony that has lost its sense of humor. He ends his ambivalent assessment of postmodernism (in which Warhol and Foucault find themselves once again linked) by asking whether there are forms of postmodern art that might be able to challenge the consumerist logic of late capitalism.[62] Clearly, the *Times* article would seem to suggest that Warhol does not—indeed, would not want to do so—and that those who perpetuate the "selling of Saint Andy" do so with his implicit *endorsement.*

Yet critics in queer theory have noted that Jameson suppresses the queer dimension of postmodern art. Building on a critique of Jameson by Mandy Merck, Judith Halberstam explains how

> Jameson's rigid identification of postmodernism with queer consumption and of modernism with heterosexual production is startling and troubling . . . indeed, his essay depends utterly on a homophobic repudiation of the superficial, the depthless, and the spectacular. In his essay, Jameson sets up a binary division between postmodernism and modernism that it in its comparison of a van Gogh painting called *Peasant Shoes* and a Warhol silk screen titled *Diamond Dust Shoes,* associates modernist work with politically urgent representations of working-class and male labor, and postmodernist art with politically anemic representations of bourgeois and female leisure.[63]

Merck, Halberstam, and Richard Dellamora insist on reading queer history back into the *Diamond Dust Shoes* silk screen. In a clever reading of queer absence and presence in Jameson's reading of Warhol's *Diamond Dust Shoes,* Dellamora notes that Jameson is anxious about the postmodern subject's loss of agency, self-presence, and historical consciousness. He explains that,

> although it is evident that Jameson deplores this loss, it is pertinent that Warhol's postmodern aesthetic develops conscious criticism of the insistence by the Abstract Expressionists on presence in their painting. Warhol's work either signifies such presence parodically, as in the oxidization paintings of the 1970s, or achieves an equivalent by erasing signs of artistic presence through banal subject-matter and mechanical technique. It is this process that I refer to when I say that Warhol exploits the position of an *unsubject* in devising what has paradoxically proven to be a remarkably indelible signature.[64]

We have already seen above how Warhol's meditations on the Time Capsules and his persona encode this play of absence and presence, but Dellamora's idea of the *unsubject* is a particularly helpful demonstration of the work of *opacity,* and the paradoxical *effect* of the "indelible" Warhol signature. He goes on to explain that Warhol "later invented the idea of the artistic signature as trademark, not the trademark of an authorial style, handling, or mythic iconography but the literal trademark of consumer products or star-images, images that convert an individual into a trademark of himself or herself."[65] Dellamora explains that, ironically, "by displacing himself as a subject in this way, Warhol has *become* a subject" such that when we see an image of a Campbell's soup can or Marilyn Monroe, for instance, we read it as "Warhol."[66] Dellamora notes a further irony in Jameson's critique of Warhol: in using an image from Warhol's *Diamond Dust Shoes* series for the cover of his book *Postmodernism, or, The Cultural Logic of Late Capitalism,* Jameson appropriates this process such that by associating the Warhol image with the author's name and "Jameson's by now well-known critique of these images, the Diamond Dust Shoes become the trademark of 'Jameson' theorist of postmodernism."[67] So it would seem that Warhol can indeed be used to endorse "anything."

While I have indicated the possibility of reading these recent developments of Warhol-as-brand as proof of Warhol's complicity with the allegedly "politically anemic representations of bourgeois and female leisure" identified by Jameson, I have also tried to indicate Warhol's challenge to the sexist and homophobic logic that dismisses the superficiality and depthlessness (coded as feminine and queer) that I have defined here as Warhol's opacity. Perhaps both possibilities are aspects of the Warhol Effect, and proof that, as Douglas Crimp insists, perhaps we all get the Warhol we deserve.[68]

Factory assistant Gerard Malanga claimed in an interview about Warhol: "It's like his life is a byproduct. He's like an institution, like Walt Disney. When he dies, there'll always be Andy Warhol films; his life exists without him whether he's here or not here."[69] As Malanga indicates, this phenomenon whereby Warhol became an institution is an effect of media technology, and this will therefore be the subject of my conclusion.

The Interview as Multi-Mediated Object

Speech is always tactical; but in passing to the written word, it is the very innocence of this tactic, perceptible to one who knows how to listen, as others know how to read, that we erase. . . . [S]peech is dangerous because it is immediate and cannot be taken back[;] . . . scription, however, has plenty of time. . . . [I]n writing down what we have said, we lose (or we keep) everything that separates hysteria from paranoia.

—Roland Barthes, "From Speech to Writing"

Their circulation, their détournement, their transferral far from the context in which they were born . . . all of these taken together, after such texts have left their authors behind but before they have been embalmed within a corpus, make up an entire erotics of thought, wayward and unpredictable. Placing these terms in contact seems to stir up dust from a bygone era.

—François Cusset, *French Theory*

THE FILM *FROST/NIXON* (2008) presents a perfect example of the interview situation as a proxy for a courtroom trial.[1] Many saw the interview as a substitute for the criminal trial that President Nixon had avoided in being pardoned by President Ford. David Frost begins the interview with the provocative question on everyone's mind "Why didn't you burn the tapes?" but realizes that he is no match for Nixon's ability to "stonewall,"[2] change the subject, and turn the interview into a nostalgic presidential monologue. Finally, the tables are turned when Frost is able to catch Nixon off guard with a piece of evidence from the tapes that had not been made public, and he obtains the confession for which everyone had been waiting.[3] Such confessional interviews are now a staple of mainstream news media

(Barbara Walters and *Larry King Live* are probably the most notable), and the audience eagerly awaits the interviewee's parapraxes (Freudian slips) and tearful breakdown, as if waiting for a breakthrough on the analyst's couch. It has been my conviction throughout the previous chapters that interviews can function as a form of confessional discourse (as well as what Freud called "wild psychoanalysis"), and I have attempted to consider alternatives, perhaps best exemplified by Warhol's interviews and *Interview* magazine. Their obsessive tape recording and ability to sabotage interviews seem to make Nixon and Warhol into "strange bedfellows" (which Warhol acknowledged in his interview with Bernardo Bertolucci in *Interview,* December 1977).[4] But there are also clear differences between Nixon's and Warhol's forms of "stonewalling" the interviewer.

President Nixon attempts mastery of discourse and welcomes the challenge of a "no holds barred" *agon* or verbal wrestling match, and his strategy for making Frost give up the fight is to launch into long monologues and run out the clock in the timed interview sessions.[5] By contrast, Warhol's "tactics" in interviews are on the fly and have the effect of making the interviewer's own speech into a monologue, thereby running out the clock in a different way (more passively, like Warhol's approach to letting the film reel run out in his "Screen Tests"). Warhol's is a "passive resistance" like Bartleby's.

A filmed interview between David Bailey and Warhol reveals a stark contrast.[6] They lie in bed together and talk, with the covers pulled up, though we can tell that Warhol is fully clothed, while Bailey has taken his clothes off. It is reminiscent of Warhol's discussion of his ideal sex life in *The Philosophy of Andy Warhol* in which couples get in bed and tell jokes ("But I'd rather laugh in bed than do it. Get under the covers and crack jokes, I guess, is the best way. 'How am I doing?' 'Fine, that was very funny.' 'Wow, you were really funny tonight.' If I went to a lady of the night, I'd probably pay her to tell me jokes." In this he resembles Woody Allen, but Warhol's speculative heterosexuality is itself a punchline).[7] Warhol is his usual noncommittal self but is quite good at turning the interview situation around, even joking about whether David is a "closet queen." Unlike the wrestling match between Frost and Nixon, Warhol de-virilizes the interview while still homoeroticizing it.

This interview is from Bailey's documentary about Warhol that was originally banned in 1973 for being "offensive," and was more readily available as a written transcript, in which the term "closet queen" is turned into "closet cleaner."[8] A reading attuned to the Repressive Hypothesis would no doubt point to the censorship and taboo clearly involved, but Foucault might help us notice the "will to knowledge" and "will to truth" that motivates Bailey and the aptly named director William Verity, but is frustrated by Warhol. Take, for example, the following exchange:

DAVID: "I suppose now we're in bed we might as well talk about your sex life."
ANDY: "Oh, OK."
DAVID: "Well do you want to tell me about your sex life."
ANDY: "What do you want to know about it."
DAVID: "All the dirt."
ANDY: "Dirt, um. I believe in fantasy."
DAVID: "um."

This is in the transcript but not in the final cut of the film, of course, which seems to reinforce the Repressive Hypothesis. But as Bailey and Warhol predicted, when audiences finally saw the documentary—the censorship scandal was of course good publicity—they were disappointed and bored, which is really Warhol's finest achievement: the art of the anticlimax.[9] I am also interested here in addressing the questions of mediation and remediation provoked by the fact that until recently this interview was available primarily as a transcript and as an excerpt in another documentary (Kim Evans's *Andy Warhol*).

In *Pop Trickster Fool: Warhol Performs Naivete*, Kelly M. Cresap argues that it is most likely that Warhol's press and media interviews were a sort of "put-on":

During the 1960s the put-on interview became like a compulsory event for many emerging careers, a backhanded way of announcing one's seriousness as an artist. The practice had precedents in earlier decades—artists such as Picasso and Salvador Dali had both dabbled in the form—but its potency in the public sphere waited until the era of hipsters and youth rebellion. Dissimulating for the press was a way of pointing up the inanity of interview questions, of thwarting an audience's search for full access and 360-degree disclosure, and of declaring one's distance from the Establishment power bloc.[10]

Cresap argues that others who adopted this stance (John Lennon and Yoko Ono, and Bob Dylan) are rather easier to decipher, finally revealing a degree of earnestness quite foreign to Warhol. Their antiestablishment motives are tied more directly to the political engagements of the decade, yet, she argues, "Regardless of the worthiness of their causes, and despite the liberating energies they unleashed, they lacked the urbane complexity and eerie clairvoyance that has sustained the Warhol mystique into the new millennium."[11] Like Cresap, my goal has been to explain how and why the "mystique" of Foucault, Barthes, and Warhol has continued into the new millennium, where the media's desire for "full access and 360-degree disclosure" is perhaps stronger than ever.

As we saw in Barthes's comments on the interview wherein the journalist is a kind of "cop who likes you" (precisely the role that Frost attempts in the Frost/Nixon interviews), the question is how to demystify the situation of the interview.[12] Barthes acknowledged the necessity of the interview as a kind of "social game" he could not refuse, despite his misgivings about journalism and the privileging of speech over—and after—writing.[13] This game is also a kind of "game of truth" that produces, as one of its "truth-effects," what Foucault called the "author function," whereby the unity of a work is located in its author, both a biographical and legal answerability.[14] One of the ironies of my own project, then, is that at times it might seem as if I have been treating these authors as people and not as figures. This is particularly ironic when dealing with the authors of "What Is an Author?" (Foucault) and "The Death of the Author" (Barthes), and the artist whom many see as killing off the idea of the artist as the unique author of the work (Warhol).[15] But again, I want to take their resistance to these author functions seriously. On my reading, Foucault (and Guibert), Barthes, and Warhol made significant interventions in the otherwise smooth functioning of "confessional discourse," the image-system, and the celebrity interview. Despite national differences (however much both France and the United States can be analyzed as "petit-bourgeois societies"),[16] they share a common postwar historical period that witnessed the rise of the "intellectual interview" and the mutual dependence of celebrity culture and media culture.

Régis Debray notes that in his earlier works, *The Scribe* and *Teachers, Writers, Celebrities*, there is not "a distinction made among mediaspheres," but he points out how "certainly in the France of today, what presents itself to view is but a milieu of sociability structured by three poles: university, publishing-editing, medias. And certainly these poles *co-exist* in any given one of them and at present, with all sorts of well-known connecting bridges between them."[17] Debray defines a mediasphere as a "*milieu*, structured by its foremost technique and practice of memory-formatting, [which] structures in its turn a type of accrediting of the discourses in currency," and he describes "the passage from hand-written and oral public communication (logosphere) to the mechanical reproduction of text (graphosphere)," and, following that, to the analogical and computer-graphic "recording of sonorous and visual signs (videosphere)."[18] The history of educational television—what was to become PBS—in the United States suggests a similar set of "connecting bridges" between the poles and mediaspheres outlined by Debray.[19]

Remediation

The Grain of the Voice: Interviews 1962–1980 includes "most of the interviews given in French by Roland Barthes," and the editor notes that "the best possible preface would have been a description by Roland Barthes himself of what an interview is."[20] Since it was published after Barthes's death, "we will never have that description now, but we do have a few pages where Roland Barthes analyzes, with admirable clarity, the passage of the spoken word to the word transcribed . . . where the stylet of writing interlaces with the grain of the voice."[21] In this prefatory text, "From Speech to Writing" (mentioned in my earlier chapter on Warhol's opacity), Barthes describes the situation as follows: "We talk, a tape recording is made, diligent secretaries listen to our words to refine, transcribe, and punctuate them, producing the first draft that we can tidy up afresh before it goes on to publication, the book, eternity. Haven't we just gone through the 'toilette of the dead'? We have embalmed our speech like a mummy, to preserve it forever. Because we really must last a bit longer than our voices; we must, through the comedy of writing, *inscribe ourselves* somewhere."[22] This concern for the process of mummification might remind us of Warhol's attention to the work of the Time Capsule, but we should also recall that Warhol preferred untidy secretarial transcription, and wanted to hang on to all the scraps of "phatic" language in conversation and interviews, which Barthes notes usually get excised in the process of transcription (the passage from speech to "the written").[23] But Barthes also wants to challenge the idea that "speech is in itself fresh, natural, spontaneous, truthful, expressive of a kind of pure interiority," noting that on the contrary, "our speech (especially in public) is immediately theatrical" and culturally coded.[24] Barthes continues this attention to theatricality when he argues that in transcription "the speaker's image-repertoire changes space" in the desire to set up an argument, "the sentence becomes hierarchical; in it is developed, as in the staging of a classic drama, the difference of roles and stage positions; in becoming social (since it passes to a larger and less familiar public), the message recovers a structure of order" and into this new order are added the typographical artifices of parentheses to indicate digression and punctuation.[25]

Barthes thus identifies and relates three practices: speech, the written, and writing. He concludes by arguing that "the development of broadcasting—that is, of a speech at the same time original and transcribable, ephemeral and memorable—now brings a striking interest" to these variations.[26] Indeed, Debray makes note of "recursive curlings," whereby mediaspheres "have not succeeded one another as substitutions, but rather as complications in a perpetual game of mutual reactivation" since there is "no zero sum game between written and oral, there being several sorts of writing and orality."[27] How then does the videosphere reactivate the problems of speech and writing discussed by Barthes?

Barthes addresses the television interview and its transcription in "Responses: Interview with *Tel Quel*":

> Jean Thibaudeau had the kindness to prepare for me a long, precise, direct and well-informed questionnaire, bearing at once (as was the rule) on my life and work, for a series of televised interviews, recorded under the generic title "Archives of the 20th Century," which will probably never appear, unless perhaps in the event of the death of the author. . . . The interview took place, but it was only possible to reproduce a few of the numerous questions asked. The responses were rewritten—which does not mean that we are dealing with writing, since, given the biographical material, the "I" (and its litany of verbs in the past tense) must be taken as if the person speaking were the same (in the same place) as the person who had lived.[28]

Barthes's humorous literal quotation of his own famous title ("the death of the author") also recalls his opening to *Sade, Fourier, Loyola*, in which he imagines the amicable return of the author and speculates that, "were I a writer, and dead," then he would love it if his life were to be reduced to a set of details, preferences, and inflections, which he names "biographemes" (clearly the justification for Louis-Jean Calvet's "friendly and detached" biography *Roland Barthes: A Biography*).[29] Yet Barthes notes that his interview with Thibaudeau was a "game" they were not very taken in by, and reminds his readers that "the quotation marks which are pertinent for any naively referential statement should thus be implicitly re-established" in the printed interview that follows.[30] At the end of the interview, Thibaudeau asks, "What is this interview? What is the 'posterity' to which, in its televisual guise, it would appear to be destined?" As noted in chapter 1, Barthes uses this opportunity to "put the interview on trial," not this particular interview, but the "everyday interview, spoken, recorded and then transcribed (but not written)," which he notes is very much in vogue (in the early 1970s, arguably still today). Barthes explains that "the reasons are presumably economical (if not directly financial): the interview is a cheap article. 'You don't have time to write a text? Well give us an interview.'"[31] Here we glimpse the political economy of the publishing industry, part of what Barthes envisioned studying in a vast schematic analysis of the activities of contemporary intellectual life (one of his many unfinished project sketches, this one was perhaps fulfilled by Pierre Bourdieu's *Homo Academicus*).[32]

Addressing the question of posterity, Barthes is nonplussed: "As for 'posterity,' what can I say? It's a dead word for me, which is giving it its dues since its validity is only established on the basis of my death." Insisting that he is "no more than a *particular contemporary*," "destined while I live to the exclusion of a large number of languages, and subsequently destined to an absolute death; buried in the archives (of the twentieth century), perhaps one day I will re-emerge, like a fugitive, one witness among others, in a broadcast of the Service for Research on 'structuralism' 'semiology' or 'literary criticism.' Can you imagine me living, working, desiring, for that?"[33] In fact, *Roland Barthes 1915–1980: Archives de XXe Siècle* was produced in 1988, featuring footage from 1970–71 of

Barthes answering the Jean Thibaudeau questionnaire.[34] Yet Barthes's rejection of eschatology as a motivation for work is perhaps inconsequential to the purposes of the archive in which he foresaw himself being buried. As we saw in chapter 5, the role of the archive is in fact always ambivalent vis-à-vis "the death of the author."

A new kind of Time Capsule is created in the form of the digital archive. My research at the Bibliothèque nationale de France in Paris revealed a different kind of digital memory with its own pleasures of playback. Carolyn Steedman notes that following Jacques Derrida's *Archive Fever* and his "speculation about the future of the archive, as the register, ledger and letter are replaced by the e-mail and the computer file," "the *arkhe* appeared to lose much of its connection to the idea of a place where official documents are stored for administrative reference, and became a metaphor capacious enough to encompass the whole of modern information technology, its storage, retrieval and communication."[35] The Institut national de l'audiovisuel (Ina) and Inathèque audiovisual archives at the BnF represent an awe-inspiring endeavor to archive the history of postwar French national broadcasting. What it allowed me to consider was the odd place—from my contemporary American point of view—of the intellectual "profile" and the intellectual "variety show" (such as *Apostrophes*). Certainly, 1960s North American culture also had its share of well-known public intellectual figures, such as Susan Sontag, Noam Chomsky, and Marshall McLuhan. But there is something unique in Foucault's and Barthes's positions as authors of "bestselling" academic books: Foucault's *The Order of Things* and Barthes's *A Lover's Discourse.*[36] This perhaps conditioned their role in the "televisual economy" of French broadcasting, which is clearly closer to British television in its state-subsidized and public educational function, comparable to the BBC broadcast of John Berger's materialist art historical intervention *Ways of Seeing.*[37]

In her important historical study, *Turning On the Mind: French Philosophers on Television*, Tamara Chaplin draws on the resources at Inathèque to challenge the common assumption that television and philosophy are antithetical, or that mass culture and intellectual discourse have no traffic between them.[38] She claims that "due to the performative nature of their discipline, founded in the Socratic dialogue and rooted in embodied oral practice, philosophers are in fact uniquely suited to the demands of television."[39] Yet she also insists that "such claims for a rapport between television, philosophy, and embodiment also require historicizing, since this connection necessarily carries historically particular effects. While philosophers may 'embody' their oeuvre on French TV (incarnating philosophy as practice), there is no doubt that by the 1970s, in response to the growing impact of the audiovisual field on the commercialization of intellectual goods, they were increasingly lured onto the small screen simply to sell books."[40] *Apostrophes* is perhaps the best example of this marketing factor in the televising of public intellectuals: "*Apostrophes* was a marketer's dream: it both encouraged the consumption of books and was itself a marketable product."[41] Host Bernard Pivot was less interested in extended Socratic dialogue and more with instigating arguments between guests specifically chosen for their divergent points of view: "It produced entertainment by producing conflict."[42] This is what Barthes identified as the French taste for debates, and this style came to dominate French television (and is arguably still the case, likewise for American television "pundits").

Chaplin discusses Foucault's appearance on *Apostrophes,* in which (as Guibert noted) he surprised audiences by not talking about *The History of Sexuality* (the book he was there to "promote") but addressing instead a recent political event known as "*l'affaire Stern.*"[43] Chaplin explains that Foucault managed to "hijack" Pivot's program, and ironically was able to use the Stern affair to illustrate *The History of Sexuality*'s larger concerns regarding the relationship between sexual discourses, the power/knowledge nexus, and the production of truth.[44] She argues that "in embracing the media, annexing the topic of discussion, and in shifting the terms of debate from a book to the discursive production of knowledge, Foucault challenged contemporaneous arguments about the growing power of television—and especially of *Apostrophes,* to dictate the contents of the intellectual field."[45] Why, then, did Pivot submit to Foucault's agenda? "Because he knew that controversy makes good drama, and good drama makes good television," Chaplin explains.[46]

Foucault made several television appearances, and Chaplin uses each of them to illustrate the range of approaches to philosophy on television from the 1950s through the 1970s (a period of varying state control of public television). In 1966, the "book show" *Lectures pour nous* (a precursor to *Apostrophes*) provided a platform for Foucault to dynamically explain *The Order of Things*. The educational television program *L'Enseignement de la philosophie* featured Foucault in dialogue with other "master" philosophers in 1965 (which, Chaplin observes, "represents philosophical thought as patriarchal, traditional, Western, and, in its universalizing evocation, fundamentally French" despite the attempt to address the postcolonial, multiracial student body in the opening credits).[47] Foucault appeared in a 1972 portrait of Gaston Bachelard on *Un Certain regard*, which contributed to the creation of a new genre for French television programming, the biographical documentary.[48] Chaplin's concluding chapter addresses the transition from public, state-controlled television to private, commercialized channels in the 1980s, but notes the interesting fact that "it was just at the moment that public television was floundering that a series titled *Océaniques* was created," which, during its run from 1987 to 1992, "presented some of the most sophisticated, compelling, and now best-known philosophical television ever produced," including shows on Foucault and Barthes.[49]

While Chaplin mentions Barthes's appearance on these programs (*Apostrophes*,[50] *Océaniques*), he is primarily listed as an example of an "*intellectuel mondaine* (worldly intellectual)" — in opposition to the "*intellectuel savant* (learned intellectual)" — during Chaplin's discussion of television's role in exacerbating "longstanding debates about the proper purview of the French philosophical field."[51] Yet Chaplin notes that French philosophy's autobiographical tradition (exemplified by Rousseau) "lent itself easily to fresh incarnations (documentary biographies, interviews, and publicity appearances) compatible with the virgin technology of television, whose focus on personality was critical to its appeal."[52] This is clearly where Barthes's biographical interview with Thibaudeau for *Archives of the 20th Century* fits in. Guibert's appearance on *Apostrophes* and the many Warhol documentaries discussed in the previous chapters are also prime examples of this aspect of television's focus on biography and personality, wherein, as Chaplin notes, they are called upon to "embody their oeuvre."[53]

Like the audiovisual archive of Inathèque, the film and video archive of the Warhol Museum acts like a Time Capsule to preserve Warhol's films and experiments with video and television. Though his films are widely respected, less attention has been given to his television soap-opera pilots; his variety show for MTV, *Andy Warhol's Fifteen Minutes,* starring Warhol beside the equally "blank" and opaque persona of Debbie Harry; and the vérité-style *Factory Diaries,* about the life of the office, featuring Candy Darling answering the phone and Warhol writing endless checks. In each of these examples, like the famous "Screen Tests," Warhol emphasizes his concern with photogenic but opaque and "blank" people, rather than psychological depth.[54]

The archives of L'Institut mémoires de l'édition contemporaine (which have moved from Paris to l'Abbaye d'Ardenne)[55] also represent an important resource for studying the work of amassing and organizing the "corpus" of Foucault, Guibert, and Barthes: the oeuvre proper, but also the manuscripts, lectures, correspondence, and fragments (such as Barthes's use of index cards, some of which are reproduced in *Roland Barthes by Roland Barthes*). Like the Warhol Museum archives, this work is ongoing and results in a number of interesting offshoots in publishing: the lecture notes for Foucault's and Barthes's courses at the Collège de France continue to be published and translated into English,[56] and each author has had an exhibition dedicated to him drawing on the manuscripts and audiovisual resources at IMEC and Ina.[57] Even more interesting is an issue of *Genesis: Revue internationale de critique génétique* dedicated to Roland Barthes, presented by Pierre-Marc de Biasi and Éric Marty. It consists of a series of "inédits" or handwritten manuscripts, including marginal notes and corrections, from the Barthes archives at IMEC, along with essays on the process of "textual genesis."[58] The audio recordings of Barthes's lectures at the Collège de France have also been published, allowing the listener to enjoy the particular "grain" of his voice.[59]

In contrast to the "open file" presented by these archives and the course notes, the function of *Œuvres complètes* (in France) is to act as a kind of capstone to this work of compilation and editing.[60] One unique effect is that interviews are "elevated" somewhat to the status of essays, and they are also removed from the original context of their publication (thus becoming unmoored from a sense of historical "timeliness": either the time of the recent publication of a book or the time of historical events and debates). But as we have seen, Foucault and Barthes both hoped to use the interview as a chance not to "traffic in opinions" but to question the role of the interview and the function of the intellectual (a label about which they both expressed ambivalence, given the history of maligning this figure in French debates).[61]

What we can see is that the "social game" of the interview is also a game between the public intellectual and "the media." But it is a game that involves a certain degree of "blackmailability" when the social subject is queer and known to have leftist politics. In *The Neutral,* Barthes describes the situation of the French intellectual after Sartre, and identifies the weariness of the position (as in "What is your position in this debate?"): "The present-day world is full of it (statements, manifestos, petitions, etc.), and it's why it is so wearisome: hard to float, to shift places."[62] Yet Barthes insists that out of weariness is created the Neutral, that "the right to weariness . . . thus shares in the *new:* new things are born out of lassitude — from being fed up."[63]

I would argue that this "new" that Barthes calls the Neutral also forms part of what I have been calling *queer opacity.* From being fed up with confessional discourse, with the epistemological games of the closet in which coming out is a disclosure at once compulsory and forbidden, we discover the possibility of "baffling" and "outplaying" the power of inquisition that is built into the interview. We also see a challenge to the biographical fixations of the author function, along with what Foucault identified as the "old prophetic function" of the intellectual. In his "The End of the Monarchy of Sex" interview, Foucault echoes Barthes's desire for the ability to shift positions and to displace oneself:

> In a general way, I think that intellectuals — if this category exists, if it should exist at all, which is not certain nor perhaps even desirable — are renouncing their old prophetic function. And by this I'm not thinking only of their claim to say what is going to happen, but also of the legislative function which they've aspired to for so long. . . . The Greek sage, the Jewish prophet, and the Roman legislator are still models that haunt those who practice today the profession of speaking and writing. I dream of the intellectual destroyer of evidence and universalities, the one who, in the inertias and constraints of the present, locates and marks the weak points, the openings, the lines of power, who incessantly displaces himself, doesn't know exactly where he is heading nor what he'll think tomorrow because he is too attentive to the present.[64]

My argument has been that queer opacity is one way of locating and marking the weak points in the system known as the "epistemology of the closet," and of finding an opening for the creation of a queer public persona that manages to resist confessional discourse. The closet would therefore represent some of the "inertias and constraints" of the present, but queer subjectivity is produced through a kind of displacement vis-à-vis the closet itself.

Acknowledgments

I WOULD LIKE TO THANK the archivists John Smith and Matt Wrbican at the Andy Warhol Museum in Pittsburgh, Martine Ollion and the staff at the Centre Michel Foucault and IMEC (Institut Mémoires de l'Édition Contemporaine) library, and the librarians at the Bibliothèque nationale de France and Inathèque for their assistance with my research. I am grateful for the generous support of a University of Minnesota Doctoral Dissertation International Research Grant and a Cultural Studies and Comparative Literature Departmental Early Dissertation Stage Summer Fellowship. I also wish to thank the organizers of the Roland Barthes Exposition at the Centre Georges Pompidou (November 27, 2002–March 10, 2003), and the colloquium "Roland Barthes, ou la traversée des signes" (January 17–18, 2003), and in particular I thank Diana Knight for her presence at the colloquium and for subsequent correspondence and assistance. For giving me the opportunity to present some of this material, I am grateful to the organizers of UCLA's QGrad conference on sexuality and gender (and for the encouragement I received from Richard Meyer there), the UCLA Art History graduate conference Migrations of Art: Scripting and Staging Subjectivities, the Technologies of Memory in the Arts conference at Radboud University in Nijmegen, as well as the Modern Language Association and Society for French Studies. I thank my students at the University of Minnesota and the University of North Florida for helping me work out some of the problems addressed here, particularly in my courses "Gay Men and Homophobia in American Culture," "Sex,

Confession, and Autobiography," "The Warhol '60s," and "The Pleasure of Roland Barthes."

I have benefited enormously from conversations with John Mowitt, especially regarding his wealth of knowledge about *Tel Quel*, and I am very grateful for his guidance with this project. Cesare Casarino's seminars on AIDS and philosophy, Foucault, Blanchot, and Deleuze have energized my thinking more than I can say. In the best possible sense, his thought has represented for me a "disturbance," and he has left here "his (multiple) traces." I learned practically everything I know about Andy Warhol from Liz Kotz, and she encouraged and contributed to my thinking about Warhol and language, for which I am very grateful. Gary Thomas has always helped to put my critique of the closet metaphor in historical and political perspective. He is a great source of inspiration and encouragement, and I am grateful for his mentorship. Tom Pepper's seminars on Freud, Lacan, Derrida, and Proust have also had a great impact on me, for which I thank him.

I could not have hoped for a smoother transition or for a more collegial department than UNF's Department of English. Many thanks go to Sam Kimball for his advice, editorial feedback, and belief in this project. I would like to thank Richard Morrison at the University of Minnesota Press for his enthusiasm and guidance. I also must thank the two manuscript readers and the copyeditor, Sue Breckenridge, for helping me in my revisions with the difficult task of transforming what was once "written at white heat . . . into a nice cold dish" (as Barthes says in "Deliberation"). I am grateful to Duane Michals and the Pace/MacGill Gallery for generously granting me permission to reproduce Michals's portrait of Andy Warhol. I also thank Greg Burchard at the Andy Warhol Museum for helping me obtain permission for the cover image of Warhol's Time Capsules. I thank Nancy and Bob Grote for their hospitality in Pittsburgh. Thanks go to John Troyer for sharing many tidbits of Warhol information with me, including a video about the Andy Warhol robot. Many thanks go to Tom Roach, Michelle Stewart, Susan Andrews, and Robert Summers for their friendship and intellectual solidarity. My parents have supported me in so many ways, for which I am grateful beyond words. Finally, I would like to thank Sam Trask for remaining steadfast in his encouragement and for traveling with me.

Notes

Preface

1. Herman Melville, "Bartleby, the Scrivener: A Story of Wall Street," in *Billy Budd and Other Stories* (New York: Viking Penguin, 1986), 3.

2. Ibid., 25–26.

3. Jacques Lacan, *Écrits: A Selection*, trans. Alan Sheridan (New York: W. W. Norton, 1977), 7.

4. Gilles Deleuze, "Bartleby; or, The Formula," in *Essays Critical and Clinical*, trans. Daniel W. Smith and Michael A. Greco (Minneapolis: University of Minnesota Press, 1997), 68.

5. Ibid., 70.

6. Ibid., 73.

7. Ibid., 88.

8. Ibid., 81.

9. Giorgio Agamben, "Bartleby, or On Contingency," in *Potentialities: Collected Essays in Philosophy*, ed. and trans. Daniel Heller-Roazen (Stanford: Stanford University Press, 1999), 247. Cf. Mordecai Marcus, "Melville's Bartleby as a Psychological Double," *College English* 23 (1962): 365–68. On "conceptual personae," see Gilles Deleuze and Félix Guattari, *What Is Philosophy?* (New York: Columbia University Press, 1994). Note, however, that there they refer to Bartleby as an "aesthetic figure" (66).

10. Ibid., 254.

11. Ibid., 255.

12. Ibid., 261.

Introduction

1. Michel Foucault, *Foucault Live: Collected Interviews, 1961–1984*, ed. Sylvère Lotringer (New York: Semiotext(e), 1996), 218.

2. Ibid.

3. Samuel R. Delany clarifies how the meaning of "coming out" has in fact shifted: "A temporal moment (and a sociological location) in the transformation from a homosexual discourse to a gay discourse may be signaled by the appearance in the 1969 fall issue of the *Village Voice* of the locution 'coming out to' one's (straight) friends, coworkers, and family (a verbal act directed toward straights) and its subsequent displacement of the demotic locution 'coming out into' (gay) society—a metaphor for one's first major gay sexual act. Between the two locutions lie Stonewall and the post-Stonewall activities of the gay liberation movement" (*Times Square Red, Times Square Blue* [New York: New York University Press, 1999], 118).

4. Michel Foucault, *The History of Sexuality*, vol. 1, *An Introduction*, trans. Robert Hurley (New York: Vintage, 1980), 59.

5. Stephen Best and Sharon Marcus explain how Sigmund Freud's model of interpretation, characterized by Paul Ricoeur in terms of the "hermeneutics of suspicion," became "a general property of literary criticism even for those who did not adhere strictly to psychoanalysis" ("Surface Reading: An Introduction," *Representations* 108 [2009]: 5).

6. Eve Kosofsky Sedgwick, *Epistemology of the Closet* (Berkeley: University of California Press, 1990). On knowingness, see Eve Kosofsky Sedgwick, *Tendencies* (Durham: Duke University Press, 1993).

7. "The Ambiguously Gay Duo" has been a recurring cartoon since 1996 on *Saturday Night Live,* created and produced by Robert Smigel and J. J. Sedelmaier, featuring superheroes Ace and Gary in a parody of the relationship between Batman and his sidekick Robin.

8. Sedgwick, *Epistemology of the Closet*, 70.

9. See Didier Eribon, "To Tell or Not to Tell," in *Insult and the Making of the Gay Self*, trans. Michael Lucey (Durham: Duke University Press, 2004), 46–55; David Van Leer, *The Queening of America: Gay Culture in Straight Society* (New York: Routledge, 1995), 123–26.

10. Sedgwick, *Epistemology of the Closet*, 70.

11. Quoted in Alexander García Düttmann, *At Odds with AIDS: Thinking and Talking about a Virus*, trans. Peter Gilgen and Conrad Scott-Curtis (Stanford: Stanford University Press, 1996), 64.

12. Roland Barthes, *The Rustle of Language*, trans. Richard Howard (Berkeley: University of California Press, 1989), 291–92; Renaud Camus, *Tricks* (Paris: Persona, 1979).

13. See D. A. Miller, *Bringing Out Roland Barthes* (Berkeley: University of California Press, 1992); and Leo Bersani, "The Gay Absence," in *Homos* (Cambridge, Mass.: Harvard University Press, 1995), 31–76.

14. Michel Foucault, *The Essential Works of Foucault 1954–1984*, vol. 3, *Power*, ed. James D. Faubion (New York: New Press, 2000), 331.

15. Augustine, *Confessions*, trans. Henry Chadwick (New York: Oxford University Press, 1998), 179. Augustine dramatizes the way in which the confession to God is meant to be overheard when he explains how moved he was when he read the Psalms, and how he wishes the Manichees (his former religious sect) could eavesdrop on his religious fervor: "As I read the fourth Psalm during that period of contemplation, I would have liked them to be somewhere nearby without me knowing they were there, watching my face and hearing my cries, to see what the Psalm had done to me. . . . Without me knowing that they were listening, lest they should think I was saying things just for their sake, I wish they could have heard. . . . But in truth I would not have said those things, nor said them in that kind of way, if I had felt myself to be heard or observed by them. Nor, had I said them, would they have understood how I was expressing the most intimate feeling of my mind with myself and to myself" (160). There is a fascinating splitting of consciousness here whereby Augustine imagines that if he were overheard by someone who knew that *he* knew he was being overheard then his sincerity would be suspect. Or, if he were aware of being watched, his response would be inauthentic. This problem is also built into the intimate journal as a subgenre of confessional discourse, wherein the words are written supposedly to express the most intimate feelings of the mind "with oneself and to oneself." This is deconstructed by Jun'ichiro Tanazaki's *The Key* (New York: Vintage, 1991), in which a married couple write journals knowing full well that they will be read by their spouse, but *as if* they are writing only for self-expression with and to the self.

16. Michel Foucault, *Essential Works of Foucault 1954–1984*, vol. 1, *Ethics, Subjectivity and Truth*, ed. Paul Rabinow (New York: New Press, 1997), 248. In this seminar, Foucault starts by addressing a central claim from volume 1, namely that "unlike other interdictions, sexual interdictions are constantly connected with the obligation to tell the truth about oneself," arguing that his "rather odd project" was to relate this prohibition to the "obligation to tell the truth" (223–24). Foucault says that "perhaps" his critics are right and he has focused too much on domination, and he hopes now to focus on the mode of action "that an individual exercises upon himself by means of the technologies of the self" (225). Foucault traces this "hermeneutics of the self" in two historically contiguous periods:

(1) Greco-Roman philosophy in the first two centuries A.D. of the early Roman Empire; and (2) Christian spirituality and monastic principles developed in the fourth and fifth centuries of the late Roman Empire. The former is the topic of the second and third volumes of *The History of Sexuality, The Use of Pleasure* and *The Care of the Self;* the latter was the topic of Foucault's unfinished project on early Christianity and *The Confessions of the Flesh.* See Michel Foucault, *The History of Sexuality,* vol. 2, *The Use of Pleasure,* trans. Robert Hurley (New York: Pantheon, 1985), *The History of Sexuality,* vol. 3, *The Care of the Self,* trans. Robert Hurley (New York: Pantheon, 1988), and *The Hermeneutics of the Subject: Lectures at the Collège de France, 1981–1982,* trans. Graham Burchell (New York: Palgrave, 2005).

17. Foucault, *Essential Works,* 1:249.

18. Ibid.

19. Jean-Jacques Rousseau, *Confessions,* trans. Angela Scholar (New York: Oxford University Press, 2000), 436. Drawing on the confessional tradition of Augustine, Rousseau explains to his reader that "the undertaking I have embarked on, to reveal myself to him in my entirety, requires that nothing about me should remain hidden or obscure; I must be continually present to his gaze; he must follow me into all the aberrations of my heart, into every recess of my life; he must not lose sight of me for a moment, for fear that, finding in my story the least lacuna, the least void, and wondering to himself what I did during that time, he should accuse me of not wanting to reveal everything" (58).

20. Paul de Man, *Allegories of Reading: Figural Language in Rousseau, Nietzsche, Rilke, and Proust* (New Haven: Yale University Press, 1979), 285.

21. Ibid., 286.

22. Ibid., 299.

23. Ibid., 298.

24. Ibid., 299.

25. Ibid., 301.

26. Foucault, *History of Sexuality* 1:61.

27. In an interview titled "What Our Present Is," Foucault explains the necessity of strategic logic: "It is a matter of making things more fragile through this historical analysis" to show that "these are only strategies and therefore, by changing a certain number of things, by changing strategies, taking things differently, finally what appears obvious to us is not at all so obvious" (*Foucault Live,* 412).

28. For an example of a queering of autobiography, see Daniel Harris, *A Memoir of No One in Particular* (New York: Basic Books, 2002).

29. It is worth noting here that not only are there differences between homosexuality and heterosexuality in terms of what counts as privacy (especially in the history of U.S. law), but that there are also national differences between France and the United States in the definition of a right to privacy. David Lindsay and Sam Ricketson explain, "The protection of privacy in France can be traced to concerns associated with the liberalisation of the press during the French Revolution. These concerns were concisely expressed by the French philosopher, Royer-Collard, in a well-known 1819 speech, in which he coined the phrase 'private life must be walled off.' From the mid nineteenth century, in a series of cases, French courts developed the concept of the 'right to one's image' (*droit à l'image*), which was eventually formulated as a 'sacred and inalienable right over ourselves, and consequently over the reproduction of our image.' From this time on, French courts continued to protect 'private life' against undue publicity, regarding privacy as a personality right. While this was initially protected through the application of general tort principles, in 1970 an express right to privacy was introduced into French law with the adoption of Article 9 of the French Civil Code, which provides that: 'Everyone is entitled to respect of private life'" (David Lindsay and Sam Ricketson, "Copyright, Privacy, and Digital Rights Management (DRM)," in *New Dimensions in Privacy Law: International and Comparative Perspectives*, ed. Andrew T. Kenyon and Megan Richardson (Cambridge: Cambridge University Press, 2006), 134. In the United States, a frequently cited statement is Samuel Warren and Louis D. Brandeis, "The Right to Privacy" *Harvard Law Review* 4 (1890): 193, available at http://www.law.louisville.edu/library/collections/brandeis/node/225. They argue, "Recent inventions and business methods call attention to the next step which must be taken for the protection of the person, and for securing to the individual what Judge Cooley calls the right 'to be let alone.' Instantaneous photographs and newspaper enterprise have invaded the sacred precincts of private and domestic life; and numerous mechanical devices threaten to make good the prediction that 'what is whispered in the closet shall be proclaimed from the house-tops.'" They note, "The general object in view is to protect the privacy of private life, and to whatever degree and in whatever connection a man's life has ceased to be private, before the publication under consideration has been made, to that extent the protection is to be withdrawn." Therefore, when celebrities in the United States sue, it is usually under the right of publicity, not the right to privacy. France is more stringent in this regard, which might explain the tendency in the texts I discuss for the "roman à clef" approach and the discreet use of initials rather than names. For an extended comparison of concepts of privacy in France and the United States, see James Q.

Whitman, "The Two Western Cultures of Privacy: Dignity Versus Liberty," *Yale Law Journal* 113 (2004): 1151–221.

30. I am aware that the term "productivity" is problematic and might be misconstrued as implying a capitalist ideology (which perhaps fits Warhol and his "Factory"). Recent queer theory has in fact explored the counterproductivity or nonproductivity of "queer." However, I am using the term here and throughout this work as a placeholder for a range of effects, consequences, disruptions, innovations, inventions, and alternatives. I am indebted to Foucault for the emphasis on discursive productivity. Here I am juxtaposing opacity as productive—meaning active/creative—with the reactive/protective strategies of the closet. The irony of the critical reaction to opacity is that it proves its productivity—that is, its tendency to further disperse rather than halt discourse.

31. Another example of such an opaque, unpossessable, impenetrable figure and a distressed narrator/interpreter/witness can be found in Gary Indiana's *Three Month Fever: The Andrew Cunanan Story* (New York: HarperCollins, 1999), about the spree killer who murdered at least five people, mostly unconnected (including fashion designer Gianni Versace), across the United States in the spring and summer of 1997 before killing himself. Indiana recognizes that whatever he does, the more he seeks out the accuracy of the truth, the more he is faced with an opaque biographical subject. His creation of fictionalized diary entries and the more experimental reverie moments of the text implicitly acknowledge that Cunanan's psychology cannot be re-created, that the motive is missing. While he uncovers the white lies that made up the Cunanan persona and reveals an individual with a background and a family history, he subverts attempts to get to the bottom of things and sort out the fact from fiction. To think one can get to the putative bottom is too ironic an undertaking when dealing with a figure like Cunanan, who reveled in self-mythologizing and detested attempts to *place* him as anything but what he said he was at a particular moment for a particular person. Indiana conceives of this posturing as Cunanan's art and must work both to show and to affirm its workings. The problem, and also the problematic, of Indiana's text, is precisely this opacity. The Cunanan myth can be undercut and reduced to a set of transparencies through the gathering of factual information, and the impulse to psychologize the murderer often devolves into a desire for recognition and reflection. (After all, don't we all know a Cunanan, and don't we all lie about money and our backgrounds?) Ironically, then, Indiana is left with what amounts to an admiration for Cunanan's own strategies of opacity, his final rejection of the biographical. If Indiana is indeed the narrator of the Cunanan story, like the narrator of Bartleby he inserts himself

at the level of an impossible attempt to write the biography he is in fact writing. Similar ironies can be found in two films that might be compared to the Cunanan case: *The Talented Mr. Ripley*, DVD, directed by Anthony Minghella (1999; Los Angeles: Paramount Home Entertainment, 2000), and *American Psycho*, DVD, directed by Mary Harron (Universal City, Calif.: Universal Studios Home Entertainment, 2000), especially the use of the close-up and voice-over in the latter.

32. See, most famously, Michel Foucault, "What Is an Author?" [1969], in *Essential Works of Foucault 1954–1984*, vol. 2, *Aesthetics, Method, and Epistemology*, ed. James D. Faubion (New York: New Press, 1998), 205–22; and Roland Barthes, "The Death of the Author" [1968], in *Image—Music—Text*, trans. Stephen Heath (New York: Farrar, Straus, and Giroux, 1977), 142–48.

33. *Velvet Goldmine*, DVD, directed by Todd Haynes (1998; Burbank, Calif.: Buena Vista Home Entertainment, 1999); *Wilde*, DVD, directed by Brian Gilbert (1997; Culver City, Calif.: Sony Pictures, 2002).

34. Tom Kalin's *Swoon* (1992) features an instance of frustrating the hermeneutic impulse directed toward the homosexual criminal. The courtroom scenes of the trial of Leopold and Loeb emphasize the categorizing and psychologizing impulse behind law proceedings that are medicalizing and homophobic. But when the two criminals leave the courthouse and are stopped on the steps by journalists seeking a confession or a motive behind their crime, they are met only with the response that Leopold and Loeb demand accuracy regarding the details of their wardrobe. Such a response, in its camp strategy, refuses the search for truth in the form of a motive, and instead reconfigures the truth as the opacity of their image. The analysis of camp and drag, which have for too long been conceptualized in terms of disclosure and transparency, of veiling and unveiling, and with an eye to the truth, might benefit enormously from a consideration in terms of their opacity. See *Swoon*, DVD, directed by Tom Kalin (1992; Culver City, Calif.: Strand Releasing, 2004).

35. Brian Winston, *Claiming the Real II, Documentary: Grierson and Beyond* (New York: Palgrave, 2008), 142.

36. Judith Butler, *Giving an Account of Oneself* (New York: Fordham University Press, 2005).

37. See Rodger Streitmatter, *Unspeakable: The Rise of the Gay and Lesbian Press in America* (Boston: Faber and Faber, 1995). In chapter 1, I will discuss Foucault's relationship to the French journal *Gai Pied*, started by Jean Le Bitoux in 1979.

38. Régis Debray, *Media Manifestos*, trans. Eric Rauth (London: Verso, 1996), 53–54. This is in the context of a "retrospective glance" in which Debray is critical

of the "self-referential dizziness" and "immoderacy" of semiology in its heyday: "for having too fully deciphered the world as sign, we forget there is a world underneath, and that the letter itself has a body" (55–56). This is also in the context of a dissertation defense, wherein he is making the case for his own "mediology" as announced on the back cover of the English translation: "Scion of that semiology of the sixties linked with the names of Roland Barthes and Umberto Eco—and affiliated trans-Atlantically to the semiotics of C. S. Peirce and media analyses of Marshall McLuhan ('medium is message')—'mediology' is in dialectical revolt against its parent thought system." Unfortunately, this dialectical revolt is sometimes as oedipal as it sounds.

39. Ibid., 26, 35; see also the mediological table, in which the *graphosphere* of printed text with its secular intelligentsia, utopias, systems, programs, and emphasis on publication is juxtaposed with the audiovisual *videosphere* with its emphasis on the young person and the star, broadcasters, and visibility (171).

40. Peter Wollen, *Raiding the Icebox: Reflections on Twentieth-Century Culture* (London: Verso, 1993), 158.

41. Ibid., 169.

42. See Roland Barthes, *A Barthes Reader*, ed. Susan Sontag (New York: Farrar, Straus, and Giroux, 1982). In fact, Sontag can be seen as a kind of "broker" of French theory, cinema, and literature in the United States (Jean Genet, for instance).

43. François Cusset, *French Theory: How Foucault, Derrida, Deleuze, & Co. Transformed the Intellectual Life of the United States*, trans. Jeff Fort (Minneapolis: University of Minnesota Press, 2008). The experience of reading Cusset's book is quite uncanny for an American academic like me, whose intellectual formation was in cultural studies, reading French theory much as Cusset describes. His acute critiques of both American and French academic life are as invigorating as a cold shower. Cusset consulted Régis Debray as an informant, and part of Debray's "sobering" tone about the immoderacy of theory seems to have carried over into his own "retrospective glance."

44. Given Cusset's sensitivity to the *détournement* and creative misreading of Foucault, Derrida, Deleuze, and Barthes, it seems only fair to point out his own occasional moments of distortion and use of admittedly extreme examples (*French Theory*, 218). While his account of queer theory is for the most part sympathetic and intelligent—for instance, he acknowledges that Foucault was used in queer theory to think *postidentity* (152–53; although "queerification" and "sexual gender" sound slightly off)—there are moments of sensationalism in his somewhat journalistic narrative about the "infectious" quality of French theory in North American

minority studies and cultural studies (152, 136; see also François Cusset, *Queer Critics: La Littérature française déshabillée par ses homo-lecteurs* [Paris: Presses Universitaires de France, 2002]). The misunderstandings surrounding "political correctness," identity politics, and the Modern Language Association's emergent subfields are treated as forms of fragmentation and communitarianism (*French Theory*, 171–77, 132), quite in line with the criticisms of conservative American critics and the French republican universalism Cusset sometimes skillfully debunks (190, 326; on this problem, see Eribon, *Insult and the Making of the Gay Self,* 10). While Cusset notes that "PC" university materials "would be quoted out of context by journalists, and were to considerably heighten the controversy," he himself does not abstain from this tactic, and his own discussion of date rape on the same page is remarkably ill-informed: "Date rape, in which 'date' refers to the already highly codified American practice of gradual, formal steps of increasing intimacy, through dinner and drinks, *before* sexual relations, while 'rape' in this case indicates that a mere indiscreet question can be viewed as rape" (173). Sedgwick's critique of PC-bashing journalism is to my mind more accurate: see Sedgwick, *Tendencies*, 15–17.

45. Marlon B. Ross, "Beyond the Closet as Raceless Paradigm," in *Black Queer Studies*, ed. E. Patrick Johnson and Mae G. Henderson (Durham: Duke University Press, 2005), 161–89. Ross argues that the "closet paradigm" has become dominant and hegemonic (a "master metaphor") for any thinking about "modern" intragender (same-sex) attraction and identity, but the fixation on the closet (what Ross calls "claustrophilia": love of the closet, closed literary canons, close reading of hidden meanings) has effectively disabled full engagement with the insights of race and class analysis. While I am not entirely convinced by his assertion that Foucault overlooks race, I agree with Ross's criticism of attempts to "analogize" sexuality and race because homophobia and racism are not discrete phenomena that can be compared (as they are experienced simultaneously by black queer men). He is primarily critical of Sedgwick's *Epistemology of the Closet* for overstating the role of an elite group of European men in defining "modern homosexuality" for everyone (something of which she is, in fact, wary: see Sedgwick, *Epistemology of the Closet*, 12).

46. In the sense explicated by Friedrich Nietzsche in *Untimely Meditations*, ed. Daniel Breazeale, trans. R. J. Hollingdale (Cambridge: Cambridge University Press, 1997)—unfashionable, but also at odds with the common sense of the present moment. There is always the possibility that this work will be seen as merely unfashionable, as Carol Mavor explains: "When a colleague recently asked me

what I was working on and I cheerfully and proudly said 'Barthes,' I received the dismissive reply, 'O-o-o-h, how retro.' Yet, my colleague's comment resonated with me in a helpful way. 'Retro' is from the Latin adverb meaning backward and hails retrospection or meditation on the past" (*Reading Boyishly: Roland Barthes, J. M. Barrie, Jacques Henri Lartigue, Marcel Proust, and D. W. Winnicott* [Durham: Duke University Press, 2007], 33). Late in his career, Barthes in fact declared in a journal entry, reprinted in of all places the avant-garde journal *Tel Quel*, "All of a sudden, it has become a matter of indifference to me whether or not I am modern" (Roland Barthes, "Deliberation," trans. Richard Howard, in *A Barthes Reader*, 489).

47. Hilton Als, "Mother," *The Warhol Look: Glamour, Style, Fashion*, ed. Mark Francis and Margery King (Pittsburgh: Andy Warhol Museum, 1997), 212–17.

48. *I Shot Andy Warhol*, DVD, directed by Mary Harron (1996; Santa Monica, Calif.: MGM Home Entertainment, 2002). For a positive feminist reading of the place of women in Warhol's world and films, see Jennifer Doyle, "'I Must Be Boring Someone': Women in Warhol's Films," in *Sex Objects: Art and the Dialectics of Desire* (Minneapolis: University of Minnesota Press, 2006), 71–96. See also Gretchen Berg's explanation to John Wilcock about how her interview with Warhol was unique: "Because I was a woman—and this is not to his discredit—but I had reason to believe that he wouldn't come on to me in the same way as he would to a young man. I felt I was perhaps at a slight disadvantage, but then I felt that I was at an advantage, just because I was a young chick and not one of his superstars. I was very straight at that time, and I was very serious, so terribly serious and interested in him that it probably amused him, and he began to react to it spontaneously, to be just as interested" (Berg to Wilcock in his ironically titled collection of interviews about Warhol, *The Autobiography and Sex Life of Andy Warhol*, ed. Christopher Trela [New York: Other Scenes, 1971; repr., New York: Trela Media, 2010], 29). Yet Berg also sympathizes with Valerie Solanas: "It was an intense reaction. Some people react differently to different things, and these reactions, I suppose, are psychotic. You have great emotion about someone, but for some reason you can't get close to them, they're not giving you what you want. I went away, she shot him. . . . It was just a different reaction. We both had the same feeling" (35).

49. See Victor Bockris, *Warhol: The Biography* (Cambridge, Mass.: Da Capo Press, 1997), 237.

50. Laura Mulvey, "Visual Pleasure and Narrative Cinema," in *Feminism and Film Theory*, ed. Constance Penley (New York: Routledge, 1988), 66.

51. *The Birds*, DVD, directed by Alfred Hitchcock (1963; Universal City, Calif.: Universal Home Entertainment, 2000).

52. As in Morrissey's song "(I'm) The End of the Family Line": "With no complications / fifteen generations / (of mine) / all honouring Nature / until I arrive / (with incredible style)" (on *Kill Uncle*, compact disc, Warner Bros., 1991).

53. On the centrality of the mother–child relation in Barthes's writing on love and sexuality, see Diana Knight, *Barthes and Utopia* (Oxford: Oxford University Press, 1997); and Mavor, *Reading Boyishly*, 129–61.

54. Roland Barthes, *Roland Barthes by Roland Barthes*, trans. Richard Howard (New York: Farrar, Straus, and Giroux, 1977), 27.

55. *Andy Warhol*, DVD, directed by Kim Evans (1987; Los Angeles: Image Entertainment, 2000); *Superstar: The Life and Times of Andy Warhol*, DVD, directed by Chuck Workman (1990; New York: WinStar Home Entertainment, 2001).

56. Andy Warhol and Pat Hackett, *POPism: The Warhol '60s* (New York: Harcourt, 1980), 276.

57. In this respect, and to demur from the usual closet reading, it might be worth comparing Warhol to, for instance, entertainers Paul Lynde or Liberace. See Margaret Thompson Drewal, "The Camp Trace in Corporate America: Liberace and the Rockettes at Radio City Music Hall," in *The Politics and Poetics of Camp*, ed. Moe Meyer (New York: Routledge, 1994), 149–81. On Warhol and gay identity, see Kenneth Silver, "Modes of Disclosure: The Construction of Gay Identity and the Rise of Pop Art," in *Hand-Painted Pop: American Art in Transition, 1955–1962*, ed. Russell Ferguson (New York: Rizzoli, 1993), 179–203; and Trevor Fairbrother, "Tomorrow's Man," in *"Success is a job in New York": The Early Art and Business of Andy Warhol* (New York: Grey Art Gallery, 1989), 55–74.

58. On Warhol's queer public persona, see Robert Summers, "Curatorial Statement," *Queer(ing) Warhol: Andy Warhol's (Self-)Portraits*, University of California–Riverside, California Museum of Photography, 2002, http://www.cmp.ucr.edu/exhibitions/warhol/essay.html.

59. David Halperin, *Saint Foucault: Towards a Gay Hagiography* (New York: Oxford University Press, 1995), 136.

60. Ibid., 57.

61. Foucault, *Foucault Live*, 326.

62. Wilcock, *Autobiography and Sex Life of Andy Warhol*, 236.

63. Michel Foucault, *Death and the Labyrinth: The World of Raymond Roussel*, trans. Charles Ruas (London: Athlone, 1986), 182.

64. On this issue, see Sedgwick, *Epistemology of the Closet*, 223, and Michael Lucey, *Never Say I: Sexuality and the First Person in Colette, Gide, and Proust* (Durham: Duke University Press, 2006).

65. Jean Cocteau, *The White Book*, trans. Margaret Crosland (San Francisco: City Lights, 1990), 8–9; *Le Livre blanc et autres texts*, ed. Bernard Benech (Paris: Passage du Marais, 1999).

66. On this, see Jacques Khalip, *Anonymous Life: Romanticism and Dispossession* (Stanford: Stanford University Press, 2009). I am in full agreement with Khalip's claim that anonymity offers resistance to the Enlightenment emphasis on transparency and self-disclosure. He also emphasizes its potential: "In abstaining from self-description . . . romantic writing on anonymity provides us with a glimpse of what kinds of aesthetic, ethical, and political projects can be imagined in the wake of the subject's withdrawal from public revelation and recognition" (14).

67. "Saint" Genet explains his approach to writing in a fascinating metareferential gesture that might productively be compared with Augustine's *Confessions* (or those of Rousseau): Genet writes, "If I try to recompose with words what my attitude was at the time, the reader will be no more taken in than I. We know that our language is incapable of recalling even the pale reflection of those bygone, foreign states. The same would be true of this entire journal if it were to be the notation of what I was. I shall therefore make clear that it is meant to indicate what I am today, as I write it. It is not a quest of time gone by, but a work of art whose pretext-subject is my former life. It will be the present fixed with the help of the past, and not vice versa. Let the reader therefore understand that the facts were what I say they were, but the interpretation that I give them is what I am—now" (*The Thief's Journal*, trans. Bernard Frechtman [New York: Grove Press, 1964], 71).

68. See Samuel R. Delany, *The Motion of Light in Water: Sex and Science Fiction Writing in the East Village* (Minneapolis: University of Minnesota Press, 2004); Yukio Mishima, *Confessions of a Mask*, trans. Meredith Weatherby (New York: New Directions, 1958); Severo Sarduy, *Christ on the Rue Jacob*, trans. Suzanne Jill Levine and Carol Maier (San Francisco: Mercury House, 1995); Quentin Crisp, *The Naked Civil Servant* (London: Jonathan Cape, 1968); Wilde is quoted in André Gide, *Oscar Wilde: A Study*, trans. Stuart Mason (Oxford: Holywell Press, 1905), 17.

69. Foucault, *Death and the Labyrinth*, 182.

70. See James Miller, *The Passion of Michel Foucault* (Cambridge, Mass.: Harvard University Press, 1993).

71. Foucault, *Essential Works*, 1:350–51.

72. Foucault, *History of Sexuality,* 1:43.

73. Jean Genet, *The Selected Writings of Jean Genet,* ed. Edmund White (Hopewell, N.J.: Ecco Press, 1993), 455.

74. For a discussion of Genet and Foucault along precisely these lines, see David Halperin, *Saint Foucault,* and *What Do Gay Men Want? An Essay on Sex, Risk, and Subjectivity* (Ann Arbor: University of Michigan Press, 2007). On the connections between Genet and Warhol, see Reva Wolf, "Artistic Appropriation and the Image of the Poet as Thief," in *Andy Warhol, Poetry, and Gossip in the 1960s* (Chicago: University of Chicago Press, 1997), 81–124.

75. Éric Marty, "La Vie posthume de Roland Barthes," in *Barthes après Barthes: Une Actualité en questions* (Pau: L'Université de Pau, 1993), 239.

76. Ibid.

77. Sedgwick, *Tendencies,* 8.

78. Sedgwick also suggests as much in one of the axioms from her introduction to *Epistemology*: "For some people, it is important that sex be embedded in contexts resonant with meaning, narrative, and connectedness with other aspects of their life; for other people, it is important that they not be; to others it doesn't occur that they might be" (*Epistemology of the Closet,* 25).

79. Moe Meyer, "Introduction: Reclaiming the Discourse of Camp," in Meyer, *The Politics and Poetics of Camp,* 3.

80. Ibid.

81. Foucault, *Foucault Live,* 326.

82. In another interview, called "History and Homosexuality," Foucault says that the problem of categorization "is still very current: between the affirmation 'I am homosexual' and the refusal to say it, lies a very ambiguous dialectic. It's a necessary affirmation since it is the affirmation of a right, but at the same time it's a cage and a trap. One day the question 'Are you a homosexual?' will be as natural as the question 'Are you a bachelor?' But after all, why would one subscribe to this obligation to choose? One can never stabilize oneself in a position; one must define the use that one makes of it according to the moment" (*Foucault Live,* 369). For more on this, see Eribon, *Insult and the Making of the Gay Self,* 46–55.

83. Sedgwick, *Epistemology of the Closet,* 68.

84. Ibid.

85. Cesare Casarino, *Modernity at Sea: Melville, Marx, Conrad in Crisis* (Minneapolis: University of Minnesota Press, 2002), 188–89.

86. Sedgwick, *Epistemology of the Closet,* 68.

87. Knight, *Barthes and Utopia,* 7.

88. Barthes, *Roland Barthes by Roland Barthes*, 87.

89. Sedgwick, *Epistemology of the Closet*, 10, 3–4, ix.

90. Eve Kosofsky Sedgwick, *Touching Feeling: Affect, Pedagogy, Performativity* (Durham: Duke University Press, 2003), 123–51. I must add here that it is with great sadness that I contemplated writing "late Sedgwick" the way I might refer to "late Foucault" or "late Barthes." But just as late in their careers Barthes and Foucault undertook a retrospective assessment of their earlier methods and texts, Sedgwick's self-reflection is immensely productive for evaluating the differences between paranoid reading, which "places its faith in exposure" (138), and the "different range of affects, ambitions, and risks" of the reparative reading position, those practices by which "selves and communities succeed in extracting sustenance from the objects of a culture—even of a culture whose avowed desire has often been not to sustain them" (151).

91. Foucault, *History of Sexuality* 1:37.

92. Ibid., 1:100.

93. Ibid., 1:95.

94. Foucault, *Essential Works*, 3:346.

95. Michel de Certeau, *The Practice of Everyday Life*, trans. Steven Rendall (Berkeley: University of California Press, 1984), xix.

96. Ibid.

97. Barthes, *Roland Barthes by Roland Barthes*, 172.

98. Ibid., 162.

99. See Réda Bensmaïa, *The Barthes Effect: The Essay as Reflective Text*, trans. Pat Fedkiew (Minneapolis: University of Minnesota Press, 1987), 51–55.

100. Foucault, *Essential Works*, 3:342, 348 n. 3.

101. Josué V. Harari, ed., *Textual Strategies: Perspectives in Post-Structuralist Criticism* (Ithaca: Cornell University Press, 1979), 38–39, 41–42.

102. Ibid., 32.

103. Halperin, *Saint Foucault*, 29.

104. Van Leer, *Queening of America*, 19.

105. Jo Eadie, "Indigestion: Diagnosing the Gay Malady," in *Anti-Gay*, ed. Mark Simpson (London: Freedom Editions, 1996), 79. Cf. Roland Barthes, *S/Z: An Essay*, trans. Richard Miller (New York: Farrar, Straus, and Giroux, 1974), 93.

106. Eadie, "Indigestion," 74.

107. The impact of Sedgwick's "Axiomatic" introduction to *Epistemology of the Closet* should be quite obvious here; see especially her list of categories including secrecy/disclosure and private/public (11).

108. Jacques Derrida, *Limited Inc.*, trans. Samuel Weber (Evanston: Northwestern University Press, 1988), 21.

109. See Judith Butler's 1999 preface to the Tenth Anniversary Edition of *Gender Trouble: Feminism and the Subversion of Identity* (New York: Routledge, 1999), vii–xxvi; and Lee Edelman, *Homographesis: Essays in Gay Literary and Cultural Theory* (New York: Routledge, 1994). I am inspired by Sedgwick's own reflection on forms of nondualistic thinking in her more recent book *Touching Feeling*.

110. Foucault, *History of Sexuality* 2:9.

111. Foucault, *Essential Works,* 2:147.

112. Ibid., 2:166.

113. Ibid.

114. Barthes, *Roland Barthes by Roland Barthes*, 142.

115. Sedgwick, *Epistemology of the Closet*, 3. The Foucault quote she excerpts is from *History of Sexuality* 1:27.

116. Foucault, *Foucault Live*, 371.

117. Ibid.

118. Ibid., 371–72.

119. Barthes, *A Barthes Reader*, 457. Originally published as *Leçon* (Paris: Seuil, 1978).

120. Maurice Blanchot, *Friendship*, trans. Elizabeth Rottenberg (Stanford: Stanford University Press, 1997), 291.

121. Foucault, *History of Sexuality,* 1:27.

122. Ibid., 1:100–101.

123. Ibid., 1:21.

124. Barthes, *A Barthes Reader*, 462.

125. Jacques Derrida, "How to Avoid Speaking: Denials," trans. Ken Frieden, in *Languages of the Unsayable*, ed. Sanford Budick and Wolfgang Iser (New York: Columbia University Press, 1989), 3–70.

126. Miller, *Bringing Out Roland Barthes*, 25.

127. Barthes, *Rustle of Language*, 291.

128. *Queer Eye for the Straight Guy*, Bravo network television program, directed by Becky Smith et al. (2003–7).

129. *Project Runway*, season 1, Bravo network television program (2004–5).

130. Reprinted in *Foucault Live*, 308–12.

131. Roland Barthes, *The Responsibility of Forms: Critical Essays on Music, Art, and Representation*, trans. Richard Howard (New York: Farrar, Straus, and Giroux, 1986), 251–52.

132. Ibid., 260.

133. Barthes, *Roland Barthes by Roland Barthes*, 117.

134. Roland Barthes, *The Neutral: Lecture Course at the Collège de France (1977–1978)*, trans. Rosalind E. Krauss and Denis Hollier (New York: Columbia University Press, 2005), 23.

135. Barthes, *Roland Barthes by Roland Barthes*, 53 (emphasis in original).

136. Best and Marcus note, "Surface reading, which strives to describe texts accurately, might easily be dismissed as politically quietist, too willing to accept things as they are. We want to reclaim from this tradition the accent on immersion in texts (without paranoia or suspicion about their merit or value), for we understand that attentiveness to the artwork as itself a kind of freedom" ("Surface Reading," 16).

137. Barthes, *Roland Barthes by Roland Barthes*, 169.

138. Eve Kosofsky Sedgwick, *Between Men: English Literature and Male Homosocial Desire* (New York: Columbia University Press, 1985), 89.

139. Barthes, *Roland Barthes by Roland Barthes*, 126–27.

140. Barthes, *Rustle of Language*, 291.

141. Barthes, *Roland Barthes by Roland Barthes*, 127.

142. I particularly admire this approach in Eleanor Kaufman's *The Delirium of Praise: Bataille, Blanchot, Deleuze, Foucault, Klossowski* (Baltimore: Johns Hopkins University Press, 2001).

143. Paul A. Bové, foreword to Gilles Deleuze, *Foucault* (Minneapolis: University of Minnesota Press, 1988), xvii.

144. Miller, *Passion of Michel Foucault*, 373.

145. Foucault, *History of Sexuality* 1:59.

146. *Factory Girl,* DVD, directed by George Hickenlooper (2006; New York: Weinstein Company, 2007). Jim Lewis's critique of the film is on the mark: "I realized at once that I wasn't watching a film about Andy and Edie at all; I was watching an allegory of the Evil Fag, who battles with the Good Man for the soul of the Lost Girl" ("A Very Nasty Portrait of the Artist: How *Factory Girl* Insults Andy Warhol," *Slate,* February 7, 2007, http://www.slate.com/id/2159245/).

147. *Andy Warhol: A Life on the Edge (A&E Biography)*, videocassette, produced and written by Jeff Swimmer (New York: New Video Group, 1996).

148. Debray, *Media Manifestos*, 61–62. Cf. Annette Lavers, *Roland Barthes: Structuralism and After* (London: Methuen, 1982), 207.

149. Debray, *Media Manifestos*, 62.

150. Melville, "Bartleby, the Scrivener," 17.

151. Friedrich Nietzsche, *Basic Writings of Nietzsche*, trans. and ed. Walter Kaufmann (New York: Modern Library, 1992), 164.

152. Barthes, *Rustle of Language*, 277.

153. Ibid., 279 (emphasis in original).

154. See Halperin, *What Do Gay Men Want?*; and Didier Eribon, *Échapper à le psychoanalyse* (Paris: Éditions Léo Sheer, 2005).

155. Michael D. Snediker, *Queer Optimism: Lyric Personhood and Other Felicitous Persuasions* (Minneapolis: University of Minnesota Press, 2009).

156. I am therefore particularly enthusiastic about the approach taken by Scott Herring in *Queering the Underworld: Slumming, Literature, and the Undoing of Lesbian and Gay History* (Chicago: Chicago University Press, 2007). Herring explains that his book "does not contribute to a hermeneutics of sexual suspicion. It does not present a collective subterranean history that gradually emerges into the light of mainstream visibility. . . . Although it draws on close reading, archival research, and the intellectual labors of prior decades, it has no particular investment in decoding bodies. . . . The closer critics examine the following texts, the less the texts reveal and the more they annoy. This is precisely their antihermeneutical point" (20–21).

157. Halperin, *Saint Foucault*, 35.

158. Oscar Wilde, "The Importance of Being Earnest," in *The Portable Oscar Wilde*, ed. Richard Aldington and Stanley Weintraub (New York: Viking Penguin, 1981), 459.

159. Ibid., 473.

160. Andy Warhol, *The Andy Warhol Diaries*, ed. Pat Hackett (New York: Warner, 1989); Hervé Guibert, *To the Friend Who Did Not Save My Life*, trans. Linda Coverdale (New York: High Risk, 1991), and *Le Mausolée des amants, Journal 1976–1991* (Paris: Gallimard, 2001); Roland Barthes, *Incidents* (Paris: Seuil, 1987), translated as *Incidents* by Richard Howard (Berkeley: University of California Press, 1992).

161. See Nicholas de Villiers, "The Retrospective Closet-effect: Jean Cocteau and Roland Barthes," *French Studies Bulletin* 1, no. 93 (2004): 14–20.

162. Barthes, *A Barthes Reader*, 460.

163. Rey Chow, "The Force of Surfaces: Defiance in Zhang Yimou's Films," in *Primitive Passions: Visuality, Sexuality, Ethnography, and Contemporary Chinese Cinema* (New York: Columbia University Press, 1995), 142–72. In her defense of filmmaker Zhang Yimou against criticisms that his films are merely superficial, Chow takes on the difficult task of valuing what she calls the "force of surfaces."

Those who want to defend his films for their profound "vitality" merely subscribe, she argues, to the very criteria that have invalidated him (depth/surface) and to what Foucault calls the "Repressive Hypothesis" about sexuality as a deep secret that must be uncovered. Arguing against Jean Baudrillard's assumption that this is a Western habit of thinking, Chow explains that "it is well known to the practitioners and scholars of Chinese literature and culture that this attitude toward deep meanings is part of a pervasive bifurcated moralism of *shi* (fullness or concreteness) versus *xu* (emptiness)," which contrasts deep/shallow and earnest/superficial, and finally deems these differences masculine/feminine (154). Therefore, feminist critics who see Zhang's melodramas about patriarchy as superficial treatments of women's problems may fall into the same self-defeating trap, which accords a negative value to the surface that is also deemed "feminine." Instead, Chow finds in Zhang a kind of auto-orientalist exhibitionism that challenges these habits of thought *at the surface*, through the defiant force of surfaces. The same could be said for the works of Wilde and Warhol discussed here in my own work. This is not merely to align myself with the pervasive preoccupation with the surface in postmodernism, however (though clearly Warhol was influential in that respect), since, like Chow, I believe there is a political stake in rejecting the Repressive Hypothesis, which has a specific urgency in the case of queer sexuality. Gay men in particular are not immune from the patriarchal values outlined by Chow, yet gay men are confronted with the double bind whereby they are seen as *both* shallow *and* as harboring a deep secret. This is why I believe that like Chow's reading of Zhang's films, the exhibitionism of the surface can take the form of defiance.

164. Ibid., 163.

165. Best and Marcus, "Surface Reading," 1.

166. Ibid., 9.

167. Ibid., 12.

168. Ibid., 6, 11.

169. Ibid., 9, 12.

170. Ibid., 12.

171. Ibid., 13.

172. Foucault, *Foucault Live*, 57.

173. Carolyn Steedman suggests that Derrida's *Archive Fever* is perhaps "the surfacing, or coming into focus, of an intermittent dialogue between Foucault and Derrida on these very topics: the archive as a way of seeing, or a way of knowing; the archive as a symbol or form of power" (*Dust: The Archive and Cultural History* [New Brunswick: Rutgers University Press, 2002], 1–2).

174. Foucault, *Foucault Live*, 57–58.

1. Confessions of a Masked Philosopher

1. Michel Foucault, *The Archaeology of Knowledge, and, The Discourse on Language*, trans. A. M. Sheridan Smith (New York: Pantheon, 1972), 17.

2. See John Mowitt, "Queer Resistance: Michel Foucault and Samuel Beckett's *The Unnamable*," *symploke* 4, nos. 1–2 (1996): 135–52.

3. Miller, *Passion of Michel Foucault*; Gilles Deleuze, *Foucault*, trans. Sean Hand (Minneapolis: University of Minnesota Press, 1988); Guibert, *To the Friend*.

4. Kaufman, *The Delirium of Praise*, 77.

5. The name "Muzil" evokes the author of *The Man Without Qualities*, Robert Musil.

6. Guibert, *To the Friend*, 13.

7. "Quel avenir pour l'homme?" *Apostrophes*, Antenne 2, December 17, 1976, L'Institut national de l'audiovisuel. For a history of *Apostrophes*, see Tamara Chaplin, *Turning On the Mind: French Philosophers on Television* (Chicago: University of Chicago Press, 2007), 130–78.

8. Guibert, *To the Friend*, 26–27.

9. Miller, *Passion of Michel Foucault*, 6.

10. Ibid., 8.

11. Ibid.

12. Ibid.

13. Ibid., 393 n. 5.

14. Halperin, *Saint Foucault*, 180.

15. Ibid., 182–83.

16. Ibid., 185.

17. Ibid. Cf. Jean-Paul Sartre, *Saint Genet: Actor and Martyr*, trans. Bernard Frechtman (New York: George Braziller, 1963). Sartre argues that "the homosexual must remain an object, a flower, an insect, an inhabitant of ancient Sodom or the planet Uranus, an automaton that hops about in the limelight, anything you like except my fellow man, except my image, except myself. For a choice must be made: if every man is all of man, this black sheep must be only a pebble or must be *me*" (587), and insists "Genet holds a mirror up to us: we must look at it and see ourselves" (599). The Flaubert quotation echoed is "*Mme Bovary, c'est moi.*"

18. See Diana Fuss, *Identification Papers* (New York: Routledge, 1995), 34–38.

19. A form of fictionalized autobiography, the term "autofiction" was coined by Serge Doubrovsky to refer to his 1977 novel *Fils, autofiction*, and is a genre associated principally with contemporary French authors. The publisher's note for Guibert's *To the Friend Who Did Not Save My Life* declares: "This is a work of

fiction. Any similarity of persons, places, or events depicted herein to actual persons, places, or events is entirely coincidental."

20. Guibert, *To the Friend*, 87–88.

21. Ibid., 91.

22. Jean Genet, *Querelle*, trans. Anselm Hollo (New York: Grove Press, 1974).

23. "Le Sexe homicide," *Apostrophes*, Antenne 2, March 16, 1990, l'Institut national de l'audiovisuel; available as a DVD extra on *La Pudeur ou l'Impudeur*, DVD, directed by Hervé Guibert (1990–91; Paris: BQHL, 2009).

24. *Silverlake Life—The View from Here*, DVD, directed by Tom Joslin and Peter Friedman (1993; New York: New Video Group, 2003).

25. Guibert, *To the Friend*, 132.

26. Ibid., 89.

27. Hervé Guibert, *The Compassion Protocol*, trans. James Kirkup (New York: George Braziller, 1994).

28. *Ex libris*, TF1, 7 March 1991, IMEC. Available as an extra on *La Pudeur ou l'Impudeur*, DVD.

29. *La Pudeur ou l'Impudeur*, DVD. It first aired on TF1, January 30, 1992.

30. Jean-Pierre Boulé, "Hervé Guibert: Autobiographical Film Writing Pushed to Its Limits?" in *Autobiography and the Existential Self: Studies in Modern French Writing*, ed. Terry Keefe and Edmund Smyth (Liverpool: Liverpool University Press, 1995), 173.

31. Barthes, *A Barthes Reader*, 493.

32. Boulé, "Hervé Guibert," 171.

33. Foucault, *Death and the Labyrinth*, 5 (emphasis mine).

34. Guibert, *To the Friend*, 185.

35. See D. A. Miller, *The Novel and the Police* (Berkeley: University of California Press, 1988).

36. Hervé Guibert, *My Parents*, trans. Liz Heron (London: Serpent's Tail, 1993).

37. Miller, *Bringing Out Roland Barthes*, 6.

38. Quoted in Ralph Sarkonak, *Angelic Echoes: Hervé Guibert and Company* (Toronto: University of Toronto Press, 2000), 15.

39. Leo Bersani, *Homos* (Cambridge, Mass.: Harvard University Press, 1995), 151 (emphasis in original).

40. Ibid., 157.

41. Ibid., 162–63.

42. Guibert, *To the Friend*, 4.

43. Jean Genet, *Our Lady of the Flowers*, trans. Bernard Frechtman (1963; New York: Grove Press, 1991).

44. Jean-Paul Sartre, introduction to *Our Lady of the Flowers*.

45. Guibert, *To the Friend*, 185.

46. Ibid., 46.

47. Ibid., 97.

48. David Macey, *The Lives of Michel Foucault* (New York: Vintage, 1995), 477.

49. Jean-Paul Aron, "Mon SIDA," *Le Nouvel Observateur*, October 30–November 5, 1987.

50. Daniel Defert, "'Plus on est honteux, plus on avoue' propos recuillis par Gilles Pail," *Libération*, October 31–November 1, 1987.

51. Guibert, *To the Friend*, 106–7.

52. Sigmund Freud, *The Interpretation of Dreams*, trans. James Strachey (New York: Avon, 1965), 153.

53. Sarkonak, *Angelic Echoes*, 27.

54. Hervé Guibert, *Ghost Image*, trans. Robert Bononno (Los Angeles: Green Integer, 1998), 16.

55. Guibert, *To the Friend*, 228.

56. Paula A. Treichler, *How to Have Theory in an Epidemic: Cultural Chronicles of AIDS* (Durham: Duke University Press, 1999), 19 (emphasis in original).

57. Fuss, *Identification Papers*, 34–38.

58. Guibert, *To the Friend*, 20.

59. Roland Barthes, *Mythologies*, trans. Annette Lavers (New York: Farrar, Straus, and Giroux, 1972), 68–70.

60. Hervé Guibert, *Mauve le vierge* (Paris: Gallimard, 1988), 103, 105.

61. Miller, *Passion of Michel Foucault*, 354–74; cf. Sarkonak, *Angelic Echoes*, 14.

62. Miller, *Passion of Michel Foucault*, 82.

63. Roland Barthes, *The Grain of the Voice: Interviews 1962–1980*, trans. Linda Coverdale (Berkeley: University of California Press, 1985), 322–23.

64. Miller, *Passion of Michel Foucault*, 257.

65. Ibid., 255–56; see also Guy Hocquenghem, *Homosexual Desire*, trans. Daniella Dangoor, preface by Jeffrey Weeks (1978; repr., Durham: Duke University Press, 1993), 25, 136.

66. Miller, *Passion of Michel Foucault*, 258.

67. Ibid.

68. From "Le Gai savoir," translated in Miller, *Passion of Michel Foucault,* 264; cf. Halperin, *Saint Foucault,* 94, 215 n. 165, 217 n. 183.

69. William Haver, *The Body of This Death: Historicity and Sociality in the Time of AIDS* (Stanford: Stanford University Press, 1996), xiv.

70. Interview conducted April 6–7, 1980, translated and reprinted in *Foucault Live* and in *Essential Works,* 1:321–28. I will quote from the latter translation. The title of my chapter combines the title of Foucault's anonymous interview with that of Yukio Mishima's *Confessions of a Mask,* which also problematizes authorial confession. In Mishima's introductory note to the novel (absent from the English translation), he writes: "Many writers, each in his own way, have set down their 'portrait of the artist as a young man.' It was precisely the opposite wish that led me to write this novel. In this novel I, in my capacity as 'the person who writes,' have been completely abstracted. *The author does not appear in the work.*" See the discussion of Mishima in Paul Gordon Schalow's introduction to his translation of *The Great Mirror of Male Love,* by Ihara Saikaku (Stanford: Stanford University Press, 1990), 5–6.

71. Foucault, *Essential Works,* 1:322.

72. Ibid.

73. Barthes, *Roland Barthes by Roland Barthes,* 53, 126.

74. Foucault, *Essential Works,* 1:325.

75. Ibid., 1:327.

76. Foucault, *History of Sexuality,* 2:8.

77. Ibid., 2:6.

78. Guibert, *To the Friend,* 246.

79. Ibid., 27–28.

80. Deleuze, *Foucault,* 94.

81. Ibid., 106.

82. Gilles Deleuze, "A Portrait of Foucault," in *Negotiations (1972–1990),* trans. Martin Joughin (New York: Columbia University Press, 1995), 108–10.

83. Guibert, *To the Friend,* 17.

84. Ibid., 18.

85. Ibid., 18–19.

86. Barthes, *Roland Barthes by Roland Barthes,* 125.

87. Guibert, *To the Friend,* 29.

88. Ibid., 202.

89. Foucault, *Death and the Labyrinth,* 9.

90. Guibert, *To the Friend,* 44.

91. Ibid., 67.

92. Sedgwick, *Touching Feeling*, 148–49.

93. Guibert, *To the Friend*, 93.

94. Ibid., 124.

95. Foucault, *Foucault Live*, 309.

96. Ibid., 310.

97. See Tom Roach, *Friendship as a Way of Life: Foucault, AIDS, and the Politics of Shared Estrangement* (New York: State University of New York Press, 2012).

98. Foucault, *Foucault Live*, 309.

99. See Roland Barthes, *A Lover's Discourse: Fragments*, trans. Richard Howard (New York: Farrar, Straus, and Giroux, 1978).

100. Foucault, *Foucault Live*, 309.

101. Ibid., 389.

102. Ibid.

103. See Sedgwick, *Tendencies*, where she grants that it is important to pluralize what counts as "family," and yet: "At the same time it seems that too much, too important ground is given up in letting the problematic of 'family' define these intimate and political structurations—'family' even in the most denaturalized and denaturalizing, the most utopian possible uses of the term. One gay scholar/ activist, Michael Lynch, said in a 1989 interview that he finds 'family' a 'dangerous word': 'I don't like the idea of the gay family, it's a heterosexist notion, I'd like a straight family to see themselves in terms of friends. I'd rather see same-sex friendship be the model to straights.' . . . Redeeming the family isn't, finally, an option but a compulsion; the question would be how to *stop* redeeming the family" (71–72). It is instructive to juxtapose this argument with Judith Butler's discussion of "kinship" in *Bodies That Matter: On the Discursive Limits of "Sex"* (New York: Routledge, 1993), 241, and her more recent "Is Kinship Always Already Heterosexual?" in *Undoing Gender* (New York: Routledge, 2004), 102–30.

104. Hervé Guibert, *Fou de Vincent* (Paris: Minuit, 1989), 70–71; translation from Sarkonak, *Angelic Echoes*, 137.

105. Guibert, *To the Friend*, 228.

2. Matte Figures

1. Barthes, *Rustle of Language*, 291.

2. Barthes, *Roland Barthes by Roland Barthes*, 117.

3. Barthes, *Rustle of Language*, 291–92.

4. Barthes, *Grain of the Voice*, 330–31.

5. Barthes, *Rustle of Language*, 292.

6. Miller, *Bringing Out Roland Barthes*, 25. I find myself returning to Miller in an attempt to understand a more recent event in the history of Barthes's reception, namely the *Roland Barthes Exposition* at the Centre Georges Pompidou (November 27, 2002–March 10, 2003), and the colloquium in conjunction with the exhibit, "Roland Barthes, ou la traversée des signes" (January 17–18, 2003). What was remarkable about this exposition, which sought to illuminate the diverse range of Barthes's career, was precisely its "discretion" and "silence" regarding the question of Barthes's homosexuality. I found myself agreeing with Miller not about Barthes's *own* repression, but that of his readers, and in this case not his detractors but rather those at pains to defend and celebrate his work, namely the organizers of the exposition. Thankfully, at the colloquium Diana Knight called attention to this closeting. See Diana Knight, "L'Homme-roman, ou Barthes et la biographie taboue," *French Studies Bulletin* 1, no. 90 (2004): 13–17. See also Nicholas de Villiers, "The Reception of Roland Barthes: The Question of the Closet," *French Studies Bulletin* 1, no. 92 (2004): 17–21.

7. Miller, *Bringing Out Roland Barthes*, 24.

8. See Louis Althusser, "Ideology and Ideological State Apparatuses (Notes towards an Investigation)," in *Lenin and Philosophy and Other Essays*, trans. Ben Brewster (1971; New York: Monthly Review Press, 2001), 121–86; and Jacques Lacan, *The Four Fundamental Concepts of Psychoanalysis, The Seminar of Jacques Lacan Book XI*, trans. Alan Sheridan (New York: W. W. Norton, 1981).

9. Jean Cocteau, *The White Book*, trans. Margaret Crosland (San Francisco: City Lights, 1990), 75–76.

10. D. A. Miller, "Foutre! Bougre! Écriture!" *Yale Journal of Criticism* 14, no. 2 (2001): 506.

11. Barthes, *Roland Barthes by Roland Barthes*, 58.

12. Miller, *Bringing Out Roland Barthes*, 6.

13. Ibid.

14. See Barbara Johnson, "Bringing Out D. A. Miller," *Narrative* 10, no. 1 (2002): 3–8.

15. Barthes's posthumous collection *Incidents*, translated by Richard Howard, was published together with Miller's *Bringing Out Roland Barthes* by the University of California Press in 1992. The jacket design by Sandy Drooker is a complex "text" in itself: Barthes's and Miller's slim white books are bound tightly together by a thick band of paper featuring a close-up of Barthes's eyes on one side and a

close-up of Miller's eyes on the other (perhaps creating a hallucinatory, cruising exchange of glances). Each book features a different photograph of a bedroom on its cover (both by Bernard Faucon): the bed is empty on the cover of Barthes's text, and occupied by two people on the cover of Miller's. The back cover of Barthes's book features a sensitive and distinguished-looking author photo of Roland Barthes by Sophie Bassouls; Arimondi's photograph of the mustached Miller on the back cover of his text visually rhymes with the other Arimondi image inside of the iconic Marlboro Man on a billboard being touched by a muscular man in a thong and leather cap (titled "Macho Man," and juxtaposed with an illustration of a flaming Erté letter "M"). All of these images connect to the themes addressed by Miller's text: the eyes and body of "the other," the gay "clone" and gay muscles, and Barthes's lonely "Soirées." It is also only fitting that Miller's engagement with Barthes mirrors Barthes's own engagement with photography (as I will discuss in chapter 4). But it also partakes in what Barthes called "the Combat of Images," especially of the author. See Barthes, *Rustle of Language*, 357.

16. Miller, *Bringing Out Roland Barthes*, 7–8.

17. Ibid., 5. See Roland Barthes, *Empire of Signs*, trans. Richard Howard (New York: Farrar, Straus, and Giroux, 1982), 34. For a more extended consideration of what it means to identify with the Barthes of *Empire of Signs*, see John Whittier Treat, *Great Mirrors Shattered: Homosexuality, Orientalism, and Japan* (New York: Oxford University Press, 1999).

18. The title of Treat's *Great Mirrors Shattered* (see previous note) is a pun on the title of Ihara Saikaku's *The Great Mirror of Male Love*. Miller himself makes a pun on the title of Yukio Mishima's *Forbidden Colors*, trans. Alfred H. Marks (1968; New York: Vintage, 1999).

19. Bersani is quoted on the inside cover of *Bringing Out Roland Barthes*.

20. Barthes, *Roland Barthes by Roland Barthes*, 60–61.

21. Ibid., 180.

22. *Le Temps retrouvé, d'après l'oeuvre de Marcel Proust*, DVD, directed by Raoul Ruiz (1999; New York: Kino International, 2001).

23. Regarding autobiography, Annette Lavers suggests that "what Barthes as narrator tells us about Barthes as character may not apply to Barthes as the model of this character, or even about Barthes the writer who lends his voice to the narrator" (*Roland Barthes*, 210).

24. Barthes, *Roland Barthes by Roland Barthes*, 109–10.

25. Ibid., 87.

26. Ibid., 125.

27. Miller, *Bringing Out Roland Barthes*, 25. For a critique of Miller's "paranoid" detective work, see Düttmann, *At Odds with AIDS*, 62–64.

28. Barthes, *Roland Barthes by Roland Barthes*, 142.

29. Barthes, *Rustle of Language*, 228.

30. Ibid., 37.

31. For a discussion of why the Nature/Nurture debate is a lose-lose situation for gay people, see Eve Kosofsky Sedgwick, "How to Bring Your Kids Up Gay: The War on Effeminate Boys," in *Tendencies*, 151–61.

32. Echoing Barthes's use of the word "boy," Foucault says: "As far back as I remember, to want boys was to want relations with boys. That has always been important for me. Not necessarily in the form of a couple, but as a matter of existence: how is it possible for men to be together? to live together, to share their time, their meals, their room, their leisure, their grief, their knowledge, their confidences? What is it, to be 'naked' among men, outside of institutional relations, family, profession and obligatory camaraderie? It's a desire, an uneasiness, a desire-in-uneasiness that exists among a lot of people" ("Friendship as a Way of Life," trans. John Johnston, in *Foucault Live*, 308–9). Foucault here raises complementary questions to those Roland Barthes addresses in *Comment vivre ensemble: Cours et séminaires au Collège de France 1976–1977* (Paris: Seuil, 2002).

33. Barthes, *Rustle of Language*, 223.

34. Barthes, *Roland Barthes by Roland Barthes*, 179.

35. Roland Barthes, *The Pleasure of the Text*, trans. Richard Miller (New York: Farrar, Straus, and Giroux, 1975).

36. Barthes, *Rustle of Language*, 225.

37. Barthes, *Roland Barthes by Roland Barthes*, 151. I would say that the same applies to the parenthetical personal anecdotes in Miller's *Bringing Out Roland Barthes*, which might appear "incidental," but are *made to signify*.

38. Barthes, *Roland Barthes by Roland Barthes*, 151.

39. The book contains four texts: "The Light of the Sud-Ouest," "Incidents," "At Le Palace Tonight . . . ," and "Soirées de Paris." For a sympathetic treatment of these texts that is critical of D. A. Miller, see Pierre Saint-Amand, "The Secretive Body: Roland Barthes's Gay Erotics," *Yale French Studies 90: Same Sex/Different Text? Gay and Lesbian Writing in French*, ed. Brigitte Mahuzier, Karen McPherson, Charles A. Porter, and Ralph Sarkonak (New Haven: Yale University Press, 1996), 153–71.

40. I am not denying that there is intense pathos to Barthes's "Soirées de Paris," especially the final entry in which Olivier G.'s remoteness causes Barthes to despair:

"I felt like crying. How clearly I saw that I would have to give up boys, because none of them felt any desire for me, and I was either too scrupulous or too clumsy to impose my desire on them; that this is an unavoidable fact, averred by all my efforts at flirting, that I have a melancholy life, that, finally, I'm bored to death by it, and that I must divest myself of this interest, or this hope" (*Incidents*, 73). But I would emphasize that the *affect* thus evoked is the result of skillful literary *effect* (for instance, Barthes's careful punctuation) rather than what Miller sees as the failure of *style* to transfigure Barthes's broken heart (*Bringing Out Roland Barthes*, 54–55).

41. Barthes, *Roland Barthes by Roland Barthes*, 149–50.

42. For a sensitive reading of the relationship between Orientalism and sexuality in Barthes's relation to Morocco and Japan, see Diana Knight, "Barthes and Orientalism," *New Literary History* 24, no. 3 (1993): 617–33. Knight emphasizes Barthes's trenchant critique of Orientalism and colonialism in his earlier *Mythologies,* but notes that his sexuality and his position as a French teacher in Morocco renders Barthes's perspective in "Incidents" more problematic. She also notes the important fact that "although Barthes made his main visit to Japan in 1966, *Empire of Signs* was actually finished in 1968–69 while he was living in Morocco. There was no way sexual relations (between Moroccans as well as between Moroccans and French) could escape alienation in a postcolonial Morocco where the French language retained its social and cultural hegemony, and there was no way that the text of 'Incidents' could fail to inscribe this alienation. But at the same time Barthes was weaving a fantasized utopian civilization which he called 'Japan,' where what had doubtless been an illusory impression of an individual 'happy sexuality' was transformed into a general principle of happy liberation for a whole society or textual system" (625).

43. Barthes, *Grain of the Voice*, 226.

44. Barthes, "Deliberation," 479–80.

45. Ibid., 481.

46. *Safe*, DVD, directed by Todd Haynes (1995; Culver City, Calif.: Sony Pictures, 2001).

47. The English edition dustjacket reads: "In 1979, just after having written skeptically on the question of whether a journal was worth keeping 'with a view to publication,' Roland Barthes began to keep—apparently with a view to publication—an intimate journal called 'Soirées de Paris.' The doubts he had entertained about the authenticity of the journal form now gave way to the necessity of, finally, giving direct notation to his gay desire in its various states of excitation,

panic, and despair." Note the rather triumphant "finally" punctuating this coming-out story "*outre-tombe*" (ventriloquized by the editor).

48. Foucault, *History of Sexuality*, 1:59 (emphasis mine).

49. See Louis-Jean Calvet, *Roland Barthes: A Biography*, trans. Sarah Wykes (Bloomington: Indiana University Press, 1994). For a defense of Calvet, see Knight, "L'Homme-roman, ou Barthes et la biographie taboue."

50. Marty, "La Vie posthume," 237, 240.

51. Ibid., 243.

52. Barthes, *Rustle of Language*, 292.

53. On the ambivalent relationship between writers and the media in the U.S. context, see Gore Vidal, "Writers and the World," in *United States: Essays 1952–1992* (New York: Broadway Books, 1993), 41–47.

54. *Questions sans visage*, television program, directed by Alexandre Tarta, 1977, L'Institut national de l'audiovisuel. This program might best be compared with the weekly American panel game show *What's My Line* (CBS, 1950–67, syndicated revival 1968–75) in which a panel of celebrity judges must try to guess the identity of a mystery guest (for instance, Salvador Dalí) by means of his or her answers to their questions.

55. Foucault, *Foucault Live*, 302–7.

56. Barthes, *Image—Music—Text*, 192.

57. Barthes, *A Barthes Reader*, 460–61.

58. Michel Foucault, "Introduction to the Non-fascist Life," preface to *Anti-Oedipus: Capitalism and Schizophrenia,* by Gilles Deleuze and Félix Guattari, trans. Robert Hurley, Mark Seem, and Helen R. Lane (Minneapolis: University of Minnesota Press, 1983), xi–xiv.

59. Antoine Compagnon, "Who Is the Real One?" in *Writing the Image after Roland Barthes*, ed. Jean-Michel Rabaté (Philadelphia: University of Pennsylvania Press, 1997), 199.

60. Halperin, *Saint Foucault*, 123.

61. Barthes, *Grain of the Voice*, 103.

62. Barthes, *Roland Barthes by Roland Barthes*, 79.

63. On this, see Lucey, *Never Say I*.

64. See Barthes, *Empire of Signs*, 7, and the review by Jan B. Gordon, "Japan: The Empty Empire and Its 'Subjects,'" *Salmagundi* 61 (1983): 102.

65. Barthes, *Rustle of Language*, 282.

66. Barthes, *Roland Barthes by Roland Barthes*, 5.

67. Barthes, *Grain of the Voice*, 223.

68. Roland Barthes, "Responses: Interview with *Tel Quel*," trans. Vérène Grieshaber, in *The Tel Quel Reader*, ed. Patrick ffrench and Roland-François Lack (New York: Routledge, 1998), 249.

69. Barthes, *Roland Barthes by Roland Barthes*, 119–20.

70. Barthes, *A Lover's Discourse*, 43.

71. Barthes, *Image—Music—Text*, 173.

72. Barthes, *Grain of the Voice*, 83.

73. I must give due credit to D. A. Miller for insisting on what is queer about the novelesque as a writing mode that offers an alternative to the typically heteronormative narrative and bourgeois family drama of the novel; see *Bringing Out Roland Barthes*, 43–51.

74. Dalia Kandiyoti, "Roland Barthes Abroad," in Rabaté, *Writing the Image after Roland Barthes*, 233–36.

75. Barthes, *Empire of Signs*, 4.

76. Noting that *Empire of Signs* was completed while Barthes was in Morocco, Knight comments that "it is almost amusing to think of Barthes actually living in one part of the 'Orient' [she cites Edward Said on this problematic notion] and using it as the negative basis on which to refantasize a better one called Japan— further off still, and where, crucially, they don't speak French" ("Barthes and Orientalism," 629).

77. Barthes, *Empire of Signs*, 9–10.

78. Barthes, *Roland Barthes by Roland Barthes*, 138.

79. Barthes, *Empire of Signs*, 9 (emphasis in original).

80. Ibid., 10.

81. See Miller, *Bringing Out Roland Barthes*, 33–42.

82. See Sarkonak, *Angelic Echoes*, 50.

83. Mavor, *Reading Boyishly*, 155.

84. Barthes, *A Lover's Discourse*, 67, 135.

85. Barthes, *Roland Barthes by Roland Barthes*, 43.

86. Ibid.

87. Barthes, *Grain of the Voice*, 119.

88. Ibid., 333–34.

89. Barthes, *Image—Music—Text*, 208.

90. Barthes, *Roland Barthes by Roland Barthes*, 162.

91. Ibid., 133. Barthes refines this in his course "The Neutral" at the Collège de France, proposing "the idea of a structural creation that would defeat, annul, or contradict the implacable binarism of the paradigm by means of a third term"

and explaining that this "temptation to suspend, to thwart, to elude the paradigm, its meaning pressure, its arrogance → to exempt meaning → this polymorphous field of paradigm, of conflict avoidance = the Neutral." Barthes also insists that the Neutral is not simply indifference: "The Neutral—my Neutral—can refer to intense, strong, unprecedented states. 'To outplay the paradigm' is an ardent, burning activity" (*The Neutral*, 7).

92. Barthes, *Roland Barthes by Roland Barthes*, 133. For an extended consideration of this passage and the problems it poses, see Knight, "Barthes and Orientalism," 626–29.

93. Barthes, *Grain of the Voice*, 123.

94. Barthes, *Roland Barthes by Roland Barthes*, 133.

95. Marty, "La Vie posthume," 239.

96. Barthes, *Roland Barthes by Roland Barthes*, 69.

97. Foucault, *Foucault Live*, 309.

98. Barthes, *Grain of the Voice*, 86.

99. Ibid.

100. Ibid., 87.

101. Roland Barthes, *The Eiffel Tower and Other Mythologies*, trans. Richard Howard (Berkeley: University of California Press, 1997), 15.

102. Barthes, *Roland Barthes by Roland Barthes*, 43.

103. Foucault, *Death and the Labyrinth*, 187.

104. Barthes, *A Barthes Reader*, 476.

105. See Nicholas de Villiers, "A Great 'Pedagogy' of Nuance: Roland Barthes's *The Neutral*," *Theory & Event* 8, no. 4 (2005).

106. Barthes, *The Neutral*, 23.

107. Ibid., 26.

108. Ibid., 27.

109. Ibid.

110. Ibid.; Maurice Blanchot, *The Infinite Conversation*, trans. Susan Hanson (Minneapolis: University of Minnesota Press, 1993), 76.

111. Barthes, *The Neutral*, 60.

112. Ibid., 61.

113. Ibid., 69.

114. Ibid., 70.

115. Ibid.

116. Barthes, *Mythologies*, 148.

117. Barthes, *The Neutral*, 73.

118. Ibid., 56.

119. Barthes, *Rustle of Language*, 355.

120. Vidal, *United States*, 123.

121. Ibid., 608.

122. Ibid., 609.

123. Pierre Bourdieu, *Homo Academicus*, trans. Peter Collier (Stanford: Stanford University Press, 1988), xxii.

124. Ibid.

125. Debray, *Media Manifestos*, 69.

126. Barthes, *The Neutral*, 56.

127. Ibid., 132. Cf. Bourdieu, *Homo Academicus*.

128. Barthes, *The Neutral*, 127.

129. Ibid., 108. See Sedgwick, *Between Men*, 89.

130. Barthes, *The Neutral*, 23, 107.

131. Wayne Koestenbaum, afterword to *I'll Be Your Mirror: The Selected Andy Warhol Interviews*, ed. Kevin Goldsmith (New York: Avalon, 2004), 396.

3. "What Do You Have to Say for Yourself?"

1. See the collection of essays *Who Is Andy Warhol?* ed. Colin MacCabe, Mark Francis, and Peter Wollen (London: BFI, 1997). "What does Andy Warhol want?" is meant to evoke Sigmund Freud's famous enigma "What do women want?" along with David Halperin's critique of psychoanalysis, *What Do Gay Men Want?* Warhol's first cameraman, Buddy Wirtschafter, explained how "you don't really know what he's about. He never really explains to you what he's about, and he, I think, somewhat surrounds himself with people who don't need to be told what's he's about or who understand it without direct communication. If you ask Andy a question like 'What is it you want?' which I have on many occasions, you'd get an answer something like 'Well, what do you think?'" in the collection of interviews about Warhol, *Autobiography and Sex Life of Andy Warhol*, 243.

2. See Kelly M. Cresap's brilliant assemblage and juxtaposition of quotes and perspectives on Warhol, "'Free Andy' Open Forum: Tracking a Man without a Rudder," in *Pop Trickster Fool: Warhol Performs Naivete* (Urbana: University of Illinois Press, 2004). See also the assortment of perspectives offered by Warhol's associates in Wilcock's *Autobiography and Sex Life of Andy Warhol*.

3. Gretchen Berg, "Andy Warhol: My True Story," in Goldsmith, *I'll Be Your Mirror*, 88, 91, 93. See also John Wilcock's interview with Gretchen Berg in *Autobiography and Sex Life of Andy Warhol*, 29–36.

4. Stephen Koch, *Stargazer: The Life, World, and Films of Andy Warhol*, 3rd ed. (New York: Marion Boyars, 1990), 16.

5. See also Bob Colacello, *Holy Terror: Andy Warhol Close Up* (New York: HarperCollins, 1990); *Andy Warhol: A Life on the Edge (A&E Biography)*, videocassette, produced and written by Jeff Swimmer (New York: New Video Group, 1996); *Andy Warhol: The Complete Picture*, DVD, directed by Chris Rodley (Los Angeles: World of Wonder, 2002). Wilcock's *Autobiography and Sex Life of Andy Warhol* is actually an "oral biography."

6. From a 1963 interview with G. R. Swenson, "What Is Pop Art? Answers from 8 Painters, Part I," reprinted in Goldsmith, *I'll Be Your Mirror*: "The reason I am painting this way is that I want to be a machine, and feel that whatever I do and do machine-like is what I want to do" (18). In fact, he starts out by saying, "I think everybody should be a machine" (16).

7. Warhol and Hackett, *POPism*, 128.

8. On shyness as nonpathological, see Christopher Lane, *Shyness: How Normal Behavior Became a Sickness* (New Haven: Yale University Press, 2007).

9. Eve Kosofsky Sedgwick, "Queer Performativity: Warhol's Shyness/Warhol's Whiteness," in *Pop Out: Queer Warhol*, ed. Jennifer Doyle, Jonathan Flatley, and José Esteban Muñoz (Durham: Duke University Press, 1996), 138.

10. See also Sedgwick and Michael Moon's discussion of Divine, "Divinity: A Dossier, a Performance Piece, a Little Understood Emotion," in *Tendencies*, 215–51.

11. Simon Watney, "Queer Andy," in Doyle, Flatley, and Muñoz, *Pop Out*, 21.

12. Van Leer, *Queening of America*, 19.

13. Ibid.

14. I realize that it might seem paradoxical to shift from the visible to the verbal when discussing someone usually considered primarily a visual artist, but I am not alone in this. Cresap proposes: "Perhaps it is a disservice to pay closer heed to an artist's words and manners than to his chosen and official métiers. Warhol, as we will see, was a good deal less confident and composed as a user of language and logic than he was as a maker of paintings and films. But in the very unstableness of his verbal utterances and social persona lies a significant, and still inadequately understood, portion of his life-work" (*Pop Trickster Fool*, 25). See also Wolf, *Andy Warhol, Poetry, and Gossip;* and Phyllis Rose, "Literary Warhol," *Yale Review* 79, no. 1 (1989): 21–33. Shelton Waldrep has also suggested a fruitful connection between Warhol and his early idol Truman Capote as both famous for their approach to "talking as performance"; see *The Aesthetics of Self-Invention: Oscar Wilde to David Bowie* (Minneapolis: University of Minnesota Press, 2004), 92–100.

15. Wayne Koestenbaum, *Andy Warhol* (New York: Viking Penguin, 2001), and afterword to Goldsmith, *I'll Be Your Mirror,* 395–97; Gavin Butt, *Between You and Me: Queer Disclosures in the New York Art World, 1948–1963* (Durham: Duke University Press, 2005); Doyle, Flatley, and Muñoz, *Pop Out.*

16. See Simon Watney, "The Warhol Effect," in *The Work of Andy Warhol,* ed. Gary Garrels (Seattle: Bay Press, 1989), 115–22.

17. Berg, "Andy Warhol," 90. This statement is also one of the most quoted, for instance on a sheet of commemorative Andy Warhol stamps issued by the U.S. Postal Service in 2001, but like the machine statement it is also rarely accepted at face value.

18. Andy Warhol, Pat Hackett, and Bob Colacello, *The Philosophy of Andy Warhol (From A to B and Back Again)* (New York: Harcourt, 1988). It is worth noting that some editions and commentators capitalize the definite article in *THE Philosophy* (perhaps ironically).

19. Frank Luther Mott, *American Journalism, a History: 1690–1960,* 3rd ed. (New York: Macmillan, 1962), 386.

20. Ibid., 444, quoting from *Nation,* July 17, 1873.

21. Cresap, *Pop Trickster Fool,* 2–3.

22. Koestenbaum, afterword to Goldsmith, *I'll Be Your Mirror,* 396.

23. Winston, *Claiming the Real II, Documentary,* 142. In this same passage, Winston clarifies that the Griersonians did not pioneer the use of the interview in film, since earlier Soviet films also featured interviews.

24. Ann Cvetkovich, "The Powers of Seeing and Being Seen: *Truth or Dare* and *Paris Is Burning,*" in *Film Theory Goes to the Movies,* ed. Jan Collins, Hilary Radner, and Ava Preacher Collins (New York: Routledge, 1993), 163. *Paris Is Burning,* DVD, directed by Jennie Livingston (1990; New York: Miramax Home Entertainment, 2005).

25. bell hooks, "Is Paris Burning?" in *Black Looks: Race and Representation* (Boston: South End, 1992), 145–56. See also Jackie Goldsby, "Queens of Language," *Afterimage* 8, no. 10 (1991): 10–11; Judith Butler, "Gender Is Burning: Questions of Appropriation and Subversion," in *Bodies That Matter,* 121–40.

26. Barthes, "Responses," 249.

27. Gerard Malanga explains his view of Warhol: "Although he is basically a voyeur and wants everybody to expose themselves completely, he won't expose himself. He likes to keep a lot of mystery going" (in Wilcock, *Autobiography and Sex Life of Andy Warhol,* 123).

28. Berg, "Andy Warhol," 87.

29. Warhol, Hackett, and Colacello, *Philosophy of Andy Warhol*, 79.

30. Ibid., 78–79.

31. Jonas Mekas, "Notes after Reseeing the Movies of Andy Warhol," in *Andy Warhol*, ed. John Coplans (Greenwich, Conn.: New York Graphic Society, 1970), 142.

32. Warhol, Hackett, and Colacello, *Philosophy of Andy Warhol*, 167.

33. Warhol and Hackett, *POPism*, 130.

34. Berg, "Andy Warhol," 96.

35. This interview is probably from around 1963, since there are *Elvis* silk screens in the background; clip in Evans's *Andy Warhol*.

36. Foucault, *Archaeology of Knowledge*, 215.

37. Foucault, *Essential Works*, 2:166.

38. Maurice Blanchot, *The One Who Was Standing apart from Me*, trans. Lydia Davis (Barrytown, N.Y.: Station Hill, 1993).

39. Foucault, *Essential Works*, 2:165.

40. Ibid.

41. Blanchot, *To the One*, 72.

42. Warhol and Hackett, *POPism*, 16.

43. Ibid., 50.

44. Foucault, *Essential Works*, 2:362.

45. Ibid.

46. Warhol and Hackett, *POPism*, 162.

47. *Uh Yes, Uh No*, compact disc (New York: Sooj Records, 1996).

48. Jordan Crandall, "Andy Warhol," in Goldsmith, *I'll Be Your Mirror*, 376.

49. Barthes, *The Neutral*, 107.

50. Ibid., 109.

51. Ibid.

52. John Wilcock, "L.A. Weekend with Warhol," *Other Scenes* 6 (April 1967), reprinted in *Autobiography and Sex Life of Andy Warhol*, 162.

53. Koestenbaum, *Andy Warhol*, 79–80.

54. Foucault, *Essential Works*, 3:346.

55. Certeau, *Practice of Everyday Life*, 37.

56. Koestenbaum, afterword to Goldsmith, *I'll Be Your Mirror*, 395.

57. This idea of Warhol as a mirror can be seen in the title of Warhol's interviews: *I'll Be Your Mirror* (after the Velvet Underground song) and is frequently expressed in Wilcock's *Autobiography and Sex Life of Andy Warhol*.

58. Barthes, "Deliberation," 487.

59. Deleuze, "Bartleby; or, The Formula," 79–80.

60. Quoted by Calvin Tomkins, "Raggedy Andy," in Coplans, *Andy Warhol*, 11.

61. See the Warhol "interviews" written by Gerard Malanga in Goldsmith, *I'll Be Your Mirror*, 47–62.

62. Emile de Antonio played an important role in telling Warhol that Jasper Johns and Robert Rauschenberg's reason for not liking him was that he was too "swish" (along with the fact that he collected other artists' work and was not ashamed of doing commercial art), which in fact contributed to Warhol's formation of a queer persona. See Warhol and Hackett, *POPism*, 14.

63. Billy Klüver, *On Record: 11 Artists 1963* (New York: Experiments in Art and Technology, 1981), 30–31.

64. *Painters Painting*, DVD, directed by Emile de Antonio (1973; New York: New Video Group, 2010). A full transcript of the interview appeared in the book *Painters Painting* by Emile de Antonio and Mitch Tuchman (New York: Abbeville Press, 1984).

65. Warhol and Hackett, *POPism*, 249.

66. Wolf, *Andy Warhol, Poetry, and Gossip*, 123.

67. Warhol and Hackett, *POPism*, 121.

68. Ibid., 248.

69. Ibid., 248–49.

70. Ibid., 199.

71. Ibid.

72. Ibid., 200.

73. *Warhol*, DVD, directed by William Verity, produced by David Bailey (1973; Enfield: Network, 2010). I will return to this documentary in the conclusion.

74. Warhol, Hackett, and Colacello, *Philosophy of Andy Warhol*, 10.

75. See Roland Barthes, "The Image," in *Rustle of Language*, 350–58.

76. Sedgwick, "Queer Performativity," 137.

77. Nat Finkelstein and David Dalton, *Andy Warhol: The Factory Years, 1964–1967* (Brooklyn: powerHouse Books, 2000).

78. Koch, *Stargazer*, 11.

79. Ibid., 10, 13.

80. For queer reevaluations of narcissism, see Earl Jackson Jr., *Strategies of Deviance: Studies in Gay Male Representation* (Bloomington: Indiana University Press, 1995); and Mark Simpson, *Male Impersonators: Men Performing Masculinity* (New York: Routledge, 1994).

81. On the Victorian equation of vanity with femininity and sexual deviance, see Bram Dijkstra, *Idols of Perversity: Fantasies of Feminine Evil in Fin-de-Siècle Culture* (New York: Oxford University Press, 1988).

82. Susan Sontag, "Notes on 'Camp,'" in *Against Interpretation and Other Essays* (New York: Octagon, 1982), 276.

83. D. A. Miller, "Sontag's Urbanity," in *The Lesbian and Gay Studies Reader*, ed. Henry Abelove, Michèle Aina Barale, and David M. Halperin (New York: Routledge, 1993), 212–20; Meyer, *Politics and Poetics of Camp*.

84. Sontag, "Notes on 'Camp,'" 276.

85. Barthes, *Roland Barthes by Roland Barthes*, 43.

86. Ibid., 132.

87. Warhol and Hackett, *POPism*, 88.

88. Ibid., 222.

89. Ibid., 8, 19.

90. Ibid., 229, 267.

91. Ibid., 37.

92. Ibid., 155.

93. Ibid., 145.

94. Ibid., 192.

95. Ibid., 293.

96. Ibid., 5.

97. Ibid., 216.

98. Barthes, "The Grain of the Voice," in *Image—Music—Text*, 179–89.

99. Barthes, *Roland Barthes by Roland Barthes*, 67–68.

100. This is also reminiscent of the comments on photography and death in Barthes's *Camera Lucida: Reflections on Photography*, trans. Richard Howard (New York: Farrar, Straus, and Giroux, 1981).

101. John Waters, *Shock Value: A Tasteful Book about Bad Taste*, 2nd ed. (New York: Thunder's Mouth, 1995).

102. Victor Bockris, "Andy Warhol the Writer," in MacCabe, Francis, and Wollen, *Who Is Andy Warhol?* 17.

103. Ibid.

104. Andy Warhol, *a: a novel* (1969; New York: Grove Press, 1998).

105. Bockris, "Andy Warhol the Writer," 19.

106. Barthes, *Grain of the Voice*, 4–5.

107. Warhol and Hackett, *POPism*, 287.

108. Warhol, *a: a novel*, 121. Note that the book is a roman à clef, with the "cast" clarified in a glossary by Victor Bockris in the 1998 edition.

109. Kaufman, *Delirium of Praise*, 23.

110. Ibid.

111. See Jacques Derrida, *Of Grammatology*, trans. Gayatri Chakravorty Spivak (Baltimore: Johns Hopkins University Press, 1998); cf. Barthes, *Grain of the Voice*, 7.

112. *Madonna: Truth or Dare*, DVD, directed by Alek Keshishian (1991; Santa Monica, Calif.: Artisan Entertainment, 1997).

113. See Cvetkovich, "The Powers of Seeing," 164–65.

114. Warhol, *a: a novel*, 145.

115. Koch, *Stargazer*, 25.

116. Warhol, Hackett, and Colacello, *Philosophy of Andy Warhol*, 26–27.

117. Ibid., 190.

118. See Mulvey, "Visual Pleasure and Narrative Cinema," 57–68.

119. Warhol, Hackett, and Colacello, *Philosophy of Andy Warhol*, 180.

120. See Callie Angell, *Andy Warhol Screen Tests: The Films of Andy Warhol Catalogue Raisonné, Volume One* (New York: Abrams, 2006).

121. Warhol, Hackett, and Colacello, *Philosophy of Andy Warhol*, 199.

122. Warhol, *a: a* novel, 115.

123. Warhol, Hackett, and Colacello, *Philosophy of Andy Warhol*, 147.

124. The Isherwood endorsement is on the dust jacket of *POPism*. On the importance of gossip in the art world, and how gossip is "full of insights," see Wolf, *Andy Warhol, Poetry, and Gossip*, 15–33.

125. Pat Hackett, introduction to Warhol, *Andy Warhol Diaries*, xviii.

126. "*Merz*" was the term coined by Kurt Schwitters for his collages from the detritus of industrial and commercial culture (the name was derived from a scrap of paper bearing the phrase "*Kommerz und Privatbank*" [Commerce and Private Bank]). See "Schwitters, Kurt—Introduction," *Twentieth-Century Literary Criticism*, vol. 95, ed. Jennifer Baise and Gale Cengage, 2000, available at eNotes.com, http://www.enotes.com/kurt-schwitters-criticism/schwitters-kurt/introduction.

127. *All About My Mother*, DVD, directed by Pedro Almodóvar (Culver City, Calif.: Sony Pictures, 1999).

128. See also Candy Darling, *My Face for the World to See: The Diaries, Letters, and Drawings of Candy Darling, Andy Warhol Superstar* (San Francisco: Hardy Marks Publications, 1997).

129. In fact, Warhol cofounded *Interview* (first called *inter/VIEW*) with John Wilcock, who had considerable experience with alternative journalism, including the *Village Voice*, *Other Scenes*, and the *East Village Other*.

130. See Gary Garrels, ed., *The Work of Andy Warhol* (Seattle: Bay Press, 1989). In *The Aesthetics of Self-Invention*, Shelton Waldrep's account of the later politics and commerce of *Interview* is emblematic: "After his near-fatal shooting by Valerie Solanis [Solanas] in 1968, Warhol retreated into the world of the jet set, replacing the factory regulars of the sixties with rich people, celebrities, and royals. One of the results was the transformation of *Interview* into a magazine almost wholly about fame, with the process of becoming famous chronicled either in the one-page bios of hunky young stars that always began each issue or in the main section, which usually included an interview with the cover star based on a 'conversation' at lunch with Andy and either another editor or a friend. . . . It was often difficult to know in *Interview* when something was an article or an ad" (97–99).

4. Unseen Warhol/Seeing Barthes

1. *Andy Warhol: The Complete Picture*, DVD, directed by Chris Rodley (Los Angeles: World of Wonder, 2002).

2. Barthes, *Camera Lucida*, 45.

3. Foucault, *Foucault Live*, 144.

4. Sedgwick, *Epistemology of the Closet*, 231 (emphasis in original).

5. Barthes, *Image—Music—Text*, 173.

6. Berg, "Andy Warhol," 90; Barthes, *Roland Barthes by Roland Barthes*, 119–20.

7. Bersani, "Gay Absence," 31–76.

8. Steven Shaviro, "Warhol's Bodies," in *The Cinematic Body* (Minneapolis: University of Minnesota Press, 1993), 201–39. See also Shaviro's chapter "Andy Warhol" in his theoretical fiction about postmodernism and popular culture, *Doom Patrols*: "It all comes down to images, and nothing but images. Warhol's art really *is* about fashion and style. It couldn't care less about what's beneath the surface. Nothing could be more 'corny,' Warhol says, than 'agonized, anguished art' that seeks to uncover hidden depths. The critical spirit finds the world to be radically deficient. Images never satisfy it; it always wants something more. But Warhol just shrugs his shoulders, and suggests that enough is enough" (*Doom Patrols: A Theoretical Fiction about Postmodernism*, 1995–97, available at http://www.dhalgren.com/Doom/ch16.html).

9. Roland Barthes, "That Old Thing, Art . . . ," in *Post-Pop Art*, ed. Paul Taylor (Cambridge, Mass.: MIT Press, 1989), 26.

10. Doyle, Flatley, and Muñoz, *Pop Out*, 6. In her later monograph, *Sex Objects: Art and the Dialectics of Desire*, Jennifer Doyle explains that "in glossing the language of criticism on Warhol, I am suggesting that we not take the queer figures that populate it for granted. They draw out some of Pop's most interesting attitudes—its curious configurations of agency that looks at once passive and active, its investment in art and sex as sites of exchange, its use of the queerness of these sites to resist monolithic narratives about what sex and art are" (49).

11. Watney, "Queer Andy," in Doyle, Flatley, and Muñoz, *Pop Out*, 21.

12. Ibid., 23.

13. Sontag, "Notes on 'Camp,'" 275–92. Cf. Meyer, *Politics and Poetics of Camp*.

14. Watney, "Warhol Effect," 115–22.

15. Ibid., 120.

16. John O'Connor and Benjamin Liu, eds., *Unseen Warhol* (New York: Rizzoli, 1996); Bockris, *Warhol*; Colacello, *Holy Terror*.

17. Watney, "Warhol Effect," 117.

18. Ibid., 119–20.

19. Ibid., 122.

20. Ibid.; we might compare this to "the *Barthes-effect*" in Bensmaïa, *Barthes Effect*, 59.

21. Robert Hughes, "The Rise of Andy Warhol," in *Art after Modernism*, ed. Brian Wallis (New York: New Museum, 1984), 45.

22. See Sedgwick, *Tendencies*, 8.

23. Warhol, Hackett, and Colacello, *Philosophy of Andy Warhol*, 81.

24. Barthes, *Roland Barthes by Roland Barthes*, 143.

25. Barthes, *A Barthes Reader*, 458, 457.

26. Barthes, *Camera Lucida*, 12.

27. On Photomats, the *Most Wanted Men*, and Jean Genet, see Wolf, "Artistic Appropriation and the Image of the Poet as Thief," in *Andy Warhol, Poetry, and Gossip*, 81–124.

28. Barthes, *Camera Lucida*, 11.

29. Sedgwick defines knowingness as "the reserve force of information about gay lives, histories, oppressions, cultures, and sexual acts—a copia of lore that our public culture sucks sumptuously at but steadfastly refuses any responsibility to acknowledge" (*Tendencies*, 222).

30. Marjorie Garber, *Vested Interests: Cross-dressing and Cultural Anxiety* (New York: Routledge, 1992).

31. Sedgwick, *Tendencies*, 223.

32. Garber, *Vested Interests*, 150; Severo Sarduy, "Writing/Transvestism," *Review* 9 (Fall 1973): 31–33.

33. Garber, *Vested Interests*, 161. For more on Warhol in drag, see Summers, "Curatorial Statement"; Doyle, *Sex Objects*, 68–70.

34. *Screen Test #2*, film, directed by Andy Warhol (1965; New York: Museum of Modern Art Film Library, 1989).

35. Douglas Crimp, "Mario Montez, For Shame," in *Regarding Sedgwick: Essays on Queer Culture and Critical Theory*, ed. Stephen M. Barber and David L. Clark (New York: Routledge, 2002), 67.

36. Richard Meyer, "Warhol's Clones," *Yale Journal of Criticism* 7, no. 1 (1994): 105.

37. See Calvet, *Roland Barthes*.

38. Warhol and Hackett, *POPism*, 199.

39. Barthes, *Camera Lucida*, 45.

40. Kaufman, *Delirium of Praise*.

41. Roland Barthes, "Fragments pour H.," *Œuvres Complètes Tome V: 1977–1980* (Paris: Seuil, 1995), 1005–6, originally published in *L'Autre Journal*, March 19, 1986; see also Barthes, *The Neutral*, 11, 215 n. 33. While not a text of "praise"—indeed Barthes gives Guibert a *lesson* in nuance ("I did not at all want 'my tongue on his skin' but only, or in another way, 'my lips on his hand'")—Guibert still introduced his publication of "Fragments pour H." with the following note: "*A Lover's Discourse*—'that chaste book' as Barthes inscribed in one copy—was published in May 1977. On December 10, answering a letter that had wounded him, Roland Barthes regaled its author with—a strange gift meant to soothe the wound the other had just inflicted—the following text titled 'Fragments pour H.'" On the relationship between Guibert and Barthes, see Sarkonak, *Angelic Echoes*.

42. Guibert, *Fou de Vincent*; see Sarkonak, *Angelic Echoes*.

43. Barthes, *Rustle of Language*, 291–95.

44. Barthes, "Inaugural Lecture, Collège de France," 457–78 [originally published as *Leçon* (Paris: Seuil, 1978)]; Michel Foucault, "Roland Barthes," *Annuaire du Collège de France* 80 (1980): 61–62.

45. Most relevant to the figures under discussion, Duane Michals's work was first exhibited in France in 1973 at Galerie Depire in Paris, followed by a number

of French exhibitions throughout the 1970s and 1980s, including an important exhibition, *Duane Michals Photographies de 1958 à 1982*, at the Musée d'Art Moderne in Paris, November 9, 1982–January 9, 1983.

46. Hervé Guibert, *L'Image fantôme* (Paris: Minuit, 1981), translated as *Ghost Image;* Michel Foucault, "La Pensée, l'émotion," in *Duane Michals Photographies de 1958 à 1982* (Paris: Musée d'Art Moderne de la Ville de Paris, 1982), iii–vii; Renaud Camus, "L'Ombre d'un double," in *Duane Michals* (Paris: Nathan, 1997); Renaud Camus, *Duane Michals* (London: Thames and Hudson, 2009).

47. Guibert, *Ghost Image*, 153–55.

48. Foucault, "La Pensée," iii.

49. Barthes, *Camera Lucida*, 59. Pierre Saint-Amand juxtaposes this ideal with the remoteness and unavailability of Olivier G.'s body at the end of Barthes's "Soirées de Paris." See Saint-Amand, "The Secretive Body," 153–71.

50. Guibert, *Ghost Image*, 113–15.

51. Sarkonak, *Angelic Echoes*, 50.

52. Translation in Sarkonak, *Angelic Echoes*, 51; the original fragment is titled "L'Homosexualité" in the table of contents of Guibert, *L'Image*, 89; a different, untitled translation appears in Guibert, *Ghost Image*, 96.

53. Barthes, *Roland Barthes by Roland Barthes*, 68.

54. Miller, *Bringing Out Roland Barthes*, 55.

55. Saint-Amand, "The Secretive Body," 167.

56. Guibert, "The Photo, as Close to Death as Possible," in *Ghost Image*, 165–69.

57. Duane Michals, *Changements* (Paris: Éditions Herscher, 1981).

58. Guibert, *Ghost Image*, 137.

59. Warhol was born Andrew Warhola in Pittsburgh in 1928 to immigrants from what is now Slovakia; Michals was born near Pittsburgh in McKeesport, Pennsylvania, in 1932 to a Slovak immigrant family as well.

60. Camus, *Duane Michals*, 1–2.

61. Ibid., 3; Duane Michals, *Homage to Cavafy* (Danbury: Addison House, 1978).

62. Foucault, "La Pensée," iii.

63. Ibid., vi.

64. See Sarkonak, *Angelic Echoes*, 16–17.

65. Guibert, *Ghost Image*, 97–98.

66. Ibid., 97.

67. Ibid., 193. Barthes's final page reads: "And afterward?—What to write now? Can you still write anything?—One writes with one's desire, and I am not through desiring" (Barthes, *Roland Barthes by Roland Barthes*, 188).

68. Barthes, *Rustle of Language*, 292.

69. Barthes, *Camera Lucida*, 49.

70. Barthes, *Rustle of Language*, 292.

71. Barthes, *A Lover's Discourse*, 60–61.

72. See Best and Marcus, "Surface Reading," 1–21.

73. Barthes, *Rustle of Language*, 36.

74. Sedgwick, *Tendencies*, 3–4.

75. Barthes, *Rustle of Language*, 42.

5. Andy Warhol Up-Tight

1. Ann Cvetkovich, *An Archive of Feelings: Trauma, Sexuality, and Lesbian Public Cultures* (Durham: Duke University Press, 2003), 244.

2. Sedgwick, *Touching Feeling*, 150.

3. Warhol, Hackett, and Colacello, *Philosophy of Andy Warhol*, 112–13. See also Peter Wollen's "reparative reading" of Warhol and leftovers, "Notes from the Underground: Andy Warhol," in *Raiding the Icebox*, 158–75.

4. Warhol, Hackett, and Colacello, *Philosophy of Andy Warhol*, 145.

5. *Citizen Kane*, DVD, directed by Orson Welles (1941; Burbank, Calif.: Warner Home Video, 2001). In an interview with Jordan Crandall, Warhol insists, "I don't really have a memory," and thus his favorite movie is "just the last one I've seen," but when asked, "What movie do you wish you were in?" he replies "A walk-on in *Citizen Kane*" (Crandall, "Andy Warhol," 350, 355).

6. John W. Smith, "Andy Warhol's Time Capsules," in *Andy Warhol's Time Capsule 21*, ed. the Andy Warhol Museum, Pittsburgh, and Museum für Moderne Kunst, Frankfurt am Main (Cologne: DuMont, 2003), 13.

7. Indeed, Smith acknowledges the irony involved in this game. There is a further irony in that, though the Warhol Time Capsules contain letters, they conform to neither the reading practices associated with the epistolary nor the situation described by Carolyn Steedman wherein "the Historian who goes to the Archive must always be an unintended reader, will always read that which is never intended for his or her eyes. . . . The Historian always reads an unintended, purloined letter" (*Dust*, 75). While surely the writers of the letters did not imagine us reading

them, Warhol's collection of everything in the Time Capsules suspends or appears to neutralize the question of original intention.

8. Watney, "Warhol Effect," 118.

9. See Pierre Bourdieu, *Distinction: A Social Critique of the Judgement of Taste*, trans. Richard Nice (Cambridge, Mass.: Harvard University Press, 1984).

10. From the *Oxford English Dictionary* definition of *effect*: "1. a. Something accomplished, caused, or produced; a result, consequence . . . b. *collective* and *abstr.* Results in general; the quality of producing a result, efficacy . . . c. *Mechanics.* The amount of work done in a given time . . . 3. a. An outward manifestation, sign, token, symptom; an appearance, phenomenon . . . 4. b. *pl.* 'Goods and chattels,' movable property. *personal effects:* personal luggage as distinguished from merchandise, etc. Also with wider meaning in phrase *no effects:* written by bankers on dishonoured cheques when the drawer has no funds in the bank; also, *to leave no effects:* to leave nothing for one's heirs" (*The Compact Oxford English Dictionary*, 2nd ed. [London: BCA, 1994], 496).

11. Watney, "Warhol Effect," 117.

12. Wollen notes that Warhol's "legacy has passed to different hands in a number of different directions. The most obvious has been assimilated into mainstream postmodernism and simulationism. But the potential of the other dimension—the underground, the camp, the Velvets is still available. It left its trace on punk and on the emergence of militantly gay art" (*Raiding the Icebox*, 172).

13. *Blow Job*, film, directed by Andy Warhol (1964; New York: Museum of Modern Art Film Library, 1989).

14. Douglas Crimp, "Face Value," in *About Face: Andy Warhol Portraits*, ed. Nicholas Baume (Hartford: Wadsworth Atheneum, 1999), 110–25.

15. Eribon, *Insult and the Making of the Gay Self,* 43, 44.

16. On this, see Delany, *Times Square Red, Times Square Blue.*

17. Barthes, *Roland Barthes by Roland Barthes*, 27.

18. This is not to underestimate the influence of Pittsburgh on Warhol (or on Duane Michals, discussed in the last chapter) or to simply make it into his closet, but to highlight what Eribon sees as a pattern of migration to the city as a chance for self-reinvention against family "interpellation" (*Insult and the Making of the Gay Self,* 24–28).

19. *Absolut Warhola*, DVD, directed by Stanislaw Mucha (2001; Philadelphia: TLA Releasing, 2004).

20. For good examples of this approach to Andy Warhol, see Koestenbaum, *Andy Warhol;* and Butt, *Between You and Me.*

21. Barthes, *A Lover's Discourse*, 135.

22. Sedgwick, *Tendencies*, 225.

23. Ibid., 227.

24. See also the Warhol interview compilation issues: "Andy-isms: Highlights from a Decade of Interviews with Andy Warhol," *Interview* (November 1989); *Interview 30th Anniversary Special* (October 1999).

25. Garrels, *Work of Andy Warhol*, 128.

26. Barthes, *Roland Barthes by Roland Barthes*, 82–83.

27. Kenneth Goldsmith introduction to Gretchen Berg's interview "Andy Warhol," 86.

28. Debray, *Media Manifestos*, 11, 17.

29. Warhol, Hackett, and Colacello, *Philosophy of Andy Warhol*, 32. See also Wollen, *Raiding the Icebox*, 165.

30. Andy Warhol interview with Bernardo Bertolucci, *Interview* (December 1977): 45.

31. One of the most interesting tapes I listened to while at the archive was in fact for the *Philosophy of Andy Warhol* chapter on "space" (labeled "AW & PH Wed. July 10/74"), where Hackett says, "Maybe you can start thinking Andy," to which he responds, "Come on, next question!" which prompts Hackett to later remark that "this is going to be a one-liner chapter . . . this chapter is so *bad* . . ." but Warhol says confidently "*you* can turn it into something." We should not forget the importance of the one doing the "redacting": it was an open secret that Pat Hackett was Warhol's ghostwriter; together with Bob Colacello she gave "Andy" a voice when mere transcription was not enough (as Colacello explains in the *Complete Picture* documentary).

32. In the digital age, however, the compact cassette tape has been recathected by nostalgia. See Tapedeck.org, the website dedicated to "analog audio tape cassette nostalgia": http://www.tapedeck.org/index.php. It is also worth mentioning that Warhol appeared in a 1983 Japanese television commercial for compact cassette and videotape manufacturer TDK.

33. Peter Krapp, "Andy's Wedding: Reading Warhol," in *Sensual Reading: New Approaches to Reading and Its Relation to the Senses*, ed. Michael Syrotinski and Ian Maclachlan (London: Associated University Press, 2001), 304.

34. Ibid., 296.

35. Swenson, "What Is Pop Art?" 18.

36. Warhol, *Andy Warhol Diaries*, 339.

37. Philip K. Dick, *Do Androids Dream of Electric Sheep?* (1968; New York: Del Ray, 1996).

38. Quoted by Sam Sloan, "SCI-FI to SCI-FACT—A Robotic Philip K. Dick," Slice of SciFi, June 23, 2005, http://www.sliceofscifi.com/2005/06/23/sci-fi-to-sci-fact-a-robotic-philip-k-dick/.

39. David Bourdon interview with Andy Warhol, in Goldsmith, *I'll Be Your Mirror*, 14.

40. Michel Foucault, *The Order of Things: An Archaeology of the Human Sciences* (New York: Random House, 1970), 386–87.

41. Sigmund Freud, "The Uncanny" [1919], trans. Alix Strachey, *Collected Papers*, vol. 4, ed. Ernest Jones (London: Hogarth, 1949), 386; E. T. A. Hoffmann, "The Sandman," in *Selected Writings of E. T. A. Hoffmann*, vol. 1, *The Tales*, ed. and trans. Leonard J. Kent and Elizabeth C. Knight (Chicago: University of Chicago Press, 1969), 137–67; *Blade Runner*, DVD, directed by Ridley Scott (1982; Burbank, Calif.: Warner Home Video, 2007).

42. Walter Benjamin, "The Work of Art in the Age of Mechanical Reproduction," in *Illuminations*, ed. Hannah Arendt, trans. Harry Zohn (New York: Schocken Books, 1969), 217–52. On the connection between Benjamin and *Blade Runner*, see Forest Pile, "Making Cyborgs, Making Humans: Of Terminators and Blade Runners," in Collins, Radner, and Collins, *Film Theory Goes to the Movies*, 227–41.

43. Barthes, "That Old Thing, Art . . . ," 24.

44. Meyer, "Warhol's Clones," 96–97.

45. *Strangers on a Train*, DVD, directed by Alfred Hitchcock (1951; Burbank, Calif.: Warner Home Video, 2004).

46. "All Is Full of Love," DVD, directed by Chris Cunningham (New York: Elektra, 1999).

47. Freud, "The Uncanny," 386.

48. *Blood for Dracula* (aka *Andy Warhol's Dracula*), DVD, directed by Paul Morrissey (1974; Los Angeles: Image Entertainment, 2005).

49. The previous two quotations are from the voice-over in the documentary *Andy Warhol: The Complete Picture*.

50. Judith Halberstam, *In a Queer Time and Place: Transgender Bodies, Subcultural Lives* (New York: New York University Press, 2005), 10.

51. *Chelsea Girls*, film, directed by Andy Warhol and Paul Morrissey (1966; New York: Museum of Modern Art Film Library, 1989).

52. Warhol and Hackett, *POPism*, 56. See also Wollen, *Raiding the Icebox*, 167–68.

53. Warhol and Hackett, *POPism*, 57, 63.

54. Ibid., 157.

55. *Flaming Creatures*, film, directed by Jack Smith (1963). See Edward Leffingwell, ed., *Flaming Creature: Jack Smith, His Amazing Life and Times* (London: Serpent's Tail, 1998). See also Wollen, *Raiding the Icebox*, 163.

56. Sedgwick, *Epistemology of the Closet*; Jonathan D. Katz, "The Silent Camp: Queer Resistance and the Rise of Pop Art," Queer Cultural Center website, Gallery 6, Jonathan D. Katz texts, http://www.queerculturalcenter.org/Pages/Katz Pages/KatzCamp.html.

57. Warhol, Hackett, and Colacello, *Philosophy of Andy Warhol*, 144.

58. *The Warhol Look: Glamour, Style, Fashion*, ed. Mark Francis and Margery King (Pittsburgh: Andy Warhol Museum, 1997), quotation from the dustjacket.

59. Ruth La Ferla, "The Selling of Saint Andy," *New York Times*, October 26, 2006, http://www.nytimes.com/2006/10/26/fashion/26warhol.html.

60. Foucault, *Order of Things*, xix.

61. La Ferla, "Selling of Saint Andy."

62. Fredric Jameson, "Postmodernism and Consumer Society," in *Movies and Mass Culture*, ed. John Belton (New Brunswick: Rutgers University Press, 1996), 202. See also Fredric Jameson, *Postmodernism, or, The Cultural Logic of Late Capitalism* (Durham: Duke University Press, 1991).

63. Halberstam, *Queer Time and Place*, 100. See also Mandy Merck, "Figuring Out Warhol," in Doyle, Flatley, and Muñoz, *Pop Out*, 224–37.

64. Richard Dellamora, "Absent Bodies/Absent Subjects: The Political Unconscious of Postmodernism," in *Outlooks: Lesbian and Gay Sexualities and Visual Cultures*, ed. Peter Horne and Reina Lewis (New York: Routledge, 1996), 28–47.

65. Ibid.

66. Ibid.

67. Ibid.

68. Douglas Crimp, "Getting the Warhol We Deserve: Cultural Studies and Queer Culture," *Invisible Culture: An Electronic Journal for Visual Studies* 1 (1998): http://www.rochester.edu/in_visible_culture/issue1/crimp/crimp.html.

69. Gerard Malanga interview in Wilcock, *Autobiography and Sex Life of Andy Warhol*, 112.

Conclusion

1. *Frost/Nixon*, DVD, directed by Ron Howard (2008; Los Angeles: Universal Studios Home Entertainment, 2009).

2. Eve Kosofsky Sedgwick notes, "Although the simple, stubborn fact or pretense of ignorance (one meaning, the Capitol one, of the word 'stonewall') can sometimes be enough to enforce discursive power, a far more complex drama of ignorance and knowledge is the more usual carrier of political struggle" (she cites the U.S. Supreme Court's legitimation of state antisodomy laws in *Bowers v. Hardwick*) (*Epistemology of the Closet*, 6).

3. In *Frost/Nixon: Behind the Scenes of the Nixon Interviews* (New York: Harper Perennial, 2007), Sir David Frost responds to the Peter Morgan play on which the film is based, and notes certain fictionalizations: "Why was Watergate now the twelfth of the twelve sessions and not—as actually happened—two sessions in the middle, at sessions eight and nine? Why did James Reston's discoveries from the Watergate tapes only reach me on the morning of the Watergate session and not eight months earlier, as had actually been the case?" Morgan's response was, "David, you've got to remember this is a play, not a documentary" (4–5).

4. Andy Warhol interview with Bernardo Bertolucci, *Interview*, 45.

5. Frost even notes that Peter Morgan pitched the stage play *Frost/Nixon* as "a sort of intellectual *Rocky*" (Frost, *Frost/Nixon*, 3).

6. Excerpted in *Andy Warhol*, DVD; David Bailey's full documentary about Warhol was rereleased in the UK as *Warhol*, DVD, directed by William Verity, produced by David Bailey (1973; Enfield: Network, 2010). The DVD insert contains an essay by Steve Rogers, "Fun with David and Andy," that explains the circumstances surrounding the banning of the documentary (a campaign launched by sportscaster Ross McWhirter after he read advance screening reviews calling the film "shocking, revolting and offensive," especially a scene where Brigid Berlin makes "breast prints" with ink on paper). It was finally broadcast on March 27, 1973, on ITV.

7. Warhol, Hackett, and Colacello, *Philosophy of Andy Warhol*, 49.

8. Here and in what follows I am quoting from the transcript of the Bailey/Warhol interview kept in the Archives of the Andy Warhol Museum, now also available with the *Warhol* DVD release.

9. See Rogers, "Fun with David and Andy," 6–7.

10. Cresap, *Pop Trickster Fool*, 3.

11. Ibid., 4.

12. Barthes, *The Neutral*, 108.

13. In his course on the Neutral, Barthes criticizes journalism's "unbearable arrogance, perhaps precisely because it is not really writing: it's fake writing (journalistic writing): no use of the 'I' (an egotistical writing is not arrogant) and yet a kind of verbal fat ('Do you recall?' 'as one would say,' etc.)," and he makes a kind of note: "To study one day this journalistic writing." (48). François Cusset explains that Gilles Deleuze similarly disparaged the "nouveaux philosophes" for inventing "a kind of 'literary or philosophical marketing' that was no more than 'journalism [considered as] an autonomous and sufficient thought within itself'" (*French Theory*, 315).

14. Michel Foucault, "What Is an Author?" in *Essential Works*, 2:205–22.

15. Barthes, "The Death of the Author," 142–48. See also Wollen, *Raiding the Icebox*, 163.

16. Cusset notes that the notion of transatlantic discontinuity, which attempts to magnify small cultural differences between France and the United States into "historical divides and conflicts of values," is ultimately "a myth invented by journalists, or at least a distortion created by ethnographers" more interested in contrasts than similarities, "which are far less exciting—and which bring up the guilt-inducing image of a homogenous 'first world,' stretching clear across the Atlantic" (*French Theory*, 273). For a helpful attempt to compare equivalent French and U.S. publications and media, see Pierre Bourdieu's introduction to the English edition of *Distinction*, xi–xiv.

17. Debray, *Media Manifestos*, 24.

18. Ibid., 26. Most relevant to the following discussion, see the mediological table on page 171 in which the division *graphosphere/videosphere* corresponds with the following oppositions: secular intelligentsia (professors) / medias (broadcasters, producers); knowledge/information; publication/visibility; "I read it in a book" (true like a printed word) / "I saw it on TV" (true like a live broadcast).

19. See David Stewart, *The PBS Companion: A History of Public Television* (New York: TV Books, 1999), in particular his discussion of the role of New York University's department of television in the 1950s, which "began seeking opportunities to place their university professors" on television (27), and his discussion of the interview show *Kaleidoscope* on KQED in San Francisco (43).

20. Barthes, *Grain of the Voice*, introductory note.

21. Ibid.

22. Ibid., 3.

23. Wollen notes that "Warhol's reluctance to edit was a constant in all his activities" (*Raiding the Icebox*, 167). I am less convinced by Wollen's reading of this as "a more social and psychological fear of rejection," than in his comparison of Warhol's approach with that of John Cage's "refusal of selectivity," and his juxtaposition of Warhol with William Burroughs, who "also tape-recorded and photographed everything incessantly, but precisely in order to edit it," noting, "Burroughs's paranoid fear of being taken over by alien words and images is the exact converse of Warhol's 'reverse-paranoid' desire to be taken over. Both recorded compulsively in order to sabotage (Burroughs) and to facilitate (Warhol) the workings of the semiotic machine" (167).

24. Barthes, *Grain of the Voice*, 3.

25. Ibid., 5–6.

26. Ibid., 7.

27. Debray, *Media Manifestos*, 35.

28. Barthes, "Responses," 249.

29. Roland Barthes, *Sade, Fourier, Loyola*, trans. Richard Miller (Berkeley: University of California Press, 1989), 8–9; Calvet, *Roland Barthes*.

30. Barthes, "Responses," 249.

31. Ibid., 265.

32. Bourdieu, *Homo Academicus*. See especially appendix 3, "The Hit Parade of French Intellectuals, or Who Is to Judge the Legitimacy of the Judges?" in which he discusses "this world where journalists write books and writers write articles and where publishers attempt to persuade journalists—especially when they write about books—to write books for them" (258). It is also worth noting that in Bourdieu's preface to the English edition he mentions "the astonishment of a certain young American visitor, at the beginning of the seventies, to whom I had to explain that all his intellectual heroes, like Althusser, Barthes, Deleuze, Derrida, and Foucault, not to mention the minor prophets of the moment, held marginal positions in the university system which often disqualified them from officially directing research (in several cases they had not themselves written a thesis, at least not in canonical form, and were therefore not allowed to direct one)" (xviii).

33. Barthes, "Responses," 266–67.

34. *Roland Barthes 1915–1980 (Les Archives du XXe siècle)*, interviews with Roland Barthes, November 23–24, 1970, and May 14, 1971, interviewer Jean José Marchand, questionnaire Jean Thibaudeau, directed by Phillipe Collin (1988; Paris: l'Institut national de l'audiovisuel, 1995).

35. Steedman, *Dust,* 4. A similarly capacious, metaphorical use of what Steedman calls "the portmanteau term 'the archive'" (4) can be seen in the "archival turn" in queer theory, especially in the work of Ann Cvetkovich and Judith Halberstam. See Cvetkovich, *An Archive of Feelings;* Halberstam, *In a Queer Time and Place.*

36. First published in French as Michel Foucault, *Les Mots et les choses: Une Archéologie des sciences humaines* (Paris: Gallimard, 1966); and Roland Barthes, *Fragments d'un discours amoureaux* (Paris: Seuil, 1977).

37. *Ways of Seeing,* four-part television program hosted by John Berger (London: British Broadcasting Corporation, 1972). See David Stewart's *PBS Companion* for a discussion of the links between educational television in the United States and the UK. Cusset acknowledges, "On several occasions, it has been a question here of an undifferentiated *Anglo-American* academic group, but this does not do justice to a largely independent British intellectual arena. There are several important features that distinguish the latter from its American counterpart when it comes to French theory: a more extensive history of public intellectuals, less of a tendency to innovate for the sake of innovation, a greater measure of clout held by Marxist academics, and, in a broader sense, the same sociopolitical paradigm of social class that exists in France" (*French Theory,* 289).

38. In her conclusion, Tamara Chaplin notes Pierre Bourdieu's critical stance: "Bourdieu has denounced the cadre of 'imposter' philosophers who engage with television as a sort of second-tier company of charlatans. According to him, the work of these 'philosopher-journalists' who 'illegally sport the philosopher's uniform' and vaunt their wares on the small screen ('you see them every day') never quite measures up to that of their more strictly academic cohorts. Bourdieu's comment epitomizes the way philosophers who interact regularly with television are often summarily dismissed as intellectual lightweights, despite Foucault's observation that one should 'never be convinced that a book is bad just because it has been on television.' However, it bears repeating that the issue here is not the caliber of what is produced but rather the potential of the product for the evolution of French philosophy, for histories of philosophy and television, and for a certain discourse of national identity in late twentieth-century France" (*Turning On the Mind,* 231).

39. Ibid., 12.

40. Ibid.

41. Ibid., 133.

42. Ibid.

43. "Quel avenir pour l'homme?" *Apostrophes.*

44. Chaplin, *Turning On the Mind*, 143.

45. Ibid., 144.

46. Ibid. See also the translator's note by Peter Collier in Pierre Bourdieu's *Homo Academicus*: "Bernard Pivot, host of the weekly television show *Apostrophes*, devoted to literary and cultural discussions, was criticized by Régis Debray, presidential adviser, and author of a book denouncing intellectuals, *Les Scribes*, in a notorious interview. Cf. also H. Hamon et P. Rotmann, *The Intellocrates. Expédition en Haute Intelligentsia*, Paris, Ramsay, 1981" (*Homo Academicus*, 279 n. 5).

47. Chaplin, *Turning On the Mind*, 111.

48. Ibid., 114.

49. Ibid., 179.

50. "Parlez-nous d'amour," *Apostrophes,* Antenne 2, April 29, 1977, L'Institut national de l'audiovisuel.

51. Chaplin, *Turning On the Mind*, 24. It might also explain the relative marginalization of Barthes in Cusset's *French Theory*, where he spends only a page on "the peculiar American avatars of Roland Barthes" (285), ironically quoting Susan Sontag: "'Of all the intellectual notables who have emerged since World War II in France, Roland Barthes is the one whose work I am most certain will endure,' wrote Susan Sontag, introducing a text written in tribute to Barthes, with whom she had become friends, and whose work she helped introduce in the United States" (285). See Susan Sontag, "Writing Itself: On Roland Barthes," in *A Barthes Reader*, iii.

52. Chaplin, *Turning On the Mind*, 24.

53. "Le Sexe homicide," *Apostrophes,* 1990.

54. See Angell, *Andy Warhol Screen Tests.*

55. See the website IMEC: Institut mémoires de l'édition contemporaine, at http://www.imec-archives.com/.

56. See de Villiers, "A Great Pedagogy of Nuance." See also the Palgrave Macmillan website dedicated to the existing and forthcoming English translations of Foucault's Collège de France lectures: http://www.palgrave.com/philosophy/foucault.asp.

57. *Roland Barthes Exhibition,* Centre Pompidou, and the colloquium Roland Barthes, ou la traversée des signes; 24 heures Foucault, exhibit by Thomas Hirschhorn, *33e édition du Festival d'Automne à Paris*, September 13–December 19, 2004: "After several previous conceptual 'monuments' to great philosophers

(Deleuze, Bataille, Spinoza), Hirschhorn commemorates the 20th anniversary of Foucault's death with a non-stop 24-hour-long series of speeches on the philosopher's work by a number of thinkers and writers, in an installation that gives a physical experience of the philosopher's mind at work" (festival website at http://www.festival-automne.com/public/2004/index.htm).

58. *Genesis 19: Roland Barthes,* ed. Pierre-Marc de Biasi and Éric Marty (Paris: Institut des texts et manuscrits modernes [item], 2002).

59. Roland Barthes, *Comment vivre ensemble: Cours au Collège de France 1976–1977,* audio CD (Paris: Seuil, 2003), and *Le Neutre: Cours au Collège de France 1977–1978,* audio CD (Paris: Seuil, 2003). See also UbuWeb: Sound, which contains mp3 files of these two courses and Barthes's "Inaugural Lecture" at the Collège de France: http://www.ubu.com/sound/barthes.html.

60. Roland Barthes, *Œuvres Complètes: Livres, Textes, Entretiens,* vols. 1–5 (Paris: Seuil, 2002); Michel Foucault, *Dites et écrits,* vols. 1–2 (Paris: Gallimard, 2001).

61. For a defense of the maligned intellectual, see Roland Barthes, "The Indictment Periodically Lodged . . ." in *Rustle of Language,* 343–44.

62. Barthes, *The Neutral,* 19.

63. Ibid., 21.

64. Foucault, *Foucault Live,* 225.

Index

NICHOLAS DE VILLIERS is assistant professor of English and film at the University of North Florida.